THE JESUS CONUNDRUM

SEARCHING FOR TRUTH BEYOND DOGMA

ERNST RODIN

www.thinktruth.com

Order this book online at www.trafford.com
or email orders@trafford.com

Most Trafford titles are also available at major online book retailers.

Printed in Victoria, BC, Canada.

ISBN: 978-1-4269-1886-5 (sc)

Library of Congress Control Number: 2009912708

*Our mission is to efficiently provide the world's finest, most comprehensive book publishing
service, enabling every author to experience success. To find out how to publish your book,
your way, and have it available worldwide, visit us online at www.trafford.com*

Trafford rev. 2/19/09

 www.trafford.com

North America & international
toll-free: 1 888 232 4444 (USA & Canada)
phone: 250 383 6864 ♦ fax: 812 355 4082

Videte, cavete a fermento phariseorum

et fermento Herodis.

Mark 8:15

Observe, guard against the leaven
of the Pharisees and Herodians.

With gratitude to my wife, Martha, who has always
placed the needs of others before her own;

Our children who have taught me what is important in life;

And to the Holy Spirit upon Whose

Advice I have relied.

PREFACE

When I sent the manuscript for critique to a number of friends and colleagues they were surprised and asked two questions, "Why did you, a physician and neuroscientist, write a book on a topic which is traditionally reserved for theologians?" and "Why should anybody want to buy it?"

Both questions are important and the first one immediately reveals how we think about our fellow human beings. We pigeonhole them by profession, hobbies and what we think we know about their families. This is the typical *pars pro toto* approach to life which will be explained further in the book. We only know some facets of a given individual which we then take for the whole, and the person in question is not supposed to step out of the slot we have assigned to him in our own minds.

The first question can best be answered as an attempt to express my gratitude to Jesus for his help throughout a long, eventful and turbulent life. The idea was born under the most unlikely circumstances and started with a dream. Not the Martin Luther King type of dream, but the nocturnal event which is part of our physiology. It occurred during a sailing trip in the Caribbean where I was island hopping on a forty footer with a friend who owned the boat and his friend, a lady pediatrician. The weather was perfect, our little crew of three most compatible, and life could not be better. It was one of those rare days when you truly have no worries. God is in heaven and there is peace on earth.

During the night I dreamt that it was late afternoon on Christmas Eve and I discovered to my dismay that I had not bought a single present for the various family members. It was a disaster. "Where am I going to get gifts now at the very last minute?" was the worried thought. But immediately came the next one, "What are we really celebrating?" "Jesus' birthday, of course." "But what can I give Jesus? He has everything he could possibly want?" The answer came back, "Souls!" Yes indeed; and if this book can help even a single soul to understand Jesus and his message better it has fulfilled its purpose.

But apart from this personal reason there was another one. In our scientific era Jesus presents us with a conundrum, in the sense of "an intricate and difficult problem." He simply does not fit into our current conceptual framework. Although his name is on our lips we don't know how to deal with him ever since the faith of the Middle Ages had given way to rationalism in what is called the "Enlightenment." This has led to the fact that some of my medical colleagues have felt the need to put a post-mortem diagnosis on him as well as Saint Paul. In the 1800s and early 1900s it was popular in learned circles to label Jesus as a paranoid schizophrenic. Albert Schweitzer, who did not agree with these opinions, wrote as his doctoral thesis *The Psychiatric Study of Jesus*, in order to provide a balanced view. But the apparent "evidence" seems just too compelling, especially when one relies mainly on the gospel of Saint John. In addition Saint Paul is nowadays regarded by many of my neurologic colleagues as "an epileptic." Thus, the two founders of Christianity carry diagnostic labels which clearly fall within the purview of my medical specialty and a study of their lives is, therefore, of professional interest.

Furthermore, having previously discussed Judaism in its historical as well as current political context in *The Moses Legacy* and *Whither Zionism?* where I could touch on Christianity only in a peripheral manner, a more detailed exposition of the philosophical differences became necessary. Most of us who are not devoutly religious only have, what may be called, a nodding acquaintance with Jesus. Some of us are in the situation of the father of the boy whose epilepsy could not be cured by the disciples. "I [want to] believe. Help my unbelief," he implored Jesus. But a more common reaction came from my oldest son who is also a physician. When I told him that I was writing this book, he said, "But you know perfectly well, Dad, that if you saw this guy in your office you'd send him to a psychiatrist." I replied, "Well, it depends on what you read and how you read it. This is why I'm writing this book."

This brings me to the next question: Why should one want to buy this book? There are already tens of thousands available from the most authoritative sources including one by the Holy Father, Pope Benedict XVI, as well as by other known authors from various walks of life. Under these circumstances the competition is obviously daunting. The reason for bringing a physician's point of view to public attention is that regardless whether you are a Christian, a Jew, a Muslim, a Hindu, a Buddhist, an agnostic, an atheist or what not, Jesus affects our lives in ways we are not aware of. The current socio-political strife, which includes the misnamed War on Terrorism, has at its basis a difference in philosophical outlook. To put it simply, the question is: does a materialistic-scientific outlook fully explain our world and what is happening in it, or is there an additional spiritual element present? We tend to smile or scoff when we read about Jesus driving out unclean spirits but how many of us are obsessed with thoughts and feelings which invade our minds, sometimes against our will, and threaten to destroy our well-being if not life altogether? We have given new names to old ills but we have solved very little thereby.

Apart from these aspects, our materialistic society is now in the process of destroying itself and what is happening in the Middle East, specifically in the Holy Land, should concern all of us because we are co-responsible for the strife and its outcome. This is why you should read this book because it is an appeal to conscience and realism. You will be introduced to a different point of view than customary. Hopefully it will make you think about your role in this world including your personal responsibility for what is happening in it.

At this point it is a pleasure to acknowledge the help I have received in the preparation of this book. For the most part this was a family enterprise. The most important support came from my wife, Martha, who kept urging me on over the years to bring it to completion, especially after earlier rejections. Our daughter, Krista, was instrumental in proofreading the document and jointly with her daughter, Alexis Joanne, the four of us came up with the title and the cover picture. Alexis also provided the first sketch which was put into artistic form by Mr. Zack Johnson.

Special thanks are also due to my friend and colleague Professor Hellmuth Petsche. He not only critiqued the manuscript and made valuable suggestions, but in addition, just like Krista, acquainted me with further relevant literature sources. Great appreciation is also expressed to Mrs. Catherine Demeter, editor of a clinical neurophysiology journal, who generously volunteered her time for additional proofreading and other editorial chores without financial compensation but simply out of kindness. Finally it is a pleasure to thank the staff of Trafford for their help in turning the manuscript into a book.

CONTENTS

INTRODUCTION

Human nature has not changed throughout recorded history and the problems of ancient Judea and Rome are still ours. We are again embroiled in wars of uncertain outcome, hate is responded to with hate, and it seems that the "Prince of Peace" has lived in vain. As average citizens we cannot change the world, regardless where, and under what government, we live. The only thing we can do is to first learn why things keep happening the way they do and then examine our attitude to what is being done in our name. If we honestly do so some of us may not be satisfied with the deceptions we are exposed to on a daily basis and instead of merely going along with what is popular at a given moment in time we may begin to espouse eternal values. In this effort the message of Jesus, when freed from sectarian overtones, is as important, if not more so, than when he lived on this earth. Our technological ability to produce and spread evil is infinitely greater than at any previous time in history and a counterbalance is urgently needed.

While the title of the book delineates the problem, the subtitle "Searching for Truth beyond Dogma" was meant to indicate that the views, which are expressed here, do not represent official doctrine, but the truth as I have come to see it. As such it is colored by professional as well as personal life experiences and makes no pretensions to absolute truth. This is in contrast to theologians, and nowadays also some politicians, who look at the world through the eyes of Gen. 3:6 where the snake told Eve, "You shall be like God, knowing good and evil, or in Latin *eritis sicut deus scientes bonum et malum*. Ever since we have passed judgment on others, and evil is exclusively reserved for the adversary. The past and current century have shown where this leads. But the word *malum* does not necessarily imply a moral judgment. It can also mean "bad," in the sense that something you do may be bad for your health. The physician does not pass moral judgments on people but only sees suffering human beings with assets and liabilities. He then tries to understand the causes that have led the patient to the current impasse and helps him/her overcome it. This is the spirit in which this book is written. Not only does it point out the potential dangers of blind obedience to dogma, be it religious or political, but it may also help in the search for a meaning in life which at times seems meaningless.

I would now like you to take a moment and answer for yourself the following Multiple Choice Test as it might appear in a quiz. It will give you an insight into your own current attitude and I shall return to it at the end of the book.

The word Jesus refers to:
a) An expletive to be used when one is angered or distressed.
b) A prophet of God.
c) A deluded itinerant Galilean preacher and miracle worker.
d) A dangerous false prophet.
e) The savior of mankind.

The fact that one can phrase a quiz in this manner makes it obvious that Jesus may be the most controversial person who has ever walked on earth. For some he was, and still is, a stumbling block which has to be rejected. For others he is the cornerstone of their belief system. Still others use his name simply as an expletive.

As the title of this book indicates this is not a theologic treatise about Jesus the Christ but a personal journey of discovery. As a physician and a scientist, with an interest in history, I have always had an urge to understand what seems to be incomprehensible in human behavior. Jesus surely represents a challenge in this regard.

I grew up in the Catholic religion but eventually found myself unable to adhere to dogmas which have been handed down through centuries. While I respect the Church, appreciate her usefulness, and wish her well in her endeavors, I cannot in good conscience subscribe to all the tenets. My scientific mind is too independent to accept hierarchical constraints and I have dutifully confessed this to a priest and received absolution. As a matter of fact it was so hilarious an experience that I am going to share it here. I had not gone to confession for several years because my major sins had evaporated with age but it was Easter; I was conflicted in a professional situation and thought it might be a good idea to hear what a priest might say. I kneeled down said my contrition and then declared, "Father, I really have only the run of the mill minor sins to confess which all of us commit in our daily lives, but my major problem is that I have difficulty with authorities." The priest, who was well hidden and whom I did not know, said something to the effect of, "go on my son." "Well, I have a problem also with the Holy Father." Whereupon the priest broke out in laughter and said, "Don't we all!" Both of us laughed together, I said my obligatory Hail Mary's and went on my way absolved.

I realize that this was an unusual priest and outside the confessional he would probably have been constrained by institutional discipline. This is a problem with organized religion of whatever denomination. All institutions, be they secular or religious, acquire a life of their own which not only needs to be protected but also expanded lest they die. This is a fact of life and must be recognized. Under these circumstances the fundamental, eternal, spiritual ideas that provided the basis for the faith may become overlaid with temporary ones and, let us be blunt, a drive for power by various factions.

But the figure of Jesus transcends specific denominations and their secular concerns. I have, therefore, followed the example of Thomas Jefferson and tried to discern from the gospels what we can learn about Jesus the person. In this attempt to reconstruct Jesus' life I was soon confronted with the fact that some of the words which are attributed to him are ununderstandable unless one is acquainted with Old Testament prophecy. In addition one must become fully aware of the religious-political conditions which prevailed in the "Holy Land" during the first century of our era. Since the Jews lived under Roman occupation at that time, we also have to know some of the facts which led up to it, as well as the forces which had shaped the Jewish religion. Otherwise key terms such as "Son of Man," "Holy Spirit," and "Kingdom of God" are simply words and a rational understanding of Jesus, as opposed to one that is strictly faith-based, becomes impossible. Furthermore, we have to know the wider intellectual climate which permeated the Roman Empire in the first century of our era. Since nowadays this knowledge tends to be limited to specialists, it is readily understandable why my son reacted in the way mentioned in the Preface, when I told him that I was writing this book. He is certainly not alone in this opinion.

In the effort to discern how Jesus might have felt and why he did what he did we are, however, limited to the narrations of the evangelists and they don't agree on key aspects. The only "fact" we know from the Gentile literature is a single sentence by Tacitus in relation to Nero's persecutions of the Christians, where he mentions that, "Christus" had suffered the extreme penalty under Pontius Pilatus. But it must also be admitted that we don't even know this much about Moses, yet he is spiritually alive not only in the Jewish but also the Christian and Muslim community. The ancient Egyptians said, "A man is not dead as long as his name is pronounced," and a wise old Rabbi declared, "it doesn't matter what really happened, what matters is what people believe has happened." This is correct and a limitation all of us have to accept. For this reason we can work scientifically with the gospels only in an "as if" manner. This means that we can accept what is written, not necessarily as absolute historical truth, which does not exist even in secular literature, but as a version of events that is regarded as such. It is in this spirit that this book has to be read.

How do we get to an understanding of Jesus' words and actions as they have been reported? The first aspect one has to realize is that we are dealing with translations of translations. We do not have Jesus' original words because no Aramaic text has ever been discovered. The gospels were written in Greek and translated during the fourth century A.D. by St. Jerome into Latin as the *Vulgata*, which means the language of the common people. The subsequent translations into the various languages of the world, and their revisions are based either on the Latin or Greek text. Since Greek was the original language the gospels appeared in, one might be tempted in one's quest for authenticity to disregard the translations altogether and simply concentrate on the Greek version. Unfortunately, the original Greek versions of the gospels no longer exist. They have been revised several times and the earliest printed version, as opposed to handwritten, dates to 1514. The Greek text that is currently available represents a 1901 revision. What are assumed to be "original" Greek manuscripts dating to the early Church exist in a museum in St. Petersburg, the British Museum in London, and the Vatican. It would surely be valuable to digitize these documents so that Bible scholars could compare them with currently existing texts. The same applies to the *Vulgata* which also exists in "Authorized" and "Revised" versions. Since revisions hardly ever cease we are not only dealing with translations of translations but also revisions of revisions.

While this makes a scientist shudder the situation is even worse for the Old Testament. The Hebrew collection of scrolls, which eventually became our Bible, emerged over a period of centuries. They contained no vowels or punctuation and are read from right to left. Bible scholars who want to glean "the truth" from early Hebrew documents, to the extent they exist, as for instance in the Dead Sea scrolls, are faced not only with a formidable but a basically unsolvable task. A given sequence of consonants can be filled in with vowels of one's choice, and sentence endings may have to be artificially constructed. For the Dead Sea Scrolls the problem is compounded by the fact that the scholars have to work, to some extent, with scraps of material which have to be pasted together in some type of logical sequence. This process is, of course, also open to bias.

In addition there is a difference between the spoken and written word which is called prosody. A little Jewish joke might illustrate this better than erudite explanations. Moshe and Shlomo had an argument during which Moshe called Shlomo a scoundrel. Shlomo was upset and took Moshe before the judge. The judge said to Moshe, "Tell Shlomo that he is not a scoundrel." Whereupon Moshe said, "Shlomo is not a scoundrel?" The judge reproved Moshe saying that this was not what was meant, whereupon Moshe replied, "Your honor, you can give me the words but I make the melody!" Yes indeed, it is the melody which counts and we try to convey it in written language by commas, exclamation marks, question marks, periods and so on. When these are missing, as they were up to the early centuries of our time, all bets are off as to the intended original meaning. This is why one can dispute interminably what a given word or sentence in a Hebrew document might have meant originally.

Compound all of this with the fact that language is not static but changes over decades let alone centuries or millennia. No one would have expected in the 1950s, for instance, that the simple word "gay" would refer to homosexual people. It seems quite possible that in another fifty years that this is all it will mean and that the Christmas Carol, "Don we now our gay apparel" will be viewed as an invitation to cross dressing. Who knows? Furthermore, words have more than one meaning in different languages and the translator has to choose the one that fits best into the concept he wants to convey. There is inevitable bias inherent in this process and it is exceedingly interesting to not only compare the various gospels, but also the different translations within the same language. If this were not enough, each translator lives in a given time period with the culture of its day and cultural bias is, therefore, practically unavoidable. We should also never forget that words are not things *per se* but symbols which stand for thoughts, feelings or visions. In this way they are always inadequate when it comes to the expression of spiritual topics.

We have to recognize also that the biblical writers were men on a mission. The authors of the Old Testament were engaged in what might be called, in modern terms, nation building. The twelve tribes of Israel were the Chosen People not only by "a god" but by "God Almighty, Ruler of the Universe" and the purpose of the nation was to be "holy." Since nations are composed of ordinary people they simply can't conform to constant holiness. This lofty ideal was never achieved and the nation was, therefore, frequently punished. The purpose of the rest of the world was to serve either for the benefit of Jacob's offspring or as the scourge of the Almighty, when they strayed. As such, the Old Testament conveys a thoroughly ethnocentric view of the world. The Jewish historians Philo and Josephus, whose writings I have previously discussed in *The Moses Legacy* in another context, were also on a mission and their goal was to convince the Greco-Roman world that the Jewish religion was the most ancient as well as noble of all. In this way they became some of the first "spin masters" on record. Aspects of their writings are included here because they lived essentially at the same time the gospels were written and, therefore, contain additional relevant information.

The evangelists and St. Paul were likewise confronted with a major task. Their goal was to legitimize Jesus as the long awaited Messiah. He was to be presented not only as the savior of the Jewish nation but as the redeemer of the entire world. Since Jews, by and large, rejected the idea that a crucified Jesus could have been the expected Messiah, conversions from Judaism to the new religion were relatively few and far between. For the "good news" to succeed it had to be brought to the Gentiles. The political problem which the Church fathers were then confronted with in the first century was that Judaism, as an established religion, had legitimacy in the Roman Empire while the newcomers were merely regarded as a sect of Judaism. Sects always have a difficult row to hoe, and even in today's world the Mormon Church, for instance, has not yet been able to achieve full recognition by some of the other traditional denominations of Christianity. To overcome this problem the gospel writers and St. Paul diligently consulted the Old Testament for prophecies which could, retroactively, be applied to Jesus. That the Jews resented this expropriation of their holy book for a, from their point of view, heretical purpose, is thoroughly understandable. Thus the hostility between "Old" and "New" was utterly unavoidable, but more about this later.

To make matters even worse in regard to our understanding of Jesus, the person, we have to realize that the current canonized version of the New Testament contains only a fraction of the literature about Jesus which was extant in the first two centuries after his death. The nascent Church was confronted not only with hostility from without but numerous schisms within and in order to survive selections had to be made. There was even a question whether or not the gospel of St. John should be included and especially the Book of Revelation, better known as the Apocalypse. Although the Church fathers relied on the Holy Spirit to guide them in the selection process it was inevitable that human motives and political considerations of the time intruded. In addition we have to be aware that all our information, from whatever source, is filtered by our brain and thereby to some extent distorted. A fuller exposition of these aspects is beyond the scope of this book but the fact needs to be recognized because it reinforces the above expressed view that we can work with the New Testament only in an "as if" manner and scientific historical authenticity cannot be achieved. Even historians and theologians have to proceed on basis of faith rather than science, when it comes to a discussion of Jesus Christ. In order to reach an understanding of what Jesus might have said and done I used as basic documents the *New Greek - English Interlinear New Testament* and for the Old Testament mainly the *Septuagint* which is the Greek translation from Hebrew. The latter is actually the oldest complete Bible, in the form we know the book today. Legend has it that the Septuagint was composed by a group of 70 (some say 72) Jewish scholars in Alexandria during the reign of Ptolemy II (283-246 B.C.). They supposedly translated the Hebrew scrolls independently of each other and when they had completed their task they found their texts to have been identical in all respects. This is myth. In fact, the Greek version differs in a number of respects from the Hebrew but this need not concern us here, because the Septuagint was the text the New Testament writers had relied on. The use of the English translations of these documents had the advantage that key Greek words could be looked up in a dictionary and their various meanings examined. *The Jerome Biblical Commentary* and *McKenzie's Dictionary of the Bible* were also of invaluable assistance. So were: *A Grammatical Analysis of the Greek New Testament. The Complete Word Study Dictionary,* and the *Novum Testamentum Latine.* Additional sources will be mentioned in the text.

Although I proceeded initially in the usual sequence of the gospels, as laid out in the New Testament, it soon became apparent that the material would not only become unmanageable but also fail to reach the desired end. I, therefore, changed the sequence by presenting the gospel of Mark first and then merely discussed the discrepancies between Mark's gospel and those of Matthew and Luke. Inasmuch as Luke provided not only the life of Jesus but also *The Acts of the Apostles* his sequence was retained. The Acts can, however, not be understood unless one is familiar with the major Pauline Epistles. They are, therefore, presented after *The Acts.* These in turn lead into St. John's gospel and subsequently the Revelation of St. John the Divine, better known as the Apocalypse, which are the most challenging to the intellect. The subsequent chapter puts the gospels into their historic context and the final one addresses Pilate's immortal question: What is truth?

As a scientist I proceeded in the same manner as for my medical investigations. I was familiar with the conventional textbook wisdom but ever so often a question arose on some specific aspect where the textbook and clinical experience did not quite agree. I then performed the appropriate experiment and reached my own conclusions. Only after I had obtained my results and was ready to prepare the data for publication did I perform a thorough literature search in order to see what others had reported. This method while limiting bias also led to major disappointments, because ever so often I found out that my efforts had merely duplicated the findings of others. But apart from hurt pride for not having been the first to make this observation I could give the previous authors credit. In addition, when one can independently confirm somebody else's results this provides them with even greater validity. The literature on Jesus is, however, so vast that nobody can read it in one's lifetime. A choice had to be made and in my search for purity I, therefore, concentrated mainly on ancient rather than recent authors. There was no slight intended and current writers should not be disappointed when their name does not show up in the bibliography, especially since this is not a theological treatise.

The literature is replete with explanations of Jesus' Divinity, but the human being with his joys and sufferings can get lost in theologic speculations. This book is an attempt at some balance. It emphasizes Jesus' human aspects and these are amenable to our understanding. Although the book will not necessarily unravel the "conundrum" which the complex literature on Jesus presents us with, it is hoped that it will show how individuals can arrive at their personal solutions. Although some readers might find certain aspects disturbing, it is worth while to remember what Seneca wrote in a letter to a friend nearly two thousand years ago on *The Subjects of Philosophy*, "What I say will benefit you even if you don't like it. Words that are not soothing must some time reach you . . ."

Finally, I would like to point out that this book was written over a period of years. It grew as insights have developed, and this is why the reader will intermittently find a comment, that a given point will be explained and discussed further in later portions of the book. I am also fully aware that this book is not the final word on a topic which human beings have pondered for millennia; it only represents insights gained so far on a journey towards personal truth. Further understanding is likely to develop which will, however, not invalidate what has been written here, but deepen our comprehension. It is, therefore, my hope that the book, as it stands today, can serve as a base for an exchange of thoughts and thereby contribute to a better world.

SAINT MARK'S JESUS

Although the Gospel of Mark tends to appear in our Bibles after that of Matthew it is generally regarded as the oldest; this is why I am placing it first. Furthermore, it is the shortest of all four, presents a human Jesus and sets the pattern for the other two synoptic gospels. The Gospel of John is largely a theologic treatise and deals with the divine nature of Christ as will be discussed later. Since both Matthew and Luke use a great deal of Mark's information it has been assumed that there existed a common source which has been called Q, an abbreviation of the German word *Quelle*. But these are fine points theologians can struggle with and need not concern us here. What is important is that Mark presents in a relatively concise form Jesus' life and teachings, and this is why I shall rely quite heavily on this document.

It is assumed that Mark accompanied Peter on his travels, where he acted as his interpreter, and wrote down what Peter taught about Jesus. The date of the gospel is somewhat controversial but it is generally thought to have been written after Peter's death between 65 and 70 A.D.. Inasmuch as Jerusalem and its temple were destroyed in 70 A.D., Jesus' prophecy of its fate in Mk. 13:3 may have been a *post hoc* interpolation. Since prophecy plays such an important role in the New as well as Old Testament it is essential to know that the authors who put these prophecies into written language had a specific purpose in mind and that they were influenced by the then current political situations. Prophecies were not uttered for the distant future, but to either threaten or console contemporaries. Unless the historical events involving the times of the various prophets are known, to the extent we have information on them, incorrect conclusions will be reached. This will be discussed in more detail later on. The main model for the characterization of Jesus was Isaiah and he was referred to in the very beginning of Mark's first chapter.

Biblical scholars have established, however, that the book of Isaiah does not come from a single author. Chapters 1-39 are ascribed to Isaiah the son of Amoz, as he called himself, while chapters 40-66 were written by an unnamed author who is referred to as Deutero-Isaiah (the second Isaiah). Some scholars believe that chapters 56-66 were written by still another author, referred to as Trito-Isaiah (the third Isaiah). This subdivision of 40-66 is not relevant for our purposes but the difference between Isaiah and Deutero-Isaiah, abbreviated 2 Isaiah, is highly important. These two sections are separated by a span of about 150 years. The scrolls of Isaiah, the son of Amoz, end with King Hezekiah in chapter 39, while the chapters beginning with 40 refer to the imminent conquest of Babylon by Cyrus of Persia and the anticipated return of the Jews to Jerusalem. Thus when 2 Isaiah started out chapter 40 with "Comfort, Comfort My people saith God" he was not talking about a distant future but an imminent event about to occur. The importance of 2 Isaiah for the Christian religion cannot be overemphasized because the Jewish people, living under Roman rule, assumed that these verses foreshadowed the end-times which were about to happen. In this way the word became flesh, to use St. John's terminology, and prophecies became in part self-fulfilling.

But the author of 2 Isaiah, in the sixth century B.C. also had, in all probability, a model which he changed to fit into the existing Jewish belief system. The Persian state religion of the time was based on the doctrines of Zarathustra, also called Zoroaster. The essence of his teachings can be summarized as follows:

Ahura Mazda (Ormuzd), which translates into the All-Wise Lord, is the supreme and only God who has created heaven and earth. He is the source of alternating light and darkness; he originated the moral order, and is judge of the world. He is also the father of twins: *Spenta Mainyu* (the Holy or Virtuous Spirit), and *Angra Mainyu* or Ahriman (The Evil Spirit), who is bent on destruction and subversion of the moral order. *Angra Mainyu's* main epithet is

Druj (the Lie). *Angra Mainyu* was expelled from heaven with his followers. They now live in hell but with access to our world where they are engaged in perverting the human race. Human beings are free to choose between following *Ahura Mazda* or *Angra Mainyu*. All thoughts and deeds of an individual are kept in a book of life. This is brought forth at time of death when the good aspects will be balanced against the evil ones. Those whose righteous conduct outweighs their sins will be rewarded by entering into a paradisiacal realm, while evildoers are condemned to regions of darkness, horror and despair. The total duration of the universe is 12000 years and life evolves in four cycles of 3000 years. The first cycle existed only in the mind of God. The second involved the creation of the material world; the third was characterized by the battle between the forces of good and evil. At the beginning of the fourth cycle Zarathustra appeared as the herald of truth who announced that the ultimate judgment was about to occur. This event would be preceded by wars, rebellions and a variety of natural disasters. At the end-time the final battle between the forces of good and evil, also described as those of light and darkness, would take place under the leadership of Astwaderata - the Son of Man - born of the virgin Eredafedhri, who is the *saoshyant* or savior. *Angra Mainyu*, the father of lies, would be overcome in a fiery cataclysm, evil would be eradicated for all time and the human race would then live in righteousness, joy, and happiness forever.

It is apparent that these ideas are closely related to Jewish apocalyptic thought, especially as expressed in the books of Daniel, Esdras, Enoch and the Dead Sea Scrolls. From them they made their way into the gospels. But let us not forget that they entered into Jewish awareness from Persia via Babylon. It is of interest to note in this connection that the term "Holy Spirit" occurred for the first time in 2 Isaiah, rather than in earlier biblical books. It should also be remembered that only a fraction of the deportees returned to Jerusalem, after they were permitted to do so by Cyrus, and Babylon became a renowned center for Jewish learning. Amalgamation of different religious ideas became unavoidable. It seems likely that the author of 2 Isaiah added Ahura-Mazda's stature to that of Yahweh who now became confirmed as the Lord of the Universe for ever more. Nevertheless, the favorite status of Israel as the Lord's Chosen People was retained and continuity could be preserved.

This was not the first time in Jewish history where another deity's properties were incorporated into the Jewish belief system as has been shown in *The Moses Legacy*. Not only did the words "Holy Spirit" occur for the first time in Old Testament writings during the Babylonian captivity, so did "Son of man" or "Son of Man." The term "son of man" shows up first and only once in 2 Isaiah 56:2 with an everyday human meaning. But Ezekiel, who also prophesied during the Babylonian captivity, is addressed by the Lord practically one hundred times as "Son of man," when he is charged with his prophetic mission. In Daniel the term shows up twice. Once in reference to Daniel's prophetic role and another time in 7:13 where ". . . one coming with the clouds of heaven, as the Son of man, and he came on to the Ancient of days, and was brought near to him . . ." when an "everlasting dominion" was given him over all nations, tribes and languages. This has clearly Zoroastrian overtones.

The excursion into Old Testament history is important because the gospel writers followed the pattern. There was strong reliance on 2 Isaiah, as well as on other prophetic, especially apocalyptic, literature. Many key phrases can be found there, except that they were now applied to Jesus as the Chosen of the Lord, rather than to the nation of Israel.

There is one more point which needs to be made. It applies to all gospels and deals with the word Jew(s), which can refer either to the inhabitants of Judea as opposed, for instance, to Galileans, or to an adherent of the Jewish religion. Some authors have failed to make this differentiation and this has given rise to confusion.

Chapter 1

After these preliminaries we can now look at Mark's gospel in detail. The first chapter not only sets the stage but also shows the method which was used. Mark starts the gospel with a quote:

As it is written in the prophet Isaiah, See I am sending my messenger ahead of you, who will prepare your way.

The voice of one crying out in the wilderness: 'Prepare the way of the Lord, make his paths straight.'

The Zondervan Amplified Bible provides references. The first sentence is attributed to Malachi 3:1 and the second sentence to Is. 40:3. Malachi when quoted in entirety states:

> Behold, I send forth my messenger, and he shall survey the way before me: and the Lord whom ye seek, shall suddenly come into his temple, even the angel of his covenant, whom ye take pleasure in: behold he is coming, saith the Lord Almighty

Isaiah 40:3 reads:

> The voice of one crying in the wilderness, Prepare ye the way of the Lord, make straight the paths of our God.

But context is always the most important aspect and is provided in the preceding verses 40:1-2:

> Comfort ye, comfort ye my people, saith God. Speak, ye priests, to the heart of Jerusalem; comfort her, for her humiliation is accomplished, her sin is put away: for she has received of the Lord's hand double the amount of her sins.

This casts a different light on the situation. The prophet reassured the Jews in Babylon that "Jerusalem," meaning the nation of Israel, had been sufficiently punished, and the Lord would now redeem her. The Jews were no longer a sinful nation which needed to fear the future but the "good news," was that the troubles were over forever. While this was temporarily the hope among the exiles, by the time of John the Baptist the Jews lived again under foreign occupation and rebellion simmered. Thus 2 Isaiah's words were given a different meaning to indicate that his "good news," the "*eu*aggélion" (Evangelium), was now about to come to pass in the person of Jesus.

Malachi is the last of the so called Twelve Prophets and his book is dated to the period of the second temple while Judea was under Persian suzerainty around 460 B.C.. The purpose of the book was to castigate the loose morals of the priesthood, which either neglected sacrifices altogether or offered impure ones. The common people who cheated, assimilated with heathens and divorced their wives were also chastised, and urged to repent. Malachi's book, when translated from Hebrew, ends in the Socino edition with the following verses:

> Behold I will send you Elijah the prophet before the coming of the great and terrible day of the Lord.
> And he shall turn the heart of the fathers to the children, and the heart of the children to their fathers; lest I come and smite the land with utter destruction [3:23, 24].

Mark, therefore, used Malachi to introduce the idea that John the Baptist was the expected Elijah who would herald the Messiah, Jesus, and the imminent Day of Judgment.

Mark continued with John the Baptist's preaching repentance and absolution from past sins. Immersion into the water of the Jordan was supposed to symbolize the cleansing (*baptison*) from sin. We are not told who John was and whether or not he had known Jesus, but I shall offer a conjecture later on. The gospel does inform us that a great many people from Judea and Jerusalem came to listen to John and to undergo baptism. John clearly saw himself as the herald of the coming kingdom of God but he emphasized that he was not to be regarded as the expected Messiah, merely his forerunner. One who was stronger and worthier was about to follow. While he, John, was washing away the sins with water, the expected one would do so with the fire of the Holy Spirit. In the immediately following sentence we are told that Jesus, a Galilean from Nazareth, came and was baptized by John. Mark provides no information about the genealogy of Jesus, his schooling, profession, or how long Jesus might have been listening to John's teachings. But something profound happened to Jesus after his immersion in the Jordan.

"And immediately upon coming out of the water, he saw the heavens opened and the spirit like a dove descending towards him. And there was a voice out of the heavens, you are my son the beloved, with you I am well pleased." The word "beloved" is in Greek *agapētós* and the Latin translation also always uses *dilectus*, rather than *amatus*. Throughout the gospels the Greek as well as Latin words which are rendered in English as love or beloved had additional meanings such as: chosen, prized, highly esteemed, which place them in a spiritual rather than physical context.

How can one try to comprehend an event of this nature? There can hardly be any doubt that Jesus was well versed in scripture and he had probably internalized a great many sayings. Memory was much more highly prized in olden days than now, and even I still had to learn major aspects of classic literature by heart during my school years. The Bible does not tell us where Jesus got his biblical education but I will offer a suggestion later on. For now it suffices to state that, as is apparent from the gospels, he was thoroughly familiar with the contents and prophecies of the Bible.

The Amplified Bible provides Psalm 2:7 and Is. 42:1 as references for Jesus' experience. The Psalm when placed in context by also quoting verse 6 states "But I have been made king by him on Sion his holy mountain, declaring the ordinances of the Lord: the Lord said to me, Thou art my Son to-day have I begotten thee." Thus the "Son" who had been begotten was either David or Israel, and the immediately following verses 2:8-9 have an ominous ring for our time, "Ask of me, and I will give thee the heathen for thine inheritance, and the ends of the earth for thy possession. Thou shalt rule them with a rod of iron; thou shalt dash them in pieces as a potter's vessel." While Christians may interpret 2:8 that Jesus' spiritual kingdom will extend to the ends of the earth, Jewish nationalists may well take these verses literally as a prophetic promise to be enacted.

Isaiah 42:1 reads in the Septuagint version, "Jacob is my servant, I will help him: Israel is my chosen, my soul has accepted him; I have put my spirit upon him; he shall bring forth judgment to the Gentiles." The Hebrew version and the English Bibles derived therefrom are more circumspect and merely say "Behold my servant ..." When one is familiar with these passages it seems likely that the gospel writer had taken them from their original context and applied them to Jesus who was henceforth God's Son, rather than to David or Israel. These verses, which are typical for how the gospel writers took Old Testament passages to make them fit new expectations, unfortunately also make it clear that a genuine accord between the

Christian and Jewish religion is not likely to be achievable. Jews will be loath to give up what they regard as their birthright and may well continue to insist that the Church has interpreted their holy writ erroneously.

Nevertheless, we have to admit that, although the details are open to question, something profound had happened to Jesus. I am inclined to believe that he was granted what Bucke has called *Cosmic Consciousness*. This experience occurs very infrequently but is at the root of all great religions. Moses experienced God in the Burning Bush. Siddartha Gautama, the Buddha, received his revelation while meditating under what has been called the Bodhi tree. Paul was visited on the road to Damascus, and Mohammed received his message through the angel Gabriel while in a cave. As mentioned, the phenomenon is exceedingly rare and tends to happen to people, who are confronted with a spiritual crisis, in their early or mid-thirties. The experience cannot be achieved by will power but is an act of pure grace. The person who is exposed to it knows all of a sudden in his whole being "oh this is what it's all about!" The universe is a beautiful orderly whole from which one is no longer "apart" but of which one is both one part as well as the whole. It is an experience of indescribable beauty, wholeness, wholesomeness, accompanied by profound joy, awe, and gratitude. Since words are only inadequate symbols for feelings this will have to suffice to provide at least a minimum of understanding. Dr. Bucke's book is well worth reading because it grants insights into a sphere most of us are not aware of and will be discussed in greater detail in another chapter and the Conclusions of this book.

The gospel writer wanted to convey that the revelation came not with a mind shattering thunderclap but instead in a kind, gentle way "like a dove." The symbol of the dove, in relation to Jesus, whose main message turned out to be not the fire and brimstone of the Old Testament but love, is most appropriate since it was also the symbol of Aphrodite in her capacity of heavenly rather than erotic love.

But Jesus was still human and shaken to the depth of his soul by what had transpired in his mind. Back on dry land he needed to be alone to sort things out or as Mark put it, "and the spirit immediately drove him out into the wilderness." We are then told that Jesus stayed there for forty days and nights but this does not need to be taken literally. All biblical authors use the number forty when a long period of time is meant. The desert near the Jordan is rampant with caves and this is where Jesus probably took refuge. During that time he was tried, also translated as tested, by Satan (adversary) but the angels (messengers of God) took care of him. What this tells us is that he was thoroughly perturbed and beset by doubts. Who was he, a poor country boy from Galilee, which was regarded by Jews (inhabitants of Judea) similar to how New Yorkers feel about Appalachia, that he should be chosen for a role which only those of noble birth and rank could aspire to? It must have been an illusion, it couldn't have been real. As is written in Buddhist literature, "Doubt is a sword that kills" and Satan is always ready to lend a helping hand. But there were also the angels who told Jesus: don't listen to your doubts, the experience was not a fantasy, this is what you were born for and we are here with you to help you carry out your appointed task. Pray diligently and you will be told at each step of the way what you are expected to do next. It appears likely that Jesus now felt he had to take up Ezekiel's mission whose orders by the Lord had been:

> Son of man, I send thee forth to the house of Israel, them that provoke me; who have provoked me, they and their fathers, to this day. And thou shalt say to them, Thus saith the Lord. Whether then indeed they shall hear or fear (for it is a provoking house,) yet they shall know that thou art a prophet in the midst of them [2: 3-5].

When Jesus had reached this understanding he joined civilization again. Mark does not tell us whether or not Jesus had an opportunity to discuss with John what had happened because it is merely stated that after John was arrested, Jesus went to Galilee to preach the good news and the imminent arrival of the kingdom of God. We are not given details but from the foregoing it is likely that he taught the message contained in Isaiah and that the predictions were now coming true. He also knew that in order for his ministry to succeed he needed helpers. The fishermen Simon (Peter) and his brother Andrew were the first to be called to his side followed by James and

John the sons of Zebedee, who were likewise in the fishing business. This small band was now to become "fishers of men."

By this time Jesus noted that he was indeed imbued with the Holy Spirit and in the synagogue in Capernaum he taught on the Sabbath with "authority" and not like the scribes. The Greek term *grammateús* is usually translated as scribe but Bible commentators feel that these people functioned basically as the "lawyers" for religious doctrinal disputes. The Pharisees had declared that oral traditions were co-equal with the "written Torah" and numerous injunctions had been levied upon the people. It was the function of the scribes, together with the Pharisees, to interpret ambiguous religious commandments and to bring the ancient written laws into conformity with the requirements of urban life. Just like the Pharisees, they were not priests but lay persons and their function was combined, after the destruction of the temple, with that of the priests, since temple services no longer existed. In this way they became today's rabbis.

Apart from teaching, Jesus now manifested his power to heal the bodies and minds of those who were afflicted with a variety of illnesses. He did so with kind, but authoritative affirmations and his personal "aura," if we may use this term, was such that people believed and did indeed feel better. Every physician knows that a great many illnesses are self-inflicted through bad habits, or they can result from faulty thinking. In modern parlance they are "psychosomatic." When Jesus "drove out evil spirits," he was the true psychotherapist *par excellence*. Most of us don't realize that a psychotherapist, if he lived up to the name of his profession, is supposed to be a healer of the soul. Our materialistic society has done away with the soul (psyche), replaced it with the mind, and charges money for what priests used to do in the confessional. We can deny the soul, just as we can deny Satan and God but they still exist and can create havoc, or bring solace to our lives. With the term "psychosomatic" we have actually re-affirmed the power of the soul over the body and if the soul can be healed by expulsion of faulty thinking patterns the body may follow suit.

Everybody has aches and pains, as well as obsessions he/she might want to get rid of. It is, therefore, no wonder that Jesus was mobbed, especially since he didn't charge for his services. Every physician who sees numerous strangers in clinical practice every day also knows how emotionally draining this type of work can be, and it is hardly surprising that Jesus intermittently had to withdraw into solitude to, figuratively speaking, recharge his batteries through communion with God in prayer.

While many illnesses show no outward manifestations and relief may, therefore, be more subjective or temporary, there are others which are more problematic and this brings us to the story of the leper with which Mark's first chapter closes. Since the story sheds some light on Jesus' feelings at the time let me paraphrase it first for content. A leper approached Jesus, fell to his knees and begged him to be cleansed with the words, "If you choose, you can make me clean." Jesus touched the man and said, "I do choose, be clean!" Then he charged the fellow not to say anything about it to anybody but to go to the priest and follow the necessary sacrifices to certify the cure. The "leprosy" disappeared but instead of doing what he had been ordered by Jesus and subjecting himself to the required ritual, as described in Lev. 14:2-32, the man started making speeches far and wide. We don't know what he said because translations vary. The Greek text says he "began to preach many things and to spread the word." Even the Latin text is ambiguous, *"coepit praedicare multum et diffamare sermonem."* This would suggest that he began not only to talk about the event but used defamatory language. We are left wondering, however, who was being defamed. Had "the man" simply pretended to have leprosy, duped Jesus, and now bragged about what he had done? Or did he argue against the priests and that the Law of Moses was no longer relevant? In either case it was a problem for Jesus who felt that he should not show himself in the towns and retreated instead to small communities. The cynical saying that no good deed goes unpunished was manifested here. But the story also shows that Jesus at that point, in the beginning of his ministry, did not scorn Mosaic Law. The matter was too serious and he did not want trouble.

Chapter 2

In the second chapter Jesus had returned to Capernaum where he stayed in Peter's house and continued with his mission of healing the sick and preaching the word of God. Large crowds arrived and they also brought someone who was paralyzed and had to be carried by four people on a litter. When they couldn't get through the crowd they lowered him down from the roof. When Jesus saw their faith he said, "Son, your sins are forgiven." The Greek text actually uses the word *téknon*, which refers to a "young one" or "little child" and leaves the gender undefined, but this is a minor point. What matters is that with the words, *"your sins are forgiven,"* Jesus had crossed another threshold. Immediately the scribes murmured: who is this blaspheming fellow? Only God can forgive sins! But there was no longer equivocation in Jesus' mind as to who he was and he told them, "Which is easier to say to the paralytic 'your sins are forgiven' or to say 'stand up, take your mat and walk?'" To make it quite clear he added, "But so that you may know that the Son of Man has authority on earth to forgive sins I say to you [the paralyzed one] stand up, take your mat and go to your home." The patient did so; the onlookers were amazed, and praised God. Another miracle had been witnessed but the fateful words "Son of Man" had been uttered, the Rubicon had been crossed and return into obscurity was no longer an option.

The next affront to the establishment came when Jesus walked alongside the lake, saw Levi, the son of Alpheus, sitting in his tax collector's office and said, "Follow me." Levi, who has subsequently been identified with Matthew, immediately got up and not only went with him but took Jesus to his house, where they feasted in company of Levi's friends, other tax collectors and "sinners." This was, of course, scandalous behavior in the eyes of observant Jews. Not only did Jesus consort with "riff-raff," the outcasts of society, and those who did the bidding of the Romans by collecting their taxes, but he also showed blatant disregard of the Jewish dietary laws, which were a cornerstone of the Law of Moses. When scribes asked Jesus why he did so he merely told them that only the sick need a physician rather than healthy people and the same applies in regard to moral life. The righteous could get along without his help but the sinners needed to be called to repentance.

Thereafter Mark reports that the Pharisees and their disciples as well as those of John observed a fast while Jesus' disciples failed to do so. When Jesus was asked why this should be the case he told them that as long as the bridegroom is present the attendants don't go about fasting, but they will do so once the groom has left. In order to affirm that a new era had dawned he added that one doesn't patch old clothes with a new piece and one doesn't pour new wine into old wineskins lest they burst. Parenthetically one might add that this is actually what happened to his message later on.

While these were relatively harmless statements the next episode was critical. On a Sabbath, Jesus and the disciples were walking along a grain field and some of them began to pluck from the stalks. The Pharisees immediately challenged Jesus with: Look at what they are doing. You know that this is not lawful on a Sabbath. But Jesus knew his Bible and quoted a precedent. In the early days of his career David and a group of his followers had come into the house of a priest asking for bread. When David was told that there was none to be had but the bread on the altar, which was holy, David and his people were allowed to eat it. Since this was a biblical quote of 1 Sam. 21:6 there wouldn't have been much of an argument but Jesus wanted to drive home a point and added that the Sabbath was made for man and not vice versa. This was clearly an affront to priestly authority and as if to add insult to injury Jesus continued with, "So the Son of Man is even Lord of the Sabbath."

Let us summarize what had happened: Jesus was regarded as having violated the oral tradition, which governed the lives of common people and was enforced by the Pharisees, on four counts. 1) He had arrogated unto himself the privilege of remitting sins, which was God's prerogative. 2) He had disregarded the dietary laws. 3) He had profaned the Sabbath. 4) He had declared himself as the Son of Man. This was a title which was regarded as belonging to the Messiah who would usher in the kingdom of God. For the religious establishment the gauntlet had been thrown down, this was blasphemy and could not be tolerated. Nevertheless, the authorities wanted to bide their time and see if Jesus would continue with this type of provocative behavior.

Chapter 3

From chapter 3 on there is not necessarily a strict chronologic order until we come to the trial and death of Jesus. There are some non sequiturs and duplications which were inevitable if Mark merely jotted down comments made by Peter as they were talking about Jesus' message and a strict chronology should not be expected. In addition the gospel writer may also have conflated other accounts. The main content of chapter 3 consists of several distinct stories. First comes the healing of a man who had a withered hand, then Jesus was mobbed by the crowd in search of healing, demons declared him the "Son of God," the twelve apostles were selected from all of the people who had followed him, his family regarded him as mentally ill, the scribes said he was possessed by the devil, and eventually his mother and the rest of the family wanted to get him out of a house where he was teaching but he ignored them.

Let us now look at key aspects. For the healing of the man with the withered hand there was a precedent in 1 Kg. 13:1-7. Rehoboam, the first King of Israel after Solomon's realm had been divided, had erected an unauthorized altar at Beth-el and was about to use it for a sacrifice. An unnamed prophet of Yahweh arrived and predicted that a child would be born out of the house of David, by name of Josiah, who would sacrifice the false priests on it. As a sign that this was true the prophet said that the altar would be rent apart and its ashes scattered. When Rehoboam heard this he stretched out his hand to order his attendants to grab hold of the prophet but immediately his hand "dried up" and the altar was rent. When the king prayed that his hand might be restored the prophet complied and it was so.

In the present context the important aspect is, however, that the healing took place on the Sabbath and Jesus had directly challenged the crowd with the question: whether or not it was lawful to do good on the Sabbath. When the crowd remained silent Jesus became angry and ordered the man to stretch out his hand, which was immediately made whole. To the Pharisees this must have smacked of sorcery, which was clearly forbidden under Mosaic law and they therefore conspired with "Herodians" how they might "destroy" Jesus. From that day on his fate was sealed and the only questions were: when and how? It is significant that already at this point the Pharisees did not want to be seen as acting on their own but began to enlist what was called in the Middle Ages "the secular arm of the Church." The most famous example is, of course, the trial and execution of Joan of Arc. The Bible does not define the "Herodians" but it is reasonable to assume that these were people loyal to Herod, who owed his throne to the Romans and here is the first hint that Roman power would eventually be used to execute Jesus. Some modern Biblical commentators point out that all anti-Jewish comments, especially those against the Pharisees are late anti-Semitic insertions. It is claimed that Jesus was actually not only a Pharisee but a zealot engaged in active anti-Roman campaigns and was crucified on account of these activities rather than for the conflict with Jewish orthodoxy. Since whoever writes about Jesus, regardless of academic degree and other accomplishments, has only the gospels to work with, I cannot agree with these opinions because support is lacking. The affront to Jewish orthodoxy was clearly sufficient to warrant a death sentence.

As mentioned previously, Jesus had referred to himself as "Son of Man" with the implication that he might be the Messiah, but when people who were possessed by "demons" called him the "Son of God," which was unequivocally the Messiah's title, he vigorously forbade them to say so. The time had not yet come because an assertion of this nature would have immediately terminated his ministry.

The selection of the twelve disciples is straight forward narrative and needs little comment. The number twelve did not only figuratively signify the twelve tribes of Israel, but there were also twelve signs of the celestial zodiac which held universal significance in the ancient world. What does require some elaboration is the general feeling by friends, family and enemies that Jesus was insane. I shall take the family first. Jesus had certainly behaved in a highly unusual manner and during the healing of the man's hand he is reported as having been quite angry with the crowd for their "hardness of heart." It takes little imagination how he might have appeared to the people at that time. Religious furor is not pleasant to watch. The family, therefore, wanted to get him to safety before something drastic happened. Who can blame them for thinking that he had lost his mind? When the family physically showed up at the house where he was teaching and wanted to be let in he refused to see them and merely pointed to his listeners as being his family. It was not blood relationship which counted. Henceforth family was to be defined by whoever does the will of God. This need not be seen as vindictive but was established practice in other religions. In order to reach Enlightenment, in Buddhism for instance, it was best to become a "homeless brother." All attachments to family, property, etc., had to be abandoned before one could join Buddha's disciples, with Buddha himself having provided the model.

For the Pharisees, Jesus was not just crazy but he was possessed by the devil, Beelzebub. This led to the famous passage that a house divided against itself cannot stand and if Satan were to make war against himself that would be the end of him. Apparently the Pharisees had accused Jesus to his face of blasphemy and this is why he retorted that all sins can be forgiven, even blasphemy, but whoever blasphemes against the Holy Spirit can never be forgiven, not in this world nor in the next. With other words: you can say whatever you want about me, but don't dare to raise your voice against the Holy Spirit. Jesus seems to be also saying that when you accuse me of having an "unclean spirit" you have transgressed this fundamental rule. You can call me mad or whatever but don't ever offend the One who speaks through me.

There is another comment that can be made before leaving this chapter. Mark shows us that Jesus was not only the meek, mild mannered individual we tend to hear about, but he was also given to occasional outbursts of anger. It will become increasingly obvious that he didn't suffer fools gladly, as the saying goes. This had been hinted at in the previous chapter because some translations state that he looked with anger rather than pity at the "leper" before he had healed him. But in the current chapter it is made explicit when he challenged the crowd with the question whether or not it was lawful to do good on the Sabbath.

Chapter 4

We are now introduced to parables; Jesus' reason for using them, and the disciples' inability to understand. The first one is the well known story of the sower who goes out and spreads the seed. Some of it falls along the road where the birds pick it up, some falls on rocky ground where it withers when the sun comes out, some falls among briers and is choked out, while other seed falls on fertile soil and brings forth an abundance of harvest. Jesus ended by saying, "let anyone with ears to hear listen." The disciples did have ears but didn't understand and had to ask what he meant. The reply is important because it can be readily misunderstood. First he told them that they were the elect to whom the secret of the kingdom of God was being entrusted, while the rest of the people were not expected to understand the meaning of the parables. "In order that they may indeed look, but not perceive, and may indeed listen, but not understand; so that they may not turn again and be forgiven." This must surely strike one as strange reasoning. If the goal of the mission was to convert sinners and bring them to God why should they be prevented from understanding the message? The reason becomes clear when one knows that Jesus was quoting Isaiah 6:9-10

Before giving the exact quote from the Hebrew translation as contained in the *Socino Chumash* the context has to be explained. Isaiah had a vision where he saw God on His throne with the seraphim in attendance. Isaiah called out in anguish "Woe is me! for I am undone . . ." The implication was that having seen the Lord of hosts, the day of judgment had arrived and that Isaiah would now be condemned for his sins. But a seraph came, touched his lips with a burning piece of coal from the altar and told him that his sins had been expiated. Then Isaiah heard the Lord say, "Whom shall I send and who will go for us?" Isaiah volunteered and said, "Here am I; send me." Then the Lord said:

> Go and tell this people:
> Hear ye indeed, but understand not; See ye indeed, but perceive not.

Make the heart of this people fat, And make their ears heavy,
And shut their eyes;
Lest they, seeing with their eyes,
And hearing with their ears,
And understanding with their heart,
Return [to Me] and be healed.

The reason for this strange statement is given in verses 11-13. Isaiah asked how long this state of affairs would persist. The answer was: until the land had been utterly devastated and the people had been removed. But there would be a small remnant left from whose "holy seed" renewal would eventually come. Thus the fall of Jerusalem and Babylonian captivity were meant here. This fate was inevitable because the people were too steeped in sin and the land had to be thoroughly cleansed. Nevertheless, eventually redemption would take place.

For Jesus the meaning of the quoted passage was obvious but the disciples, who were not yet imbued with the Holy Spirit, were bewildered. Jesus had overestimated their capacity for understanding and asked, possibly somewhat annoyed: don't you understand what this parable means? If you can't even understand this simple one how can you understand all the others? He then patiently explained that the seed is the word of God. In most people it finds no resonance and does not lead to permanent results. But when the recipient understands what is meant, the word would bear abundant fruit. The choice of the word "seed" is also important. In the Old Testament "seed" refers to blood related offspring. It has a material meaning and Isaiah also used it in this sense. Jesus, on the other hand, was a thoroughly spiritual person. To understand him we must leave the material sphere and turn to that of the spirit.

This is why Jesus told the apostles: pay close attention to what you hear and try to understand it. All will be revealed in time because there is nothing hidden that will not be brought to daylight. Unless one does so the next sentence can also readily be misunderstood, "For to him who has, will be given and from whom who has not even what he has will be taken away." With other words: once you begin to comprehend what the kingdom of God really is, your understanding will grow; but those who have only a dim awareness and act on that will lose it all in the end. There is actually a parallel in the Dhammapada, the Pali translation of Buddha's words:

> Even though throughout his life
> A childish one attends on a wise person,
> He does not perceive [thereby] dhamma,
> As a ladle, the flavor of the dish.

A childish individual, one who regards himself as clever without being so, will never understand the true teaching; just as a spoon which stirs the pot will never know the flavor of the soup. This is but one example of numerous others that could be cited to show the essential congruence of Jesus' and Buddha's words.

Jesus went on to explain that for the kingdom of God to take root and bear fruit in their souls they must be patient. Just as the farmer has to be before he can reap the harvest. With the mustard seed parable, which is the smallest of all seeds yet produces a large tree useful for birds to nest in and providing shade, he might have told the people: Don't be arrogant and disdainful, all great things have small beginnings.

In the evening, to get away from the crowd Jesus told the disciples: let's go sailing! A little flotilla went out, but he was exhausted and went to sleep in the stern of one of the boats. A storm came up and the sailors became afraid that the boats would be swamped. They awakened him; he looked around, "rebuked" the wind and said to the waves "be still." Wind and waves abated to the utter astonishment of the disciples, who wondered how Jesus could have power even over the elements. But for him, to put it colloquially, it was no big deal. "Why are you afraid have you still no faith?" The ending of the chapter with a major miracle over the forces of nature sets the stage for the next one in which only miracles are brought to our attention.

Chapter 5

We are now confronted with a major challenge to our scientific era because this chapter deals exclusively with supernatural occurrences. To achieve even a modicum of understanding of what might have transpired we have to keep human nature and the mission of the apostles in mind. As far as human nature is concerned all of us know that exaggerations are a daily fact of life. The fish which has been caught gets bigger with each retelling and so do the difficulties one has successfully overcome when told to an audience years later. Not only is memory fallible but the need to gild the lily is a universal fact of life and even scientists have to guard against it.

In addition we have to recognize the purpose for which Mark wrote his gospel. He had to convince the Greco-Roman world that the crucified Jesus was not only the Jewish Messiah, who had risen from the dead, but was also the Son of the Ruler of the Universe and thereby the redeemer of all humanity. This was certainly a tall order and the later statement, "*credo quia absurdum*" by Tertullian, "I believe because it is unreasonable," is not likely to have carried much weight among the intelligentsia. As Goethe wrote, "*Das Wunder ist des Glaubens liebstes Kind*," the miracle is faith's most beloved child. There had to be miracles to achieve credibility. It is as simple as that: no miracle, no Christianity. But there were precedents, just as for everything else. Jewish written and oral tradition was replete with miracles. Practically everybody knows of Moses parting the Red Sea, Manna arriving from heaven, a staff turning into a snake and back again as well as numerous other examples which demonstrate Yahweh's power. We are, however, less familiar with the glorious deeds of Abraham, Moses, and Jacob as related in the oral legends of the Jewish people. These have been preserved in the Talmud.

For instance, how many of us know that Abraham had to undergo several tests, before he became worthy of the benefits the Lord provided him with as related in the biblical prophecies. The first one occurred immediately after his birth because the secular powers in charge of the country wanted to kill him. Abraham hid himself under the earth for thirteen years and saw neither sun nor moon. When he emerged he could immediately speak the holy language (Hebrew), experienced a profound distaste for the worship of idols in the country and sought refuge with the creator. The second test was that he was thrown into jail for ten years. After that he was to be burned to death in a kiln, but the Almighty stretched out his hand and rescued him. The third test was that Abraham had to leave his home and move to Haran where his parents died. The narrator added, "Harder than everything else is to be homeless." Subsequently we are told that it was "the godless" Nimrod who had thrown Abraham into the kiln and it was Gabriel who told the Lord that he would go down and rescue Abraham, the just. The Lord, however, said, "I am unique in my world and he is unique in his, therefore, it is appropriate that a unique one, rescues another unique one." Another variant of the story relates that when the Lord was ready to come down in person to rescue Abraham, His host said, "Lord of the world! This one you want to save? Just think how many godless ones will be descended from him. But the Lord said: for Jacob his son's sake, who will be derived from him, will I save him." The narrator explained: The crown of the just one is his grandchildren.

There are numerous other examples of this type of legends in the Talmud. For instance: when Isaac was born, many deaf people regained hearing, many blind people regained sight and many who were insane became normal. Also the sun shone 48 times brighter on that day. On the other hand the cruelties of the Egyptians before Moses was born were truly appalling. After Pharaoh's well known edict to kill all newborn males, the pregnant Hebrew women went into the fields to give birth and then returned home leaving the newborns in the field. But God sent an angel who washed each child, anointed it, wrapped it in sheets and gave each one two stones. From one of them the child sucked milk and from the other honey. The mercy of the Lord then ordered the earth to open her mouth and they remained underground. The Egyptians plowed the fields but couldn't harm the children who prospered underground until they emerged fully grown into daylight to return to the homes of their fathers.

During the years of persecution the Egyptians were even more cruel. Whenever there were not enough bricks the overseers tore Hebrew babies from their mother's breasts and the fathers had to use them instead of bricks. Moses was likewise endowed with supernatural powers above and beyond those reported in the Bible. For instance when he and Aaron first came to see Pharaoh to ask for the release of their people the door to the palace was guarded by two young, fierce, chained lions. If Pharaoh wanted to see someone he sent his magicians down who whispered to the lions and thereby tamed them. Moses, on the other hand, simply waved his staff over the lions, released them from their chains and they bounced after him like happy puppies. No wonder that Pharaoh was deeply impressed; even more so because Moses' and Aaron's faces shone like angels from God. Nevertheless, he did not accede to their request to let the Hebrews go, but just told them to come back the next day.

These stories have been collected in *Die Sagen der Juden* (Legends of the Jews) which is a sizeable volume of 1167 pages. They were the Jewish folk milieu the gospel writers were familiar with. When one is aware of them, Jesus' miracles seem far less elaborate and are certainly a great deal less vindictive.

Let us take the first one where the madman's evil spirits were sent into the Gadarene swine who threw themselves, like lemmings, off a cliff. The locale of this miracle varies between translations. The King James Version has Gadarene while the Greek and Latin text has Gesarines. Gadar as well as Gesar were towns southeast from the Sea of Galilee. But since Gadar is only about 6 miles from the shore and Gesar about 35 miles, it is more likely that the event took place in the vicinity of Gadar. As far as the demon possessed individual is concerned, who had addressed Jesus as the Son of the Most High God; he had his counterpart in any of our psychiatric wards prior to the discovery of tranquilizers. These noisy unfortunates had indeed to be shackled, which created further howls of distress and there was no treatment available. In the days when body, mind and soul were one, the idea that the person was possessed by a demon was hardly far fetched. The only cure was exorcism and that is what Jesus did. But in this particular instance the unclean spirit was not simply evicted but given to a herd of swine which promptly committed suicide by drowning themselves. One could spin numerous fantasies over the mechanisms or meanings of this event but I must humbly confess to ignorance since my limited information about the spirit world does not lend itself to a rational approach. The only aspect of the miracle which can be rationally understood is that in this instance Jesus did not tell the cured one to be quiet about it but rather to proclaim the miracle openly. This could be done safely in Decapolis because this loose confederation of ten cities reported directly to the Roman governor of Syria and was not under Jewish jurisdiction. Romans were notoriously liberal in religious matters and another miracle worker would not have been of concern to them.

The second and third miracles namely Jesus feeling "power" going out of him when his robe was touched by the woman with a long standing uterine hemorrhage, and the raising of the daughter of a synagogue chief, are connected and deserve some discussion. What they suggest is that Jesus was not only a psychotherapist *par excellence* but also a supreme clairvoyant. Psychotherapy has already been discussed but we do need to look at clairvoyance and not simply brush it off as nonsense, because the overwhelming majority of people do not have this ability. I believe the phenomenon exists in certain gifted individuals, although they themselves don't know how it comes about. I shall now relate a personal encounter.

Several decades ago I visited the Parapsychology Institute at the University of Utrecht and was told by the Chairman of the Department about his most prominent paragnost Gerard Croiset. Professor ten Haeff, who was a dedicated scientist, said that the people he works with in the field of telepathy and clairvoyance tend to be specialists and in some the faculty develops after a life threatening event. For instance Croiset nearly drowned in childhood and his specialty was locating missing persons, especially drowning victims. In this capacity he had helped the Dutch police on several occasions to recover missing individuals. In addition he had the gift of healing people by what might be called, for lack of a better word, personal magnetism. Later that day, I had the opportunity to meet Croiset in his "office," where a number of people were gathered to be freed of a variety of ailments. I watched him lay his hands on the sufferers and saw satisfied people leaving. When he was done and we were alone I asked him how he did it. Our conversation was handicapped by the fact that he spoke neither German nor English well, and my Dutch was non-existent. Nevertheless, he explained that when he is engaged in healing he experiences a surge of energy as if the water had suddenly been turned on in a garden hose. I did not have any ailments at the time so I didn't ask for a cure and I was also too polite to question the duration of the results. In regard to clairvoyance he explained that when he is asked to look for a victim he sees the location, as if in a dream, but it corresponds to reality. He could not explain it any further than that but he impressed me as a sincere and religious person who does not deliberately lie to people. While I have mental reservations about the "cures" of serious illnesses, I don't doubt that people felt better after having seen him.

Let us now look at the clairvoyance aspect. The fact that he couldn't explain the phenomenon, even if he had been able to use either German or English to perfection, is actually quite reasonable when we consider the following scenario. Let us assume for a moment that we meet with a visitor from outer space who comes from a highly developed civilization. These people are similar to us in all respects except that they don't dream at night. If he were to ask me what I do in order to dream I would have to say I have no idea, the dreams just come. Even with all my neurophysiologic training, which locates the ability to dream to certain brain structures, I still can't turn dreams on or off. Dreams are for us a mystery and the outer-spacer might think we are just making up stories. Thus a good dose of humility is called for when it comes to phenomena beyond our daily experience and this applies also to Jesus' miracles.

If we use the Croiset analogy of the garden hose it is not unreasonable to assume that Jesus could indeed have felt something when that woman intruded unauthorized into his energy field, or the aura, clairvoyants are talking about. James van Praagh wrote a nice book about extrasensory phenomena and from his exposition I get the impression that he is just as sincere a person as Croiset was. Van Praagh explains that he can see the aura around a given person in vivid colors and depending upon the color he gets an impression of what ails an individual. About the claim that he can also see dead relatives standing next to the individual he is counseling, I have to be more skeptical. Whether these are truly the spirits of the departed or is van Praagh reading mental images from his client in a telepathic manner I have no way of knowing.

If van Praagh can discern auras around a person which depend on the state of health of the individual there seems to be no reason why Jesus could not have done so likewise. Thus when he said that the child is not dead he may have had a mental image of the twelve year old, and her "aura," although impaired, was not that of a dead person. The transfusion of one's energy field into that of another person, who is in dire need of it, exists currently only in science-fiction movies but maybe Dr. Crusher's magic wand of Star Trek fame may become reality centuries from now. Let us admit, therefore, that we simply don't know what happened and move on.

Chapter 6

This chapter contains a conflation of several stories. In Nazareth, Jesus' home town, he was greeted with derision and unable to perform major miracles, apart from relieving minor ailments by laying on of hands. Then Jesus sent out the disciples to preach the gospel. When the apostles returned and reported on the major news which included the murder of John the Baptist and the story of how Salome had enticed Herod to have John's head presented to her on a platter. Subsequently comes the miraculous feeding of the five thousand and Jesus walking on the water towards the apostles' boat when they had already shoved off from shore.

There are several interesting aspects. When Jesus taught authoritatively in the synagogue the listeners, who knew him well from former days, were obviously amazed as well as annoyed at what they must have regarded as him having assumed airs which he was not entitled to. "Is this not the carpenter, the son of Mary and are not his brothers and sisters here with us?" they asked. The Greek word *téktōn* is usually translated as "carpenter" but it can also mean joiner or master builder. This is why the Latin version reads, "*nonne iste est faber, filius Mariae . . . ?*" *Faber* is a generic term for any one who works with hard materials and it was usually qualified by another specific term. For instance carpenter would have been *faber lignarius*, a blacksmith *faber ferrarius,* etc. Since neither the Greek nor the Latin version provides a qualifier, Jesus' original occupation cannot be ascertained from the text, but it is really irrelevant. It is not important what one was but only what one becomes!

Of greater interest is why he could not perform miracles in his home town which led to the famous statement that: a prophet is not without honor except in his home country and in his own home. Familiarity breeds contempt we say now and it has always been so. Jesus' miracles depended on faith in God who had to make the audiences' hearts and spirits receptive to His message. What we are told is: No faith - No miracle. This is why Jesus kept saying, "Your faith has healed you!"

There is, however, another aspect which deals with Jesus' paternity. It is unusual for biblical authors not to name the father. Abraham was the son of Terah, Moses was the son of Amram, Joshua was the son of Nun, David was the son of Jesse, Solomon was the son of David and so on. Mark had followed the custom whenever genealogy was mentioned. For instance the Apostles John and James were the sons of Zebedee, and Levi the son of Alphaeus. Yet Jesus, as far as Mark is concerned, was the son of Mary. This is a departure from tradition and suggests that the identity of the biologic father may have been uncertain, which will be discussed further later on.

After his failure in Nazareth Jesus retreated into the country and it is likely that he may have experienced serious doubts about his ministry. Nazareth had been a major setback and there was no sense denying it to himself. It seems that he needed to be alone again and this is why he sent the apostles out to teach for the time being, rather than to continue personally. Only communion with God in solitude could give him the needed sense of direction for the future. After he had given the apostles power and authority to drive out unclean spirits he ordered them not to take anything on the road with them except for sandals, a single tunic and a walking stick. They should not be taking a knapsack, and not even bread or money on their trip. Instead he told them that they were to enter people's homes and remain there for some time, while they taught and healed. But if they were not accepted and listened to they should shake the dust off their feet as a testimony against the people living there. The potential significance of this passage will become apparent later.

Subsequently, Mark tells us that the apostles were successful in driving out unclean spirits and healing the sick and that the people regarded Jesus as the re-incarnation of Elijah. But Herod had become concerned that Jesus might be the resurrected John the Baptist whom he had ordered to be killed on the request of Herodias, his wife. When the disciples returned with the news, Jesus wanted to discuss the situation with them alone and they went by boat to what they thought was a solitary place. But the crowd had followed and Jesus could not resist teaching until the evening. When there was no food available except for five loaves and two fish Jesus performed the miracle of breaking the bread into small pieces, which the apostles distributed and the hunger of the multitude was satisfied. The number five thousand is in all probability an exaggeration and from the next episode it seems that the miracle was not of the major proportion that has been assumed by posterity.

When the crowd had left, Jesus went up into the hills to pray while the disciples took off in the boat. A headwind came up and they had trouble rowing. Then they saw Jesus walking on the lake as if he were an apparition and they were thoroughly frightened. But he told them in the Greek version, "have courage, I am, do not be afraid." The Latin version says,"*confidite, ego sum, nolite timere.* I am using both versions here because I AM in capital letters, as written in *The Amplified Bible,* would indicate that Jesus had arrogated unto himself the divine name. The King James Version is more modest and translates *ego sum* with "it is I." As soon as Jesus entered the boat the wind died down. The point to be made here is, however, that the disciples were infinitely more impressed with this event than the previous miracle because Mark says that they were dumbfounded and, due to the hardness of their hearts, had not understood the miracle of the loaves. The skeptic might argue that if one feeds five thousand people with five loaves of bread this should have made a greater impression than Mark reports. These stories are obviously later inserts into the life of Jesus and can safely be regarded as just that, namely stories. The major point of the chapter is that Jesus had experienced rejection by his own and now had to reappraise his future conduct.

Chapter 7

Here we find some non sequiturs as well as a duplication which suggests that the text has been corrupted. The important aspect is that Jesus was challenged in regard to his apparent neglect of the oral law by Pharisees and scribes, some of whom had come from as far as Jerusalem. Jesus not only refuted their argument but called them hypocrites on top of it.

To understand the context one must realize that the oral law had regulated every aspect of a person's life to minute details and whenever the oral law conflicted with the written one the scribes and Pharisees performed legal acrobatics so that the words of the law might be preserved while its spirit had been violated. For instance, the abstention from work on the Sabbath has already been mentioned previously, but the religious lawyers debated the meaning of the term "work." While it seems obvious to anyone who is not burdened with a legal mind, it was not so for the orthodoxy. There was even a question whether or not an egg which a hen had laid on the Sabbath was allowed to be eaten. The lighting of a fire was also forbidden as being work, and this led to the practice of hiring the *Shabbes goy*. A Gentile was paid to perform essential functions of daily living. That this practice was expressly forbidden in the written law was winked at by the authorities. This was the type of hypocrisy Jesus condemned.

In the chapter under consideration, dietary regulations were involved. The disciples had not washed their hands prior to eating and it seems that the cooking utensils may also have been cleaned less rigorously than the oral law required. While Jesus still adhered to the spirit of the written law he disdained some of the oral elaborations as man-made which nullified the spirit of God. In order to chastise the challengers he quoted Isaiah 29:13 to them, "This people draw nigh to me with their mouth, and they honor me with their lips, but their heart is far from me." Isaiah, who referred to God's grievances with the people of Jerusalem, continued the sentence with, "but in vain do they worship me, teaching the commandments and precepts of men." Verse 15 of the same chapter is also relevant because it was likewise adopted by Jesus at some point. "Woe to them that deepen their counsel, and not by the Lord. Woe to them that take secret counsel, and whose works are in darkness, and they say, Who has seen us? and who shall know us? or what we do?" All of us including government officials would do well to ponder theses sentences.

In the current context of Jesus' argument with the Pharisees and scribes he continued his lecture with an example of how they directly violated Mosaic Law by making exemptions which were unwarranted. Verses 11 and 12 are difficult to understand unless one knows the pharisaic practices of the day. The commandment "Honor thy father and thy mother" is straightforward. Not only should one not bad-mouth one's parents but one is also under obligation to help them whenever they are in need. The Pharisees had found a way around it. The child, usually the son, could say he had given his property to God, thereby making it sacred: *Corban*. Nevertheless, he was still allowed free use of it for himself but was no longer under any obligation towards the parents because it was already God's property. These were the type of legalities Jesus objected to. When he then told the interlocutors that nothing that goes into a man defiles him only what comes out the disciples were again unable to perceive the meaning and he had to explain. What you eat or drink just goes in and out *per vias naturales*, and does not defile you, "but from the heart proceed evil thoughts, adulteries, fornications, murders, thefts, covetousness, wickedness, deceit, lasciviousness, an evil eye, blasphemy, pride, foolishness." It is not so important how you clean the outside but rather that you clean up your mind and thoughts only then you will serve God in the proper manner. This is also what Buddha taught when he insisted that one needs to rid one's mind of stains and defilements.

The battle lines between Jesus and the religious leadership had again been drawn and he continued with healing the sick and exorcizing evil spirits. If we are to trust Mark's chronology, it would be noteworthy that Jesus again removed himself to Gentile lands after this unpleasantness with the authorities. First he went to the Mediterranean seashore, Tyre and Sidon, and subsequently to Decapolis where he was out of reach from religious law. Yet there is a paradox. We can readily assume that he didn't just go sight-seeing but when a gentile woman asked him to heal her daughter he supposedly refused with the words, "Let the children be fed first, for it is not fair to take the children's food and throw it to the dogs." These were surely harsh words and suggest a rather marked chauvinistic streak. Did he just regard himself as a temporary refugee from religious law and didn't want to have anything to do with Gentiles? But the woman persevered with: even dogs get the crumbs from the dinner table, and Jesus relented. In the Decapolis province Jesus healed a deaf mute, but this time he charged the people not to say anything about it. There seems to be no particular reason for the request. He was out of Jewish jurisdiction and in the previous episode where he had sent the evil spirits from the violently insane man into the Gadarene swine he had no objection to the miracle being proclaimed far and wide. The explanation might be that he had arrived furtively this time because the Gadarenese had asked him not to come back after their herd of swine had been lost to a watery grave. But these are details theologians can argue about.

Chapter 8

This chapter continues with miracles and since we are told that Jesus now fed four thousand with seven loaves and a few fish it seems likely that this is a duplication of the previous story, except that the situation is even more miraculous because the remains of the meal filled seven baskets. The reason for Mark presenting the story at this point seems to be that he wanted to indicate that Jesus was now teaching to the Gentiles in the Decapolis area and was moved with pity towards them. Since the chapter ends with Jesus foretelling his passion and death it seems likely that the feeding of a non-Jewish multitude may be a lead-in towards the eventual conversion of Gentiles.

Mark continues with Jesus returning to Jewish territory and the Pharisees asking of him a sign from heaven which would testify to his authority, but Jesus refused to do so. A similar event is presented in more detail in Matthew 16:2, 3 and I prefer it because the quote is a sailors' adage. In Matthew's version Jesus did not just refuse to give the requested sign but prefaced his refusal with the equivalent of: red sky at night, sailors delight; red sky in the morning, sailors take warning. Jesus then rebuked them as a wicked and adulterous generation, which was unable to read the signs of the time. This was another insult the authorities could not ignore.

To the disciples Jesus added: beware of the leaven of the Pharisees and of the Herodians, while Matthew reports the saying as beware of the leaven of the Pharisees and Sadducees. Both versions say essentially the same thing. Don't trust the power structures; they misinterpret God's word to suit their needs. This is made more explicit at the end of the chapter. But before then he restored sight to a blind man and again ordered him to be quiet about the miracle. Although he knew what was in store for him it seems that he still did not yet want an open irremediable break. This is why he first asked the disciples, "Who do the people say I am?" I believe that this was not just a rhetorical question. He really wanted an answer. When they said: John the Baptist, Elijah, or one of the prophets, Jesus followed up with but, "who do *you* [emphasis added] say I am?" At that point Peter blurted out, "You are the Christ!" From that moment on Jesus accepted the role of the Messiah with all the lethal consequences.

Nevertheless, for now he still charged them to be quiet about this insight and told them what it meant. The prophecy of 2 Isaiah 53:3-12 was now to be fulfilled. Jesus was to become the suffering servant of whom it had been said:

"He is despised and rejected of men; a man of sorrows, and acquainted with grief; and we hid as it were our faces from him . . . we esteemed him not. Surely, he has borne our grieves, and carried our sorrows: yet we did esteem him stricken, smitten of God and afflicted. But he was wounded for our transgressions, he was bruised for our iniquities . . . and with his stripes we are healed. All we like sheep have gone astray; we have turned every one to his own way; and the Lord hath laid on him the iniquity of us all. He was oppressed, and he was afflicted, yet he opened not his mouth: he is brought as a lamb to the slaughter, and as a sheep before her shearers is dumb, so he openeth not his mouth. He was taken from prison and from the judgment . . . he was cut out of the land of the living: for the transgressions of my people was he stricken. And he made his grave with the wicked and with the rich in his death; because he had done no violence, neither was any deceit in his mouth. Yet it pleased the Lord to bruise him . . . when thou shalt make his soul an offering for sin, he shall see his seed, he shall prolong his days and the pleasure of the Lord shall prosper in his hand. He shall see of the travail of his soul and shall be satisfied: by his knowledge shall my righteous servant justify many; for he shall bear their iniquities. Therefore will I divide him a portion with the great, and he shall divide the spoil with the strong; because he hath poured out his soul unto death; and he was numbered with the transgressors; and he bare the sins of many, and made intercession for the transgressors."

Although Jewish authorities interpreted the "suffering servant" passages as referring to the nation of Israel as a whole, Jesus took them personally. Had he not been despised and rejected by the authorities and even his family? Had they not said that he was mad, smitten by God with an unclean spirit? It had all come true in his life so far and now was the time to complete the rest of the prophecy.

Jesus, therefore, told the disciples that the Son of Man had to be rejected by the elders, chief priests and scribes, had to be killed and after three days arise from the grave. When the thunderstruck Peter said in so many words, to use today's colloquialism, no way are we going to allow this, Jesus rebuked him in the sternest way possible, "Get behind me Satan! For you are setting your mind not on the things of God but the things of men." Calling Peter "Satan" may strike one as uncalled for but what Jesus meant to say was: stop talking this way, don't raise doubts about what has to be done. To drive home the point he insisted that whoever wanted to follow him must deny himself and take up his cross, whoever wanted to save his life would lose it, but whoever loses it in the defense of the gospel would achieve eternal life. "For what will it profit them, to gain the whole world, and forfeit their life? . . . . Those who are ashamed of me and of my words . . . of them the Son of Man shall also be ashamed when he comes in the glory of his Father with the holy angels."

The words *Ypage satanâ*, go away adversary, occur three times in the gospels. In Matthew 4:10, where Jesus utters them after the third temptation and in Mt. 16:33 where they are identical with Mark's version in regard to the rebuke of Peter. They can actually serve as an important mental mechanism whenever one is beset either by temptations to veer from the straight and narrow, or if one were to find oneself in spiritual distress. The human being can, on rare occasions, not only feel the presence of God but also that of unmitigated evil. I experienced this in a dream several decades ago. It consisted of a feeling of a presence in the room which was utterly and disastrously evil. There was no sound, no vision, no smell, no touch just a knowledge of pure and unadulterated evil which was about to encompass me. In my distress the words *Ypage satana* came out from my throat and the hoarse sound awakened me. The experience was extremely real, because all dreams are real until one wakes up. Dreams of this type should not necessarily be dismissed as "just another dream," but as possible harbingers of the existence of another dimension we neither are aware of, nor have control over. They have growth potential for one's personality

But let us return to Jesus' tragic situation. He had made the decision and knew that his human life was about to end in a most cruel manner. The terrible price the disciples were now asked to pay for having followed him was surely not what they thought they had bargained for. But even today, the words: what shall it profit a man to gain the whole world at the price of his soul, contain an important message. Wealth or power, unless used for the healing of wounds and for feeding the hungry, is bound to corrupt mind and soul. How much misery could be avoided if our "Christian" politicians heeded this saying?

Chapter 9

The first verse is a direct continuation of Jesus' admonitions and could have two meanings. The Greek version reads, "Truly I tell you, that there are some standing here who will not taste death, until they see that the kingdom of God has come with power." This could be taken to mean that some of the disciples would still be alive by the time the messianic kingdom became a physical presence on this earth. If one subscribes to this interpretation one must say that

Jesus was either deluded or mistaken. But the Greek word *dúnamis* for power can also mean ability, might, miracle, meaning, worth or value. The Latin translation used the word *virtute* which signifies manliness, moral excellence, ability, virtue, or bravery. Furthermore when one reads the sentence in the context of what transpired next, namely the transfiguration of Jesus, it can make perfect sense. One might paraphrase the statement as: a few of you will see the power of God with your own eyes, before you die.

Mark continues his narration with Jesus' transfiguration. Jesus took his three most trusted disciples: Peter, James and John to a high mountain where his appearance was transformed in front of them. His garments shone exceedingly white as no bleacher could do and they saw Jesus converse with Moses and Elijah. The terrified Peter who didn't know what to say offered to make three tabernacles: one for Jesus and the other two for Moses and Elijah respectively. But a cloud came and they heard a voice from heaven, "This is my beloved Son, listen to him!" The word beloved is expressed in Latin as *carissimus*, dearest. As soon as the disciples looked around no one else but Jesus was present any longer. He admonished them not to mention to anyone what they had witnessed until, "the Son of Man had risen from the dead." They promised to do so but had difficulty understanding what "risen from the dead" meant. They also questioned Jesus why the scribes and Pharisees insisted that Elijah had to return before the Messiah could arrive. This assumption was based on Malachi 3:23 (4:5 in Christian Bibles), "Behold, I will send you Elijah the prophet before the coming of the great and terrible day of the Lord," which has been mentioned previously.

The figure of Elijah had at the time of Jesus assumed mythical proportion. His achievements are reported in Kings 17-22 and 2 Kings 1 and 2. In essence, Elijah whose ancestry is never mentioned, was a zealous prophet of the Lord who performed numerous miracles which included: a prediction of years of drought until Elijah would bring rain with the Lord's help, making a small amount of flour and oil last for a long time, raising a child from the dead, confounding 450 prophets of Baal in a challenge as to who was mightier: Yahweh or Baal, and then when the Lord's power had been demonstrated by fire from heaven which kindled the altar, he had all the prophets of Baal killed. On two occasions Elijah did not take orders from a captain whose fifty men were to bring him before the king but instead he killed them with heavenly fire. He was despised by King Ahab and his wife, Jezebeel, and had to flee twice from their wrath; once into Gentile territory for several years and on another occasion to Judea. After the killing of Baal's prophets he had to flee to Mount Horeb (Sinai). The journey lasted for forty days and nights and he was sustained only by what he had eaten prior to departure. On the mountain he hid in a cave where the Lord appeared to him not with wind and fire but as a gentle whisper. His designated successor Elisha inherited Elijah's powers by dividing the waters of the Jordan when he struck them with Elijah's mantle. The prophet himself did not die but was carried to heaven in a chariot of fire.

These stories are in the biblical text but the oral tradition had elaborated on his departure from earth. We are told that the Lord had created heaven strictly for Elijah's sake so that he could enter therein, but the angel of death did not agree and asked permission to go to earth and do his job. The Lord relented, but the moment Elijah saw him he stepped on the angel of death and tried to drive him out of the world altogether. This was, however, not permitted. Elijah, therefore, ascended to heaven with the angel of death in tow. The reason why there was no ancestry given for Elijah was that before he had come to earth he had already resided in heaven and he simply returned there after his mission on earth was completed.

Unless one is aware of this context the miracles of Jesus and the emphasis on Elijah cannot be readily understood. There is, however, another aspect to the Elijah story which requires comment, namely the question: who wrote the books of Kings? *The Jerome Biblical Commentary* points out that the historical books of the Bible were written in their present form during the Babylonian exile. The purpose was not history *per se*, but theology. The point had to be made and reiterated that Yahweh, the Lord of the Universe, had chosen the nation of Israel as His special people; they had failed to honor Him; they had gone "whoring" after other gods and were, therefore, repeatedly punished. The Lord used other nations to accomplish this object. But if and when Israel repented, He would show mercy again and punish instead those nations whom He had previously used for His purpose. This was the message. The method to get the message across was to show by means of prophecy and miracles that Yahweh's power exceeded that of all the idol deities among which the Chosen People lived. Thus the prophecies were a theologic device which post- rather than pre-dated the events. Instead of predicting the future, they were used to justify the past. Jesus reversed the situation because he took the prophecies at face value, applied them to himself, and as such used the past to enact the future. Elijah had already returned in the person of John the Baptist and it was time to move on to the fate the Son of Man had to suffer.

There are numerous parallels and symbolic allusions to the Old Testament in the circumstances surrounding the transfiguration. Moses had received the Ten Commandments on a mountain and Jesus received official recognition by the Lord, as well as by Moses and Elijah, on a mountain. When Moses came down his face was radiant so was that of Jesus. Moses found a multitude dancing around the golden calf, while Jesus found a group of people arguing with the disciples who had stayed behind. The reason for the commotion was that they had been unable to drive a "dumb spirit" out of a boy. The subsequent description of the boy's illness makes it clear that he had suffered from epilepsy.

In Jesus' time epilepsy was called *morbus sacer*, the sacred disease. The word *sacer* denotes, however, not only holy but also "accursed" and "devoted to destruction." Anyone who has seen a major epileptic seizure knows that this is a highly dramatic event with marked emotional impact on witnesses. It is hardly surprising that people were thoroughly frightened by it. The sudden onset, the unpredictability of the time of occurrence and the apparent violence of convulsions accompanied by a piercing scream, followed by absence of breathing, foaming at the mouth, and frequently loss of bladder control is an event one cannot readily forget. Thus there were good reasons for the common folk to talk of demonic possession, although Hippocrates had already declared five hundred years earlier that epilepsy was no more divine than any other illness. He had furthermore stated that the disease was curable, "except when for passage of time it has become stronger than the remedies applied." This dictum is still true in some cases in spite of the most modern medical treatment.

When the child was brought to Jesus he asked, like any good physician, how long the boy had been suffering from the malady. The father then proceeded to describe a case of a severe form of childhood epilepsy. A rather characteristic exchange preceded the cure. When Jesus was told that the disciples had been ineffective he grew angry, complained about the faithless generation and wondered how long he would have to put up with them. The father's request, "if you are able to do anything, have pity on us . . . ." annoyed him even further and he said to the father, "all things can be done for the one who believes." The distraught parent then cried in tears, "I believe, help my unbelief!" After this plea Jesus ordered the deaf and mute spirit to leave the boy and not ever to return. The child recovered and the disciples wondered why they could not have done the same. Jesus replied that with this spirit nothing avails but prayer and fasting. In the Greek text fasting is omitted although it shows up in the Latin version. As an aside I might mention that intense fasting, if not followed by binge eating, can on occasion help some epilepsy patients and there exists also a diet, low in carbohydrates but rich in certain fats, which is at times helpful.

The rest of chapter 9 is devoted to Jesus reiterating to the disciples his impending fate. They were unable to understand and had already begun to discuss among themselves the glory they would reap in the coming kingdom and who would be the most favored. Jesus had to disappoint them again. Anybody who wanted to be first would be last and the servant of all the others, he told them. He then took a little child in his arms and said that, "Whoever welcomes one such child in my name, welcomes me, and whoever welcomes me, welcomes not me but the one who sent me." He added that someone who deprived any of these children of their faith would be better off if he were thrown into the lake with a millstone around his neck. Jesus then proceeded to admonish his flock that nothing is more important in this world than to keep one's faith. Even if one's own bodily part were to make one falter and stray from the path it should be cut off, because it was better to enter crippled into heaven than going to hell on account of one's lusts.

There are, in addition, two apparent *non sequiturs* in the chapter which seem to be out of order. Sandwiched between receiving the child in his name and the fate which shall befall one who deprives a child of faith is an anecdote where the disciples complained about a man who was casting out demons in Jesus' name but didn't even belong to their group. This is likewise an allusion to Moses having been confronted with the same situation in Num. 11:27 and who had said, "Would that everyone were a prophet in Israel." Jesus told them not to be concerned about it because, "for he who is not against us, is with us!" Jesus explained further that anyone who performs miracles in his name can no longer talk evil about him and is, therefore, to be welcomed.

The chapter ends after the mentioned encouragement to sacrifice even body parts, when necessary, to avoid hell fire, with a somewhat cryptic passage. Jesus told the disciples, "For every one will be salted with fire. Salt is good, but if salt has lost its saltiness, wherewith will you season it? Have salt in yourselves and have peace with one another." For the explanation of these verses we have to keep two aspects in mind. One is that salt was of major importance to keep food, especially meat, from putrefaction and the other its religious, ritual role. For the latter we have to consult the Old Testament again. In Leviticus 2:13 the Israelites were ordered that all meat offerings to the Lord had to be salted. "And every oblation of thy meat offering shalt thou season with salt . . . with all thine offerings thou shalt offer salt." In II Chron.13:5 we are told that the "Lord God of Israel gave the kingdom over Israel to David forever, even to him and to his sons by a covenant of salt." The "purifying" powers of salt were demonstrated by Elisha when he used it for cleansing the Jordan River in II Kings 2:21-22. The metaphors cited above in Jesus' admonitions mean not only that the disciples had to give up even that what they cherish most if it detracts them from the right path, but that this needed to be done in the spirit of performing a sacrifice for God. Thus Jesus' comment meant that they must consider their entire conduct to be a holy sacrifice to the Lord, while at the same time not becoming argumentative among them as to whose actions were the most worthy.

Chapter 10

We are now starting on the road to Calvary. In the beginning of the chapter Pharisees were again testing Jesus; this time in regard to divorce which was allowed in the Law of Moses. But Jesus had stricter ideas. Once you married in the sight of God you became one flesh and the marriage was indissoluble. To strengthen the statement further he also told them that re-marriage of a divorced man or woman constituted adultery.

When women started to bring their little children to Jesus for a blessing, the apostles were annoyed and began to shoo them away. They wanted Jesus for themselves in order to learn about the kingdom of heaven, their role in it, and what was going to happen next, rather than those ominous predictions of death and resurrection. One can readily imagine the scene. There were constant interruptions and some of Jesus' "bodyguards" may well have said to these mothers with wailing infants, "oh come on, leave the master alone; get lost!" When Jesus saw this he became angry and it was time for another lesson as to what the kingdom of Heaven was really like. He told them in the words of the King James Version, "Whoever shall not receive the kingdom of God as a little child, he shall not enter therein."

There is a reason why I have used the King James Version because the great Bertrand Russell had a serious problem with this phrase. In the book entitled, *"Why I am not a Christian"* which consists of a number of speeches and essays by this eminent philosopher and mathematician, he wrote:

> The church's conception of righteousness is socially undesirable in various ways - first and foremost in its depreciation of intelligence and science. This defect is inherited from the gospels. Christ tells us to become as little children, but little children cannot understand differential calculus, or the principles of currency, or the modern methods of combating disease.

Here is an example of what happens when spiritual information is imparted to a person who is thoroughly materialistically oriented and willfully denies the existence of anything above and beyond what can be experienced with our external senses. Under those circumstances even an outstanding logician can fall into the group of having eyes and ears but not perceiving. I shall discuss this further when it comes to the death of Jesus and the process of dying.

What Jesus obviously meant to convey was that your mind must be as open and receptive to the experience of God's realm just as a little child's is, whose faith has not yet been corrupted by doubt and criticism. This point, as well as the insistence on giving up not only one's cherished notions, but also physical property and acceptance of the role of servant rather than master, was driven home further in the subsequent conversations among Jesus and his little band of followers on the journey to Jerusalem.

While they were walking a stranger approached them and asked of Jesus, "Good teacher what must I do to inherit eternal life?" Jesus immediately objected to being called "good" because there is no one good but God, thereby clearly affirming his human nature. Then he proceeded to list the commandments: don't commit adultery, don't kill, don't steal, don't bear false witness, don't defraud, and honor your father and mother. When the man said, "Teacher I have kept all these since my youth," Jesus added, " . . . go sell what you own, and give the money to the poor, and you will have treasure in heaven; then come, follow me."

This type of sacrifice was too great and the man went away deeply troubled because he was very prosperous. Jesus pitied him and told the disciples, "It is easier for a camel to go through the eye of a needle than for someone who is rich to enter the kingdom of God." What did he mean by that metaphor? Some theologians argued that the text is corrupted and should have read *kámīlos* (cable) instead of *kámēlos* (camel). Others thought that "eye of a needle" referred to a particular narrow entrance gate in Jerusalem. But this is not important. Jesus clearly wanted to make a strong point by using paradoxical language. I believe he intended to get across to his people: you have to make a choice, either your heart is in this world with its riches or in the next. But entrance to the kingdom of God is not a right! You have to pay for your ticket and that has to be done here, in this life, by helping others in need, rather than by hoarding money.

The disciples were stunned by this uncompromising attitude on Jesus' part and asked themselves: could anybody be saved under these circumstances? Jesus answered them with the cryptic statement, "With mortals it is impossible, but not for God: for with God all things are possible." What he may have meant was that God can, figuratively speaking, send even a camel through the eye of a needle, and in his infinite mercy admit rich people, but only as an act of grace rather than on merit. Even Peter became concerned, however, and told Jesus in so many words: but look, we have left behind everything and followed you, so what's with us? What do we get out of it? Jesus reassured him: once you have voluntarily given up everything you valued, you will receive even in this life more than you have given away, in addition to eternal life in the next. This could have been regarded as a good deal if the words *"cum persecutionem,"* and persecutions, had not been added to what they would have to endure for his sake, prior to gaining eternal life.

Persecutions were obviously not to their liking so the disciples ignored it and began to concentrate on which one of them would get preference in the coming kingdom. These were common folk for whom the kingdom of God had very material properties. The seed of pride had been sown into their souls. *They* were now the elect of God and not those highbrow fellows in Jerusalem. In their opinion, and who can blame them, it was the apostles who would now rule the roost. The sons of Zebedee, James and John, therefore, approached Jesus with the request for the most coveted seats of honor, to the left and right side of him, in the kingdom. He probably looked at them and then asked in so many words: Are you really capable of taking upon yourselves all that will be asked of me? They eagerly said yes but little did they know what was really meant. Nevertheless, Jesus had to tell them that it was not up to him to distribute seating arrangements, this privilege the Lord had reserved for Himself. In addition he had to tell them again: don't be like the Gentiles where one rules over others, but if anyone of them wanted to achieve greatness he should serve the others, just as Jesus himself had not come to rule but to serve. He might have added, "Humility, my friends, is a virtue and pride a sin!"

Mark ends the chapter with a blind man referring to Jesus as "Son of David," and begging him to have mercy on him. Jesus no longer bade the man to hush up and not to use the messianic title in front of others, but instead asked him what he wanted. The man requested to have his sight restored and Jesus complied, telling him, "Your faith has made you well." They journeyed on and the previously blind individual followed them. There was to be no more hiding from the public as to who Jesus really was. Restoring sight to the blind was expected from the Messiah according to Isaiah's prophecy. The world might as well now know that Jesus had shouldered the burden and would carry this message into the very heart of Jerusalem regardless of the consequences.

Chapter 11

On the approach to Jerusalem, at the foot of the Mount of Olives, Jesus sent two disciples into town to bring him a colt so that he could enter the city in the manner prescribed by scripture. The gesture was understood and he was received with royal glory. Garments and tree branches were spread out on the road while people shouted, "Hosanna! Blessed is the one who comes in the name of the Lord! Blessed is the coming kingdom of our ancestor David! Hosanna in the highest heaven!" The savior had arrived; the deliverer from Roman yoke; the Lord's Chosen People would once again regain their sovereignty in the land of their inheritance, and their enemies would be crushed. That is what the people thought on that day.

Jesus knew better. He went to the temple, looked around and then went back with the twelve to Bethany. The next morning while returning to Jerusalem the famous fig tree episode took place. Jesus may not have had breakfast and was hungry. When he saw a fig tree in the distance he thought that there would be fruit to eat. But he had been misled by the leaves of the tree and there were no figs. "For it was not the season for figs!" Jesus became furious with the tree, although this surely was not the tree's fault, and cursed it so that no man might ever eat of its fruit thereafter. This episode gave Bertrand Russell the opportunity to prefer Socrates or Buddha over Jesus because a temper tantrum towards an innocent living entity does not behoove a wise man, let alone a Son of God. Theologians have previously pointed out that this scene should not be taken literally but represents an allegory to condemn the wayward Jews. Israel was the fig tree which had seemed to bear fruit but had rejected Jesus' message and was, therefore, doomed to be barren forever. This may well be so but the story might also be understandable from a more mundane perspective.

Let us remember the circumstances. Here was a human being who knew that his life would soon be cut short for doing the will of God. On the previous day he had seen what the conditions in the temple were really like. He may well have stewed over it during the night and didn't get much sleep, in addition to having had nothing to eat. When one is hypoglycemic the fuse shortens and anger outbursts occur. This may also explain his rude behavior in the temple immediately after his arrival. He was in no mood to tolerate the noisy bargaining of the money changers. Only temple money could buy the required sacrificial animals and some of these "service providers" may well have cheated their customers. In addition, there were the agonized shrieks emanating from animals about to be slaughtered, as well as crowds and confusion everywhere. In short, pandemonium reigned and Jesus became incensed. His Father's House was being violated and he acted accordingly. He drove out those that were selling and buying, overthrew the tables of the money changers, the seats of the sellers of doves and he, or more likely his praetorian guard the disciples, did not let anyone carry anything around on the temple grounds.

The Messiah had arrived and taken charge of his Father's House. "Is it not written 'My house shall be called a house of prayer for all the nations'? But you have made it a den of robbers," he yelled at them. The Latin version uses the words *speluncam latronum*, den of thieves, but that doesn't matter the meaning is clear. The Jewish rulers had dishonored the temple and Jesus would clean house. What do authorities, regardless whether they are religious or secular, do under those circumstances? They devise means how to get rid of this trouble maker at the earliest moment and in the most expedient way. What did Moses do when his authority was challenged in Numbers 25:6-9? Phinehas had to get rid of the malcontent. The story had been fleshed out by Josephus and was presented in *The Moses Legacy*. What did Henry II say when Beckett got on his nerves? "Will no one rid me of this turbulent priest?" Jesus had signed his death warrant.

Jesus left in the evening, and when they passed the fig tree next morning on the way to Jerusalem it had withered. While Peter was thoroughly amazed Jesus merely explained that if you have faith you can move mountains. Therefore, when you pray for whatever you need and believe that you will receive it, it shall be done. But when you pray you must forgive whoever has wronged you so that your heavenly Father will also forgive you the wrongs you have done. If you do not forgive, you will not receive forgiveness either.

When the little group of the faithful arrived again at the temple, the priests and scribes were ready. Who authorized you to do what you are doing? they asked Jesus. But he refused to be trapped and told them if you just answer one question for me then I shall answer you. "Did the baptism of John come from heaven or was it of human origin?" Now he had put them in a bind. The challengers deliberated and thought: if we say from heaven Jesus will retort: why didn't you believe him? If we say it was a human endeavor, we'll have a riot on our hands because too many of John's followers were around. So they told Jesus we can't tell and he replied, "Neither will I tell you by what authority I am doing these things."

Chapter 12

This chapter continues with Jesus teaching in the temple and being challenged by the religious authorities. First we find the parable of the planter of a vineyard who had done everything he could so that it might prosper and not be a prey to robbers. He then appointed some of his servants to take care of it in his absence. After some time the owner sent a messenger to look after his property but the servants killed the emissary. Undaunted the owner kept sending six other messengers in succession but all were either manhandled or killed by the unruly servants. Finally the owner sent his own son, whom he dearly loved, in the hope that they would now listen. But the servants had taken over the vineyard and also killed the son because they felt that the heir of the owner would dispossess them. Jesus then asked what do you think the owner of the vineyard should do next? He would come and destroy this unruly people and give the vineyard to others. Then Jesus added: have you not read the scripture, "The stone that the builders rejected the same is become the head of the corner. This has been done of the Lord; and it is wonderful in our eyes?" He had quoted Psalm 118 verses 22, 23, which in the Septuagint version as reproduced here, are in Psalm 117. The implications for the assembled religious hierarchy were obvious. All former prophets had suffered a dire fate and now they were confronted with a Galilean who acted as if he were the Messiah. They were hurt to the quick and wanted to arrest Jesus, but there were too many of his followers around and action had to be postponed.

The verses from the mentioned psalm were subsequently taken by the apostles, and later on the Church, to indicate that the Jewish nation had forfeited its right to the divine inheritance and Jesus' teachings were now to be the cornerstone of the New Covenant. This leaves us, however, with the origin of this somewhat cryptic passage. To whom had it originally been addressed?

The Psalms and Proverbs of the Bible have a long tradition and some of them can be found even in Egyptian and Mesopotamian wisdom literature. Although many of the Psalms are attributed to David this must not be taken literally. Just as the "five books of Moses," the Pentateuch, Torah, were not written by Moses but considerably later and do not have a single author. In antiquity Jewish religious authors could not sign their own names because they would have lacked credibility. Their statements, therefore, had to be predated either to Moses or David. The prophets likewise, did not speak in their own names but used the phrase, "Thus saith the Lord." Even Jesus kept re-iterating: it is not I who is speaking to you but the Father, by means of the Holy Spirit. The psalms were joined together in their current form after the Babylonian exile. Thus it is impossible to put a date on a specific psalm because they are in essence an anthology from a variety of sources and different time periods. They first appear in their current form in the Septuagint which originated in Alexandria during the third century B.C.. The context of verses 19-26 from Psalm 117 (118, in the Christian Bibles) is as follows:

> Open to me the gates of righteousness: I will go into them and give praise to the Lord. This is the gate of the Lord; the righteous shall enter by it. I will give thanks to thee: because thou hast heard me, and art becoming my salvation. The stone which the builders rejected, the same is become the head of the corner. This has been done of the Lord; and it is wonderful in our eyes. This is the day which the Lord has made: let us exult and rejoice in it. O Lord save now: O Lord send now prosperity. Blessed is he that comes in the name of the Lord: we have blessed you out of the house of the Lord.

We don't know who the psalmist was but the context suggests that it was written around the time when the exiles had returned, and the second temple had been re-dedicated with much hope for the future.

It does not take a great deal of fantasy to realize how the religious authorities might have felt when Jesus threw these verses at them. To make matters worse he did so in their temple precinct. From their point of view they were confronted with a pretender to messianic glory who did not even come from Judea but from Galilee and who had accused them only a couple of days earlier to have turned "my Father's house" into a den of thieves. There was no choice; Jesus had to be done away with.

Yet, as mentioned, they had to be cautious to avoid a riot. They, therefore, chose a strategy to embarrass him before the crowd. This was done with three questions: one in regard to money, while the other two involved religion. The money question: whether or not it was legal to pay taxes to the Romans clearly had political overtones. If Jesus said yes he would have been regarded as a traitor to his people and if he had said no they could have accused him of raising sedition. In his wisdom Jesus asked them to show him a coin and then to tell him whose picture was on it. When they said Caesar's he spoke the now famous words, "Give to Caesar what is Caesar's and give to God what is God's." This unexpected turn of events left the onlookers amazed.

But now it was time for the Sadducees to level a religious challenge. In contrast to the Pharisees, they did not believe in a resurrection of the dead, since scriptural authority was lacking. They, therefore, tried to trip up Jesus who was preaching a final judgment when the dead would rise. The question was: whose wife is it in the resurrection if a widow had survived seven husbands? Mosaic Law had ordained that if a husband died and had left no offspring, the brothers had to marry the widow until children were born. If any one of the six others had produced a child by this widow the question would have been moot because that one would have been the only legitimate husband. But since they all had failed, to whom was this woman legally married in the resurrection? While polygamy had been condoned in the days of the patriarchs there was no precedent for polyandry. Thus the question was legitimate and tricky. Jesus simply answered that in the resurrection there is no marriage, "They are all like angels." One might add that the resurrected don't have to procreate sexually, which was in those days still the purpose of marriage. Jesus also brought to their attention that when God spoke from the burning bush to Moses, He said, "I am the God of Abraham, and the God of Isaac, and the God of Jacob. He is God not of the dead but of the living and, therefore, you are quite wrong." The point here is that Jesus told them: if Abraham, Isaac, and Jacob were dead God would have said "I was" the God of these patriarchs. But for and with God there is no past or future only the eternal present: I am!

Now the Sadducees were also trumped and it was time for the scribes to try their mettle. The question was: which is the prime commandment? For an answer Jesus recited Deuteronomy 6: 4, 5, "Hear, O Israel, the Lord our God, the Lord is One. And you shall love the Lord, your God, with all your heart, and with all your mind, and all your soul, and with all your strength." To this he added, "And the second one is: You shall love your neighbor as yourself. There is no other commandment greater than these." With this addition Jesus quoted the second part of Leviticus 19:18. The word "neighbor" inevitably brought up another question: "who is my neighbor?" as related in Luke's parable of the Good Samaritan. To understand that question we must give the full text of Lev.19:18, "Thou shalt not take vengeance, nor bear any grudge against the children of thy people, but thou shalt love thy neighbor as thyself: I am, the Lord." Thus the context makes it clear that the verse restricts the commandment to members of Jacob's tribe. There are some modern authors who gloss over this difference between the Old and the New Testament by citing only the last half of the verse. They, thereby, want to give the impression that Judaism was always a religion of love towards all. This was not the case. It was Jesus who changed the concept and he deserves the credit. The parable of the Good Samaritan which highlights this point was provided by Luke and will be discussed further in the appropriate chapter.

The scribe who had asked the question was impressed and agreed. Whereupon Jesus told him that he was not far from the kingdom of God. It was now time for Jesus to ask questions, "How can the scribes say that the Messiah is the son of David? David himself, by the Holy Spirit, declared 'The Lord said to my Lord, "Sit at my right hand, until I put your enemies under your feet."' David himself calls him Lord; so how can he be his son?" While Jesus' earlier statements are readily understandable by anyone, this question seems to defy an answer. Let us, therefore, look at the context of Psalm 109:1 (King James, 110) by presenting the Psalm in its entirety:

A Psalm of David

The Lord said to my Lord, Sit thou on my right hand until, I make thine enemies thy footstool. The Lord shall send out a rod of power for thee out of Sion, rule them in the midst of thine enemies. With thee is dominion in the day of thy power; in the splendors of thy saints. I have begotten thee from the womb before the morning. The Lord sware, and will not repent. Thou art a priest for ever, after the order of Melchizedek. The Lord at thy right hand has dashed in pieces kings in the days of his wrath. He shall judge among the nations, he shall fill up the number of corpses, he shall crush, the heads of many of the earth. He shall drink of the brook in the way; therefore shall he lift up the head.

This is obviously a complex statement. Let us start with the title. The words "of David" can be taken to mean either "written by David" or "about David." The Greek word *"to"* which is translated as "of" can also mean, "therefore," "then," or "in this case;" which does not help much in understanding the first sentence. Who is this Lord the Lord wants to honor in this manner? The pharisaic interpretation assumed that the Lord who did the talking was God and the Lord who sat at his right side was the Messiah whom David, as the author of the verses, anticipated. This may or may not be what had been meant originally. *The Jerome Biblical Commentary* provides another explanation, as put forth by Rowley, and centers on the name Melchizedek. This person shows up only twice in the Old Testament. The first time in Genesis 14:18-20 and the second time in the Psalm under discussion. The Genesis account refers to Abraham's meeting with Melchizedek the King of Salem (Jerusalem) who was also the priest of "God the Most High" who gave Abraham bread and wine and said, " 'Blessed be Abraham of God Most High, Maker of heaven and earth and blessed be God the Most High, who hath delivered thine enemies into thy hand.' And he [Abraham] gave him a tenth of all." The name Melchizedek translates into "My king is righteousness" and the encounter took place after Abraham had defeated a number of tribal leaders and liberated his nephew Lot who had been captured by the king of Sodom. Rowley assumed that if Zadok was the speaker (priest of Jerusalem when David had captured the city) he addressed David and confirmed his kingship in the name of Yahweh.

Instead of engaging in theologic disputes let us return to Jesus and try to discern why he brought up this obscure detail in the first place. I believe he did so precisely because of its obscurity and to demonstrate how the "sages" can manipulate words to suit their desires. Jesus had poked fun at their worldly wisdom and the crowd enjoyed it. That is why, "the people heard him gladly." This conjecture seems to be confirmed by the immediately following sentences of Jesus where he warned the audience, "Beware of the scribes, who like to walk around in long robes, and to be greeted in the market place, and to have the best seats in the synagogues and places of honor at banquets. They patiently devour widows' houses and for the sake of appearance say long prayers. They will receive the greater condemnation." The Greek word which has been translated as devours means to eat up and in this context refers to extracting the last dime from a poor widow's household for prayers on behalf of the deceased. This is also probably the reason why Jesus commended a poor widow to his disciples whom they had watched giving the equivalent of a farthing to the temple. While the rich had given from abundance, he told them, this poor widow still gave from what little she had.

Chapter 13

Jesus continued his discussion with what was to happen at the end of days. When the disciples admired the beautiful building of the temple, Jesus was not impressed and told them that not one stone would be left standing upon the other. They left the city and Jesus sat down on the Mount of Olives. While looking at the temple Peter, James, John and Andrew asked him privately when the end was going to come and what sign there would be to announce it. Jesus warned them not to be deceived. There will be many who will come and say I am the Messiah and they will mislead many. When the disciples hear of wars and rumors of wars they shouldn't be concerned, this was not yet the end. Nations will rise against each other and so will kingdoms. Earthquakes in various places, famines and other calamities will take place, but this was just the beginning. More important is what will be happening to them. They will be turned over to the authorities; they will be beaten and taken before governors and kings for proclaiming Jesus' message. But when they testify before the courts they should not worry about what to say, because the Holy Spirit will speak for them. They will be hated and detested by everybody on account of Jesus. Families will be torn apart, brother will hand over brother to be killed, so will a father turn over his child and children will turn against the parents. But those who persevere and endure these tribulations will be saved.

As to the time when these disasters would occur we find the cryptic remark in regard to a prophecy of Daniel. The Greek text says, "when you see the abomination of desolation having stood where it ought not (the one reading take note) then let the ones who live in Judea flee to the mountains . . ." *The New English Bible* says, "'But when you see "the abomination of desolation usurping a place which is not his . . ." What is this "abomination of desolation," the disciples were supposed to be concerned about? Inasmuch as our current "millenniarists" put great stock in this prophecy we need to examine it in some detail and as always translations and context are important. What has been translated as "abomination of desolation" from the Greek and *abominationem desolationis* in the Latin is in the literal sense "that detestable thing which makes waste," or "lays desolate."

Since Jesus quoted Daniel in this passage we need to know what Daniel had prophesied. Dn verses 11:31 and 12:11 are the most relevant ones but context is essential. In chapter 11 verses 28, 29 Daniel discusses how a king from the north would come down, perform great deeds and then go home again but "his heart shall be against the holy covenant." The subsequent verses 29-32, as presented in the Septuagint version, are important because they provide historical information

> At the set time he shall return, and shall come into the south, but the last expedition shall not be as the first. For the Citians issuing forth shall come against him, and he shall be brought low, and shall return, and shall be incensed against the holy covenant: and he shall do thus, and shall return, and have intelligence with them that have forsaken the holy covenant.
>
> And seeds shall spring up out of him, and they shall profane the sanctuary of strength, and they shall remove the perpetual sacrifice, and make the abomination desolate. And the transgressors shall bring about a covenant by deceitful ways: but a people knowing their God shall prevail and do valiantly.

When one removes the poetic language and looks at the past rather than the future we have an excellent description of the cause of the Maccabean wars which had transpired about two hundred years before Jesus' time. The book of Daniel was not written in the fifth or fourth century B.C. but during the Hasmonean dynasty (164- 64 B.C.) which had re-established a theocratic state largely within the borders of David's ancient kingdom. The evil king from the north was Antiochus IV who had led two expeditions to Egypt. The first one was reasonably successful but when he wanted to annex Egypt he was put in check by the Romans (Citians or Kittim). The Roman ambassador Pompilius Laenas drew, literally, the first proverbial "line in the sand." He took his walking stick made a circle around Antiochus and told him that by the time he stepped out of the circle he had to declare whether he wanted peace or war with Rome. Antiochus was in no position to win a war against Rome and opted for peace.

Needless to say he was thoroughly furious over this humiliation, especially since his title was Epiphanes, God manifest. In addition to this put-down at the hands of the Romans he was also confronted with a civil war among the Jews of Jerusalem. One group favored assimilation with the Gentiles and preferred Greek ways over the laws of Moses, while the orthodox group insisted on literal fulfillment. En route back to the capital at Antioch the king vented his anger on the hapless Jews. His troops devastated Jerusalem, and put numerous inhabitants "to the sword." One of the renegade priests who had fought against the orthodox faction then led Antiochus through the temple where the latter helped himself to some of the treasures. Subsequently he had a statue of himself, in the guise of Zeus, set up in the temple. Jewish religious law was forbidden and the seeds for the Maccabean wars were sown. I have presented what one may call a Reader's Digest version of these times in *Whither Zionism?* because this era is now being re-enacted over two thousand years later, with even higher stakes. When the book of Daniel talks about, "have intelligence with them that have forsaken the holy covenant," he refers to those Jews who had taken to the Greek's way of life.

Verse 12:11 at the end of the book provides a time frame:

> And from the time of the removal of the perpetual sacrifice, when the abomination of desolation shall be set up, there shall be a thousand two hundred and ninety days. Blessed is he that waits and comes to the thousand three hundred and thirty five days.

One thousand two hundred and ninety days amount to about three and a half years. The ban of the Jewish religion occurred in 167 B.C. and the temple was re-dedicated at the end of December 164 B.C.. The additional 45 days may refer to the victory celebration which was subsequently commemorated as the feast of Hanukkah. The miracle of the minute quantity of holy oil having lasted for eight days is not recorded in the Bible and is a legend from the Talmud. The origin can probably be found in Elijah's stay with the Phoenician widow who likewise had too little oil for the lamp, but it kept burning while Elijah resided with her.

The historical facts in regard to Daniel's prophecy are well known now and the books of Daniel have been dated to around 100 B.C. Jesus, on he other hand, is not likely to have had this information at his time and, therefore, took the "prophecy" at face value. We must also remember that Mark's account was written either just before or immediately after the Jewish war, which was a major catastrophe for Jerusalem and Judea. Furthermore, in 40 A.D. the Roman Emperor Gaius, better known as Caligula, who had succeeded Tiberius, had decreed that not only should he be venerated as a god while he was still alive, a privilege which was reserved for exceptional emperors after their death, but in addition that his statue be set up in the Jerusalem temple. For the Jews this was, of course, not only an abomination but also a catastrophe of the first magnitude and a replay of Antiochus' ban of the religion. Caligula was persuaded by his friend the Jewish King Agrippa to rescind the edict, but had Caligula not been murdered in January of 41 the Jewish war against Rome might well have broken out 25 years earlier. While Jesus, who was crucified during Tiberius' reign, could not have known about Caligula's plans, the country was in sufficient turmoil that any reasonable person would have been aware that a catastrophic war was in the offing.

Jesus' warning of false Messiahs who were to come was correct. The final, even more disastrous, war of the Jews against Rome from 132-135 A.D. was led by Bar Cochba, who had been hailed as the Messiah by the highly respected rabbi Akhiba. On the other hand the darkening of sun and moon as well as the falling of the stars did not happen in the real world. Neither did the Son of Man come in the clouds with great power and glory, as the then living generation was led to expect. But the statement that Jesus' words would persist throughout the ages was true. The warning to be attentive to the signs of the times was also good advice and we should heed it, especially now!

As mentioned above Daniel's "abomination of desolation," was a statue of Antiochus IV which desecrated the temple; but is there possibly a modern equivalent? We still speak of Palestine as the Holy Land, but it is being desecrated at this time by an Israeli regime which cannot find peace with its neighbors and even its own native Palestinian population. In search for security, the state has armed itself with a massive arsenal of weapons of mass destruction of atomic, biologic and chemical nature. The state is also determined to use these if it were to feel a vital threat to its existence. These weapons are truly an abomination; they bring desolation and are in a place where they should not be. Since Jesus' words are eternal, this is a sign of the time we are warned against lest the *dies irae, dies illa, solvet saeclum in favilla;* the day of wrath, that day which shall dissolve our age into poisonous dust, becomes an awful reality.

Chapter 14

The tragedy now begins in earnest and what had been expected takes its course. Passover was at hand. The Jewish authorities wanted to avoid a riot during the holy days and intended to wait until all the crowds that thronged through the streets of Jerusalem had dispersed. But they received unexpected help from Judas Iscariot who promised to deliver Jesus into their hands. Public arrest during daytime was out of the question on account of the crowds. But only the disciples knew where Jesus spent his nights and it was Judas' task to identify him in the darkness. Judas' motives have been discussed by numerous authors. They range from him having been a crook, who did it for money, to having been a Jewish nationalist who wanted to force Jesus to issue a call to arms and be the militaristic Messiah everyone expected. Let us not forget that the name Jesus is merely the Latin rendering for Jeshua, also spelled Joshua (Yahweh is salvation), who had conquered the Holy Land for the Hebrews after Moses' death. It is therefore reasonable that he was expected to live up to this example. A pacifist Messiah who would go like a lamb to slaughter was unthinkable, not only for Judas but everyone else. People must do what is expected of them, but Jesus proved them wrong. Bar Cochba and all the subsequent Messiahs throughout Jewish history are dead but Jesus lives on in the hearts of hundreds of millions around the world.

The rest of the story is so well known that it can be summarized except for some key passages. When the unnamed woman poured precious oil over Jesus' head she was rebuked by some for wasting money which could have been given to the poor. But Jesus told them that the poor would always exist and she had only come to anoint his body before burial. The Last Supper followed thereafter. When Jesus broke the bread, gave it to the disciples with the words, "Take, this is my body" and repeated the formula with a cup of wine, "This is my blood of the covenant, which is poured out for many," they were probably dumbfounded. Subsequently, they went to the Mount of Olives where Jesus predicted that Peter would deny him three times before the night was over. Peter protested violently but neither he nor the others could stay awake although Jesus had hoped that they would pray with him. Deeply distressed he fell to the ground and prayed fervently that the cup should be taken away from him, "yet not what I want, but what you want" shall be done. Here we are confronted with the thoroughly human Jesus who knew that inevitable pain and death were at hand. He would have liked to avoid it and hoped for a miracle, but was resigned to his fate if it did not materialize.

When he got up and found Peter, his rock, asleep with the others he was disappointed. He awakened him and asked him to pray. The passage, "pray that you may not come into temptation," is rendered in *The New English Bible* as, "that you may be spared the test." If one puts oneself in Jesus' place at this supreme time of trial these translations may not do the situation justice. He knew that the hour of ordeal had come for all of them. It was time to stand up and be counted. He was about to die, the hope was that the disciples would carry on with the work in his name, and he furthermore knew that they would be persecuted for doing so. Therefore they needed to be vigilant and strong. The Latin text says: *Vigilate, et orate ut non intretis in tentationem. Spiritus quidem promptus est, caro vero infirma;* be vigilant and pray (for strength) that you do not fall into temptation. The spirit indeed is ready (available) but the flesh truly weak. *Tentatio* also means "test" or "trial." What Jesus was telling them was that they would now be sorely tested. Therefore, they needed to remain awake and pray for strength. The spirit would help them but there was danger that they would not be strong enough to endure.

Jesus had overcome the flesh and there was for the moment only spirit, but the disciples had not yet reached that stage. The exhortations didn't work, the flesh was too strong and when it is mind over matter, for most of us, matter wins hands down. The disciples kept on sleeping and Jesus resigned himself to the situation. Judas came with an assortment of variously armed people, called him Master, kissed him, and Jesus was arrested. There may have been a scuffle because someone drew a sword and cut off the ear of one of the high priest's servants. Jesus was led away and there is the curious story of a young man who had come dressed only in a linen cloth and who ran away naked when someone tried to get a hold of him.

Up to that time only Jewish authorities were involved and Jesus was led to an assembly of the religious leaders. False witnesses were brought against him leveling a variety of charges, but initially he remained silent. Eventually the high priest asked directly, "Are you the Messiah the Son of the Blessed One?" Now the chips were down, and Jesus told them, "I am and you will see the Son of Man seated at the right hand of the Power, and coming with the clouds of heaven." This assertion was the ultimate blasphemy and the death sentence was inevitable. It was duly pronounced and the crowd began to physically, as well as mentally, torment him.

Peter had, in the meantime, quietly followed the throng from a safe distance and when he was discovered by his Galilean accent as one of Jesus' disciples, he denied the assertion three times. Only after the cock had crowed did he remember the prophecy and felt deeply conscience-stricken. But there was now nothing he could do to help, so he went away thoroughly ashamed of his cowardice.

Chapter 15

The death sentence had been proclaimed and this chapter provides the information how it was carried out. Jewish law required stoning for the sin of blasphemy, but this was no ordinary case. You cannot possibly stone someone in public who had been hailed by the crowd only a few days earlier as the Son of David, the Messiah. It just couldn't be done without creating a major upheaval, especially during Passover. The foremost of the religious power structure then debated what to do. If they kept Jesus in prison there was danger that an unruly mob might free him; if they secretly killed him the matter would become known, and they would forever be tainted by his murder. Obviously the simplest and most effective solution would be to turn him over to the Romans who would have no problem in crucifying him for being a troublemaker. This expedient was, of course, a superb idea because in this way the Jewish authorities could "wash their hands" of the affair and it was Rome's problem. If Jesus' followers were indeed to take up arms they would have the Roman legions to contend with rather than the puny temple guard. No sooner said then done; Jesus was bound and taken to Pilate. But the procurator didn't quite know what to do with the man. He had not raised a revolt nor engaged in any other anti-Roman conduct so what was the charge? Pilate couldn't care less about blasphemy or any of the other religious squabbles of the Jews whom he detested. The only question was whether or not Jesus was a danger to Rome.

The Jews, as opposed to the Galileans, did not have a king at that time. They had forfeited that privilege voluntarily. Herod the Great's successors had proven themselves incompetent and the Jewish priesthood had asked Augustus to appoint a procurator so that the province could be governed directly by Rome. All the Romans wanted was peace and quiet in their Empire so Augustus acceded to their request and the Jews were saddled with a variety of provincial administrators who did their best to bleed the country of resources so that they could retire to greener pastures when their tour of duty, in what they regarded as a miserable patch of earth, was over.

Thus for Pilate the only charge that could be leveled against Jesus was: had he assumed royal privileges? Therefore the question: Are you the King of the Jews? To which Jesus replied diplomatically,

"You say so." This is a situation were written language is ambiguous and everything hangs on prosody. Was the emphasis on *You* or on *say so* ? In the first instance it would have been merely Pilate's opinion while in the second it would have amounted to a: Yes!

Pilate had to resolve this ambiguity, but Jesus remained silent from then on. The procurator was obviously in a quandary so he tried to shift the blame back to the Jewish leadership and their followers. Supposedly there was a custom at Passover that an act of leniency was called for and a prisoner could be released. Barabbas, a zealot, had been incarcerated for acts of violence against Rome, so Pilate asked the crowd whom they wanted to have freed: Barabbas or "the King of the Jews?" The crowd who loved their "freedom fighters" demanded Barabbas and to Pilate's question what he should be doing, "with the man whom you call the King of the Jews?" the answer was "crucify him!" With a little poetic license and considering the times, one might have added the unspoken thought: do what you always do; crucify him! Pilate complied; Jesus was scourged and led away.

The subsequent verses 16-20 which deal with Jesus being mocked by soldiers are exceedingly well known. Practically unknown, except to some Bible scholars, is a historic event which had taken place in Alexandria during 38 A.D., within less than a decade after Jesus' death. For this reason let me first mention Mark's verses. Pilate's soldiers led Jesus away, clothed him with purple, put a crown of thorns on his head, saluted him as King of the Jews, smote him with a reed, spat upon him, bowed their knees and worshiped him, before he was given his own clothes back and led to crucifixion. An exceedingly similar story can be found in Philo's chapter on Flaccus.

Philo, of whom more will be said in the chapter on St. John, was an eminent Jew of Alexandria, who led the Jewish deputation to Gaius (Caligula) in the hope of being able to make him abandon his effort to place a colossal golden statue bearing his likeness in the Jerusalem temple. Philo's deputation did not achieve its goal, but as mentioned before, Caligula's long time friend Agrippa, to whom he had just recently given the crown of Judea, was successful with his intervention. Basically, Agrippa had told Caligula in so many words: if you want a war I can't hinder you, but if you have any sense please forget about this project. As mentioned Caligula was killed within a few months thereafter, Claudius became Emperor and the problem was moot. In 38 A.D. when Agrippa was on his way to Judea in order to assume his regal duties, he stopped off in Alexandria. On his arrival he showed bad judgment in a city where long-standing anti-Jewish sentiments had risen to fever pitch. Let me quote from Philo as to what happened when Agrippa showed up:

> But the men of Alexandria ready to burst with envy and ill-will (for the Egyptian disposition is by nature a most jealous and envious one and inclined to look upon the good fortune of others as adversity to itself) and being at the same time filled with an ancient and what I may call innate enmity towards the Jews were indignant at any one's becoming a king of the Jews, no less than if each individual among them had been deprived of an ancestral kingdom of his own inheritance.

This provides the background, and anyone who has even a nodding acquaintance with psychoanalytic doctrine will immediately suspect that there was a degree of projection involved in Philo's description of the Egyptians. Freud used the term to indicate when one's own opinions or desires are attributed to the therapist. It is probably fair to say that the ill-feelings were mutual. Agrippa was not only resented for the above given reasons but he also had made an ostentatious display of power and wealth. As Philo stated, "He attracts all eyes towards himself when they see the array of sentinels and bodyguards around him and adorned with silvered and gilded arms." This spectacle irritated the Alexandrians, especially since it was known that Agrippa lived on borrowed money. Alexander, Philo's brother, had loaned him 200,000 drachmas and another 300,000 had come from Antonia, the mother of the future Emperor Claudius. In response to Agrippa's parade the mob got hold of a "certain madman named Carabbas," who apparently was mentally retarded rather than violent. He used to spend his time naked in the road regardless of the weather and as Philo wrote was:

> the sport of idle children and wanton youths; and they, driving the poor wretch as far as the public gymnasium, and

setting him up there on high so that he might be seen by everybody, flattened out a leaf of papyrus and put it on his head instead of a diadem, and clothed the rest of his body with a common door mat instead of a cloak and instead of a sceptre they put in his hand a small stick of the native papyrus which they found laying at the way side and gave it to him; and when like actors in theatrical spectacles, he had received all the insignia of royal authority, and had been dressed and adorned like a king, the young men bearing sticks on their shoulders stood on each side of him instead of spear bearers, in imitation of the bodyguards of the king, and then others came up, some as if to salute him, and others making as though they wished to plead their causes before him, and others pretending to wish to consult him about the affairs of the state.

Then from the multitude of those who were standing around there arose a wonderful shout of men calling out Maris, and this is the name by which it is said they call the kings among the Syrians; for they knew that Agrippa was by birth a Syrian and also that he was possessed of a great district of Syria of which he was the sovereign.

Philo then states that Flaccus, the governor of Alexandria, should have dispersed the crowd and put the fellow in jail. Instead he did nothing and allowed a major pogrom to take place.

This story represents a curious coincidence. Had Jesus' mocking of less than a decade earlier made history in Alexandria or had the gospel writer known about it and inserted the story? Although Philo was a contemporary of Jesus his extant works give no evidence that he knew anything about him, although he reports one of Pilate's misdeeds which provoked the citizens of Judea and may have led to his recall. It must be admitted, however, that Philo can hardly be regarded as an objective observer of the scene as is apparent from the earlier quote and throughout his writings.

Jesus was then led to Golgotha, and Simon, "a Cyrenian," was forced to carry the cross. The English translations render Golgotha as "place of *a* skull" or "place of *the* skull" but the Greek term is *kranion topos,* without a definite or indefinite article. There is a reason why I am making a point of it. During a stay in Jerusalem some years ago I visited, of course, the Church of the Holy Sepulcher but failed to see how this little elevation within the church could have been Golgotha. On the other hand, right outside the Damascus Gate there is a sizeable hill which indeed does resemble a skull with empty eye sockets. It is clearly outside the city walls but close to them and might well have served as a crucifixion site in Roman times. Nearby is also the so-called "Garden tomb" and the British general Gordon, who had later on been decapitated by the Mahdi in Khartoum, had regarded it as the genuine burial site of Jesus. The garden and tomb, including a huge round stone, which could be rolled into place to cover the entrance, were well kept up by Protestant missionaries. This quiet scene, which was not overrun by tourists to the extent the official tomb was, provided, at least for me, more of a spiritual experience than could be attained at the officially recognized site. But this is in the domain of Biblical archeologists and they can argue over who is right; the Protestants or the Catholic, Armenian and Greek orthodox priests, who are responsible for the care of the official site.

Mark details how Jesus refused a drink of wine mixed with myrrh, which was apparently meant as an analgesic. Jesus did so because he probably wanted to present this sacrifice to the Father in possession of his full mental powers rather than in a drugged state. This is in contrast to the gospel of John where Jesus did accept such a drink. The reason for the difference of the three synoptic gospels, which are unanimous on this point, and that of John, will be discussed further in the appropriate context. Mark also relates how the soldiers gambled for his clothes and that two miscreants were crucified to his left and right side. This was taken as fulfillment of scripture and may or may not have happened that way. That passers-by including priests and scribes jeered and mocked him to come down from the cross so that they could witness the miracle, does have a ring of truth to it. There was supposedly an eclipse of the sun for three hours but this is not attested to by other sources. At the ninth hour Jesus called out "*Eloi, Eloi, lema sabachthani*" which is translated as "My God, My God why have you forsaken me?" Measured against these words the rest of the chapter with the bystanders' reactions, the temple curtain being torn in two, the centurion's declaration that Jesus was the Son of God, Joseph of Arimathea's request of Pilate to be allowed to bury the body and after having received permission did entomb him in a sepulcher cut from a rock, is surely anticlimactic.

Let us imagine the scene. In Gethsemane Jesus had prayed that the cup of suffering and death might pass by him, but if not he would empty it to the bitter end. It came on the cross. When he was hanging there, deserted by his disciples, hungry, tired and racked with pain; flies licking his open wounds from the nails, the scourging, and the crown of thorns; his human nature came through in the desperate cry: "My God, my God why have you abandoned me?" The heavens had not opened; the angels had not come down to rescue him. There was no miracle, it had all been a delusion! He had reached the utter depth of human despair. When it is said that in so doing he was "merely" reciting the 22nd psalm this is true. But it is also the most appropriate one under the circumstances. Unless one has felt this utter and total abandonment in one's soul, words are useless to explain it. Patients will tell the physician that when one is in a manic state the entire world is in one's power, but the worst part is what is called "the lucid interval." It comes about either spontaneously during extreme stress or as a result of medication. The realization that one has been mad is the most devastating experience of all.

Jesus was not to be spared this last ordeal. It was necessary. If he had been truly God, in the fullest sense of the word, at the time of crucifixion, the entire event would have been a sham, because he would have known that this was merely a temporary inconvenience. Just like the actors in a drama who when they get killed know that they will take their bow to the applause of the audience a short while later. It would have immensely cheapened his sacrifice. No; it is my firm belief that he was one of us who felt just as we do and he no longer addressed God as Father who would do favors for His son but simply as the deity whose purposes we cannot fathom.

But were those words really his final thoughts? Let me now look at the situation as a physician who is familiar with what happens to people when they die. There is no moment of death, organs decay depending upon their oxygen requirements. When a comatose person is on a respirator and the instrument is disconnected it takes about five minutes for brain electrical activity to cease. Regardless of the cause of death when the last breath has been taken the brain becomes deprived of oxygen; carbon dioxide as well as nitrogen build up and voluntary thought is no longer possible. We don't know the final thoughts of a person who has truly died, rather than having had a "near-death experience," but we do know what happens when an individual is deprived of oxygen for a shorter period of time. Since I have discussed this in the medical literature two decades ago I shall be brief here. When the oxygen flow to the brain is seriously restricted critical judgment disappears first. Jesus was right, and Bertrand Russell was wrong. In the last moments of our lives, regardless who we are, we will "become as little children" who take what we see and hear as the full truth. Questions are over and done with, now we know! But what we know bears no relationship to what we are used to in our waking lives. The patently false can become full truth, and the eminent Bertrand Russell may have discovered with joy and relief why two and two really make five. Joy and a feeling of power are frequent accompaniments of hypoxia, which in turn is inevitable when we die. On the other hand there is no guarantee that our final thoughts and these are really the only ones that count, because they might determine how we spend eternity, are pleasant. They might also be profoundly distressing. Just as we cannot direct the contents of our dreams according to our will, so are we going to be unable to wish ourselves out of a potential nightmare. Heaven and hell are not geographic locations. They are mental states. Eternity is not merely an interminably long time but also an experience where time simply does not exist, where there is no past or future but simply the eternal now. If one finds oneself caught in this situation when there is no awakening from a nightmare, one can indeed be in deep trouble. But depending upon the life we have led, we may be able to shape our nocturnal dreams and thereby, possibly, our dying moments. If one has lived on this earth with faith in the goodness of God the final thought may well be "Lord have mercy, *kyrie eleison.*" If one firmly believes this, one is not likely to be disappointed. In this way death has lost its sting, even if there were to be no physical resurrection, or some other "afterlife." When one lives in the world of spirit the material one loses a great deal of its luster anyway.

So when Jesus cried in agony why Lord have you abandoned me? these were still words. But there comes a time when words cease and pictures take over. Of these only he was privy to but judging from his life, one can be reasonably certain that he may well have seen the heavens open again and being received by a loving Father.

Chapter 16

On Sunday morning Mary Magdalene, of whom we are told Jesus had driven out seven demons, Mary the mother of James, and Salome, came to the tomb to anoint the body. They found that the stone had been rolled away and inside was an angel who told them not to be afraid but to inform Peter and the disciples that Jesus had risen and gone ahead to Galilee, where they would meet him. The text then states that the women, "fled from the tomb, for terror and amazement had seized them; and they said nothing to anyone, for they were afraid." Although the disappearance of Jesus' body is indeed mysterious, the mystery in regard to Mark's gospel deepens.

There are two endings to chapter 16. A short one consisting of only two sentences after verse 8 and the longer version of verses 9-20. For a scientist the short version, which does not even appear in the Latin text, is a welcome relief. The unskilled handling of poisonous snakes and drinking toxic juice in the name of Jesus while remaining unharmed, just smacks a little bit too much of what Jesus had warned against. "Beware of the leaven of Pharisees and Herodians," has become one of my favorite maxims. Instead of verses 9-20 the short version states, "And all that had been commanded them they told briefly to those around Peter. And afterwards Jesus showed himself and sent out through them, from east to west, the sacred and imperishable proclamation of eternal salvation. Amen."

What happened here? *The Jerome Biblical Commentary* provides the explanation. The extant manuscript ended with verse 8 and whatever Mark had reported subsequently, is now lost. It is regarded as highly unlikely that Mark would have ended his account with trembling women. This would have been out of character with all the preceding messages of faith and hope so there must have been some type of ending. But since none could be found, the Church fathers had a problem on their hands. They had to choose from the two different endings which were available at the time although none of them are in Mark's style and diction. They opted for the long version as it now exists in our Bibles, although even Eusebius (c. 260-339), one of the most eminent members of the Church, had already declared the long version as inauthentic. It was a decision by committee to encourage more conversions from the less educated who are more likely to respond to miracles than to a doctrine which emphasizes merely spiritual values rather than material rewards.

In essence, verses 9-20 tell us that Peter and the disciples didn't believe the women's report. Jesus then appeared first to Mary Magdalene and "in another form" to two disciples. Nevertheless, disbelief persisted until Jesus showed himself to all the eleven, upbraided them for their lack of faith and charged them to preach the gospel of salvation far and wide. He who believes would be saved; he who does not would be condemned. The believers would in his name: cast out demons, speak with "new tongues," pick up snakes with their hands and heal people. Jesus was then received into heaven, sat on the right side of God; the disciples went forth preached everywhere and their words were confirmed by the mentioned signs from the Lord.

Even a lay person can detect that this version is out of character with the preceding chapters. Nevertheless, there is an important statement which is probably authentic, not only because it appears in other gospels but because it carries an essential element of Jesus' message. He appeared to the disciples "in another form." The meaning of this passage will be taken up later.

In addition to these two versions there exists still another gloss which has also been regarded as belonging to Mark's book. It resides in the Freer Museum of the Smithsonian Institute in Washington and consists of an insert after verse 14 to soften the impact of Jesus' scolding the disciples for their unbelief. The translation provided by Edward J. Mally reads:

> And they [the disciples] excused themselves, saying 'This age of lawlessness and disbelief is under Satan, who does not permit the true power of God to prevail over the unclean things of the spirits. Therefore reveal your righteousness

now.' Thus they addressed Christ, but Christ said to them in reply, 'The term of the years of Satan's authority has been fulfilled, but other terrible things draw near, even for the sinners for whom I was handed over in death, that they might return to the truth, and sin no more, that they might inherit the spiritual and incorruptible glory of righteousness which is in heaven.'

It seems exceedingly unlikely that fishermen would have addressed Jesus in this manner nor would he have answered in such a convoluted style. Thus, there was good reason for the Church to reject it. But as mentioned the current long version is problematic enough and I was very happy to read that it is not authentic.

In conclusion it is apparent that everything Jesus stood for is contained in Mark's gospel which one might subtitle: How Jesus of Nazareth became Christ. The other two synoptic gospels add some of Jesus' words but they also try to "gild the lily." Conspicuously absent from Mark's gospel are: genealogy, virgin birth, the Sermon on the Mount and the famous "woe to scribes and Pharisees" diatribe. Thus Mark presents a human Jesus we, or at least I, can understand and identify with.

Let me return now to the statement of my son, as quoted in the Introduction. What would I have done had I been a physician in Galilee and the family had brought this "obviously deranged" Jesus to me? I would have sequestered myself with him and on a one to one basis would have done in a covert fashion what is called a "mental status examination." I would have listened to his speech pattern and how he answered my questions when put forth in an interested, non-threatening manner. This would have allowed me to determinewhether his mental processes were either: disorganized, grandiose, fearful, or spiteful; or whether I was confronted by an individual who genuinely believed that he was called by God to bring people back to Him from their aberrant ways. I would have concluded that he was not mentally ill but obsessed with what he regarded as his mission in life. I would have told him: Well Jesus, you know that if you continue with this type of behavior the power structures will kill you. He would have said: I know, but this is what I was born for: To suffer and to die in the attempt to bring the people back to the heart of God's message for humankind. If he had a smattering of Greek he might even have quoted Socrates to me, "Anytus and Meletus can kill me; they cannot harm me." I would have nodded and said, "I will grieve for your suffering and dying but if it comes true what you so fervently believe in, I'll rejoice with you."

Saint Matthew's Jesus

As mentioned previously, the gospels of Matthew and Luke depended heavily on Mark and present much of the same material in expanded form. For this reason I shall cover only those aspects of Jesus' life and teachings which did not appear in Mark. The author of the document is unknown but it is believed that it could not have been the apostle Levi, the tax collector who had been renamed Matthew, because the gospel does not show full familiarity with Palestinian geography. Furthermore, it was written originally in impeccable Greek rather than representing a translation from Aramaic. The date for our current version is assumed to have been after the Jewish war and the destruction of the temple. Its purpose was to present the incipient Jewish-Christian community with a concise outline of Jesus' life and teachings. The essential point Matthew was trying to make was that Jesus was the new Moses and the promised Messiah. The Law was not abrogated, but has been fulfilled. The onerous rules of the oral law which were useful and necessary while growing up were now outdated as adulthood had been achieved. Instead of the rituals the main commandments for the community were to love God and each other, and to conduct themselves accordingly throughout their lives. This is, however, an oversimplification as the, in part, contradictory text shows.

In order to convince the readership of Jesus' messianic stature, Matthew had to present a genealogy which shows him as descended from David, and on account of Micah's prophecy the birth had to be placed into Bethlehem:

> And thou, Beth-lehem, house of Ephratah, art few in number to be reckoned among the thousands of Judah;

> Yet out of thee shalt one come forth to me to be a ruler of Israel;
>
> And his goings forth were from the beginning, even from eternity [5:1].

On the other hand Matthew also relates that during betrothal, but prior to the actual marriage, Mary "was found with child of the Holy Ghost." One cannot fault Gentile, or Jewish, readers when they asked: well, which way was it? Was Joseph the natural father or had God performed a miracle? The subsequent stories of Joseph's dream in which he was told that he should not reject Mary because she was carrying the savior, the visit by the "Wise Men, " Herod's attempt to kill the baby, the flight of the family to Egypt and eventual return to Galilee, had theologic reasons and need not be taken literally. Joseph's dream mirrors that of Amram, Moses' father, who in oral tradition, as related by Josephus, had been assured that the child would bring untold blessings to Israel. Virgin birth was regarded as necessary on account of the Is. 7:14 prophecy. Matthew's information about the Old Testament came from the Septuagint and the appropriate quote is, "behold a virgin shall conceive in the womb, and shall bring forth a son, and thou shalt call his name Emmanuel." But the Greek word *parthenos*, which is translated as "virgin" can also simply mean maiden. Supernatural birth would not necessarily have been required but it was probably felt useful since many of the heroes and demi-gods of antiquity, including the Buddha, had been so conceived. The slaughter of the innocents by Herod mirrors the fate of the Hebrew children at the hands of Pharaoh in Moses' time and the flight to Egypt was necessary to fulfill the statement in Hosea 11:1 "And out of Egypt I called My son."

In chapters 3 and 4 Matthew follows Mark rather closely although John the Baptist had recognized Jesus as his superior and was loath to perform the baptism. But Jesus encouraged him to do so anyway in order to "fulfill all righteousness." The temptation by Satan was refused with the famous words: that man does not live by bread alone, that one should not tempt God, and only God should be served.

Chapters 5-8 are a departure from Mark because they present the Sermon on the Mount where blessings are bestowed on the afflicted.

The sermon contains apparent paradoxes because misfortunes are regarded as blessings which would lead to rewards. The first verse, "Blessed are the poor in spirit: for theirs is the kingdom of heaven" has puzzled me for quite some time. Who are these poor in spirit? The question is not irrelevant because, especially in my profession, the phrase could be regarded as referring to people with limited intellectual endowment. The solution seems again to lie in the translation. Although the word *ptōchoí* does mean poor it can also mean distressed. Under these circumstances it would make perfect sense for this verse to introduce all the rest of the beatitudes. Those distressed individuals who beg for the Holy Spirit to come into their lives will indeed receive it and reside in the kingdom of Heaven.

Numerous other sayings of Jesus which have become famous are also contained in these chapters. Jesus had not come to destroy the Law but to fulfill it in the spirit it was originally meant. Agree with your adversary quickly, do not swear an oath, "Let your words be Yes, Yes; No, No: anything more than this comes from the evil one." Do not pray with ostentation and many words but pray in secret and simply. Do not lay up treasures on earth where they are liable to corruption, but with good works which will be rewarded in heaven. Keep your eye single, namely devoted to do right, and be steadfast. No one can serve two masters: God and mammon; do not put cares for your property and the future ahead of regard for the righteousness of God, which should be the true goal. Judge not because you will be judged the same way by others, whoever hears the teachings and follows them will be like the wise man who builds his house on a rock.

Verse 5:44 has become a hallmark of the Christian tradition: love your enemies and pray for those who persecute you. This is obviously difficult to put into practice because it runs counter to human nature. There is simply no way that we could hug and kiss Osama bin Laden, for instance, although it might be possible to pray for him, that he mends his ways. But the Latin words are, "diligite vos inimicos et orate pro persequentibus vos." This throws a different light on the situation. Although *diligo* does mean love it has nothing to do with amorous love, and means in this case to prize or esteem. We don't have to hate our enemy. He is meant to be a learning experience; we can find out what motivates him, help him overcome his false ideas and if we have to defeat him we need to recognize that we have to live with the defeated people in peace thereafter. This is why *diligite vos inimicos* is superior to Old Testament teachings.

Chapter 6 verses 9-13 contain what is called the Lord's Prayer and deserve closer scrutiny. Although most every one knows the words, I shall take them sentence by sentence. In contrast to John's gospel where Jesus always refers to God as "My Father," Matthew uses, up to chapter 7 the term "your" father when Jesus is addressing a crowd. This was in keeping with the culture of the time where the chief god of every society was considered the father of gods and men. The introductory statement of the prayer, "Our father who art in heaven" has actually a corollary in the Iliad (book 3, 267). On the plains of Troy Agamemnon started his prayer with, "Father Jove who rulest in Ida, most glorious in power . . ." The subsequent difference in the prayer is that the Greeks and the Trojans, who used a similar appellation (book 3, 310), prayed for a specific earthly benefit while Jesus asked mainly for spiritual blessings.

Verse 11, "Give us this day our daily bread" seems incongruous. It is sandwiched between the request that God's will be done on earth as it is in heaven, and the forgiveness of sins. When the entire prayer deals with matters of the spirit why should we suddenly be concerned about our stomachs? The answer to this apparent incongruity may lie again in the translation. The Greek word which has been translated into "daily" is *èpioúsion,* and is a neologism that does not exist anywhere else in Greek literature. It is a compound word of *èpi* and *oúsia* which means essence or substance, while *èpi* has several meanings, depending upon context. Some of these are: "on" or "upon" when referring to a place; "on," "at," or "during" when it refers to time, but it can also be used metaphorically in a variety of ways. Thus the combination of these two words is obviously a translation from some other language and its exact meaning has been debated by scholars. For instance *The Jerome Biblical Commentary* mentions a suggestion by K. Stendhal that the word refers to the messianic banquet in the kingdom of heaven. The Latin text does not help much either because the word is translated in Mt. 11:6 as *supersubstantialem.* This is likewise a neologism which does not show up in Latin dictionaries, but the same word *èpioúsion* when it occurs in Luke 11:3 is translated into Latin as *quotidianum* which indeed means daily. If Jesus had said "daily," Matthew would not have had a problem translating it. But in the context of Jesus' prayer *supersubstantialem* seems to fit much better because he was not necessarily concerned with the material bread but the bread from God which is enlightenment by the spirit. Thus I believe that Jesus may have asked us to pray for receiving God's word, the supernatural bread, rather than merely the one derived from the earth. This should, however, not blind us to the fact that there are still literally millions around the world for whom even ordinary bread is not available and ought to be provided.

There is, however, an additional way how to read this most important of all prayers. It transcends sectarian barriers and can be used even by atheists if one were to omit the introductory statements about the Lord granting these requests. The prayer can be taken as rules for everyday conduct. For instance "Thy will be done" can signify that when we are confronted with a reasonable request from someone else and it is in our power to grant it we should do so. "Give us this day our daily bread" orders us to feed the physically as well as spiritually hungry. "As we forgive those who trespass against us," can mean that intermittent flash floods of anger are part of the human condition when we feel ourselves wronged, but to carry a long term grudge is harmful and should be avoided. "Lead us not into temptation" is perhaps the one aspect our society needs to heed the most. What it means, for instance, is that we should not let valuables lie unguarded in open view so that others might be tempted to steal them. But since the most important temptation for a great many of us tends to be sexual, our culture needs to be reformed. Modesty in clothing, language and visual imagery would go a considerable distance to reduce the sexual promiscuity which has become the norm and rips families apart. So would a change in the constant repetition of violence, now even by women who have become Amazon warriors, on TV and the movie screens. The deleterious effect on our civilization cannot be overemphasized and daily reminders in our prayer that we should abstain from such incitements would be most appropriate.

The words, "But deliver us from evil," require somewhat more extensive discussion. In the sense of the prayer as used here they can be taken to order us as not to voluntarily inflict misfortunes on others for our own perceived gain, and if we are indeed harmed let us use our inner resources to minimize the impact. There is, however an additional interpretation possible when we consider that "evil" in the prayer has only lately become an abstract noun. Initially the meaning was: deliver us from the Evil One, Satan. In olden times the forces of nature were personified and this was achieved by naming them, according to their assumed main attributes. Satan means adversary or accuser and as such had been assigned the role of prosecutor when the human soul is judged by God. But this prosecutor is not impartial; he needs to win his case and his prime tool is the Lie in any and all of its forms.

There are numerous other names for "the devil" but a German one, "der *Leibhaftige*," although no longer in common use, is most descriptive and appropriate. Literally translated it means he who clings to the body. In the allegorical sense it can be taken to mean the ultimate materialist, for whom spiritual values not only do not exist, but must be combated. This makes him the enemy of God. Once he clings to your body and convinces you that he only has your best interest at heart your soul is in dire straits. You are then like Faust who has made his pact with the devil, loathes it, but finds his companion indispensable. The Catholic Church has found a way out of this dilemma via exorcism. It need not be mumbo-jumbo and may not even need a priest only the firm resolution, spoken to oneself repeatedly on various occasions: "I reject Satan and all his works." This allows one in Jesus' words: to be in the world, but not of it.

The concluding verses of the prayer, "For thine is the power . . ." are not found in the Greek or Latin version of the gospel and represent a later interpolation. When we look at the prayer from this vantage point its silent recitation on a daily basis can indeed remind us of our duties towards others, whomever they might be.

Let us also remember that it was Jesus who introduced this prayer to us and he, therefore, was likely to have used it himself. What was the temptation he was concerned about? Sexual promiscuity was probably not a major problem, neither were gambling, alcohol abuse, gluttony or any of the other common vices. I believe that the major temptation may have been doubt: Was he really qualified to assume the role he thought he had been chosen for or was it all a phenomenal mistake? He could not have been human unless he had been beset by doubts which had to be banished.

In chapter 8 we find the story of the centurion who had asked Jesus to heal one of his servants who was paralyzed and in a great deal of distress. When Jesus said that he would come to the house, the centurion uttered the famous words, "Lord, I am not worthy to have you come under my roof, but only speak the word and my servant will be healed [8:7-8]." Jesus marveled at the centurion's answer and commented that he had not found anyone among the Israelites with such faith. The story is recounted with some elaborations in Luke 7: 2-10. I am making a point of it because it has been used to indicate that Jesus had no objections to war. This will be explained further in the chapter on St. Luke.

Chapter 9 presents essentially medical miracles and only chapter 10 represents significant departures from Mark. There is no mention of Jesus being humiliated by the crowd in Nazareth and that his family had regarded him as mentally unstable. These aspects were regarded as disrespectful details and, therefore, omitted. Nevertheless, they are probably genuine, as Mark had reported them, for precisely that reason. In Matthew's version the disciples were sent out simply because as it says at the end of chapter 9, "The harvest is plentiful, but the laborers are few." The instructions to the twelve were also more detailed. They were not to go into the lands of the Gentiles or the Samaritans but rather, "to the lost sheep of the house of Israel." They were to heal the sick and preach that, "the kingdom of heaven has come near." Their conduct was to be "wise as serpents and harmless as doves," and they were warned that persecutions were going to be at hand. Another departure is that from now on Jesus keeps referring to God always as, "my Father" thereby separating himself from the rest of the people including the disciples. The term does not occur in Mark. In Luke it is used only once after the resurrection when Jesus promised to send the Holy Spirit (24:49) On the other hand, John employs it routinely when Jesus talks about God. The later chapters of Matthew might, therefore, be seen as a bridge between these two gospels.

Chapter 11 deals with the relationship of John the Baptist's disciples to those of Jesus but also shows that Jesus' message had not been received well even in Galilee because three of the major towns of his mission were singled out for destruction on account of their unbelief (11:20-24). This is typical Old Testament rhetoric and is not found in Mark or Luke.

The subsequent verses 25-30 appear to be a theological interpolation because they do not relate to the foregoing but have become the underpinning of the Mysterium Christi. Jesus thanked the Father for having revealed to him what was hidden from the wise; that all things were delivered unto him as the Son of the Father; that no one could know the Father but the Son and those to whom the Son would reveal it. An offer was also extended to all who were burdened to come to him because with him the soul could find its rest. The last sentence, "For my yoke is easy, and my burden is light," is, of course, in the literal sense contradicted by subsequent expectations of martyrdom. In the present context it probably was meant to indicate that the burdensome Law of Moses (commonly referred to as the yoke) has been superceded and faith in Jesus was all that was required. Chapters 12 and 13 do not present information which is essentially different from what is contained in Mark, except for some additional brief parables in regard to the kingdom of heaven. It is likened to a treasure in a field and a pearl which when found is worth more than anything else. These parables are non-specific because they occur also in Buddhist teaching. On the other hand there is also the apocalyptic vision of separating the good and the evil at the end of time where the wicked will suffer eternal hell fire, which is shared, as mentioned previously with the followers of Zarathustra.

Chapters 14-17 contain essentially similar information as Mark's gospel, except that in 16:18 Jesus tells Peter that he will be the rock upon whom he will build the Church. This statement occurs only in Matthew rather than in Mark or Luke. When Peter had answered the question in these two gospels who he thought Jesus was with, "you are the Christ," Jesus had merely replied with the admonition not to mention this to anybody. The word "Church," also appears here for the first time and the use of the Greek word *ekklēsía,* is a clear departure from precedent. While *synagoge,* from which the term synagogue was derived, means nothing else but assembly, gathering or congregation, *ekklesia* had a deeper connotation. It was derived from "having been called out" and denoted the assembly of a body of free citizens who had been called out by a herald. In the current context it refers to the faithful having been called forth by Jesus and they were thereby relieved from the yoke of the law. By the time the gospel was written, Christian churches had already been founded and the gospel writer needed Jesus' authority to confer on Peter the apostolic succession. The tension between Peter and Paul as symbols for Jewish Christianity versus Hellenistic Christianity is palpable in the Acts of the Apostles and Paul's epistles. This change in language lends further credence to the opinion that the author of Matthew's gospel came from the Jewish rather than Gentile membership of the Church.

The existence of the Church is also mentioned in 18:17 where Jesus supposedly ordered that a recalcitrant offender who did not listen to the admonitions of witnesses should be brought before the Church, "but if he neglects to hear the church, let him be unto thee as a Gentile and a tax collector." This statement clearly refers to circumstances after Jesus' death. They are also out of character with Mark's description of a Jesus who had readily mixed with, and been entertained by, tax collectors. Thus 18:17 can only be understood in the context of the nascent Church which found itself beset by doctrinal conflicts. Expulsion from the Church was the remedy used to settle disputes. The immediately following statements (18:21-22) in regard to the forgiving of trespasses, "until seven times seven" can probably more readily be attributed to Jesus, although in the subsequent parable of the unmerciful debtor Jesus refers to God again as "my heavenly Father." It would seem that an editor might have been involved who combined different documents in a somewhat arbitrary manner.

Chapter 19 brings no new information but chapter 20 contains the parable of the laborers in the vineyard which had political significance for the new Church. A man hired workers in the morning for his vineyard and promised to give them a penny for the day's work. Throughout the day the man kept hiring more workers at the same pay of one penny, even those who were hired last and had hardly done any work at all got as much as the ones who had worked since the morning. When the men who had put in a full day's work complained about the apparent injustice they were told that they had agreed to it when they signed up and the owner was free to decide how much he wanted to pay to whom. In the context of the times this parable, as well as frequent statements that "the last shall be first," was meant to indicate to the Jewish people that, although they had worked in the Lord's vineyard considerably longer than the converts to the new religion, they had no claim for preferential treatment by the Lord.

In chapter 22 we find the parable of the king's marriage feast which provides the same message. The invited guests made excuses for not attending, therefore, the king told the servants to gather people from wherever they could find them. The meaning is obvious: the Jews had rejected the invitation by the Lord so it was now offered to the Gentiles regardless of their previous conduct. But there is more to it because verses 5-7 have been taken to indicate that the parable originated after the fall of Jerusalem. While some of the originally invited wedding guests had simply declined and gone on with their business others "seized his [the king's] slaves, mistreated them, and killed them. The king was enraged. He sent his troops, destroyed those murderers, and burned their city." Thus the destruction of Jerusalem, which is referred to here, was regarded as divine punishment for the Jews. They not only had rejected Jesus as the Messiah but also murdered him and some of his followers. However, even among the new guests there was one man who "was not wearing a wedding robe." The king was astonished and then bid his servants, "Bind him hand and foot, and throw him into outer darkness; where there will be weeping and gnashing of teeth." This type of punishment is clearly out of proportion. It differs markedly from the forgiving Jesus and is much more in line with the utterances of the Old Testament prophets. The last sentences of the parable can also be taken to indicate that even within the new Church there were some who did not toe the line and who would be expelled with dire warnings.

Chapter 23 contains an elaboration of Mark's discourse against the religious authorities who preached the Law but did not follow it. They were hypocrites who loved to be honored and respected but it was all for show rather than having come from the heart. The new congregation should be humble, not exalt itself, even to the extent of not calling anyone "your father on earth, for you have one Father—the one in heaven." Biblical authorities agree that this chapter with the numerous denunciations of the ruling Jewish circles was written to separate the new Church from Judaism, but it is not yet clear whether the Law was still to be followed in a more honest manner or whether it was already regarded as obsolete. As mentioned, the Acts of the Apostles and Paul's epistles give ample evidence of this discord in the early Church. On the other hand, the imprecations against hypocrisy in general and the admonition for humility are timeless. They should be taken to heart even in our generation regardless of religious belief system.

Chapter 24 deals with the impending destruction of Jerusalem and its temple but, as mentioned, the described events had already occurred. The persecution of the faithful was also in progress, but the hope for the immediate return of Jesus, and with it the arrival of the messianic kingdom, had to be kept alive. For this reason his followers would have to remain faithful and not yield to the siren songs of false prophets. The threat of "weeping and gnashing of teeth" is again Old Testament rhetoric, albeit in a shorter version. The sayings of the Prophets are replete with warnings of this type and the full flavor of disasters which would befall the Jewish people when they did not follow Moses' laws can only be appreciated when one reads the curses in Deuteronomy 28:15-68. They should be required reading for anyone who feels that the gospel writers had been too harsh on "the Jews." Jewish authors prefer to read and quote the preceding 13 verses of blessings which the nation would reap when it adhered to the Law; but the curses had become reality three times by the middle of the second century. First, during the Babylonian conquest, and subsequently in 70 and 135 A.D.. When one considers the conduct of Israel's current political leaders, another re-enactment of Moses' curses seems to be a definite possibility.

The parable of the ten virgins, in chapter 25, re-emphasized the need to be watchful and observant. The five wise virgins had the oil for their lamps ready when the bridegroom came unannounced. The foolish ones had not prepared themselves and they wanted to beg some from the wise ones but were turned away. Again the message by the Church to the Jewish people was obvious: join us now, or the door will be shut in your faces. Sayings like these tell us more about the political struggle of the early Church than about universal ethics, apart from the advice to be prudent and to be prepared for all eventualities. But this simple statement was, of course, common sense and would not have needed a parable.

The rest of the chapter deals with the parable of differing amounts of money being given to a number of people according to their abilities. The ones who had doubled the amount they had received were rewarded, while the one who had simply stored it and subsequently gave it back was not only chastised but also, "cast into outer darkness: there shall be weeping and gnashing of teeth," which seems to have been a favorite refrain of the author.

There is a remarkable difference between Mark and Matthew in this parable. Mark used the verse, "For every one that hath shall be given, and he shall have abundance: but from him who hath not shall be taken away even that which he hath" in relationship to the spiritual bread of heaven which reveals the kingdom of God. Matthew was much more explicit and declared that the Lord was a venture capitalist who liked to receive unearned income, "You ought to have invested my money with the bankers, and on my return I would have received what was my own with interest." Not only did the debtor have to give the "talent" to someone else, who had invested wisely but the Master also said, "As for this worthless slave, throw him into the outer darkness, where there will be weeping and gnashing of teeth." Although one can draw a spiritual inference, namely that one should use one's God given endowments to the fullest, the emphasis on money in this parable as well as its brutal ending make it unlikely that it came from Jesus' lips in this form.

The chapter ends with the Final Judgment where the sheep will be separated from the goats. The latter will be cast into everlasting fire. But in the concluding verses of the chapter we also find the commandment to be helpful and considerate towards the needs of others in whatever form they may appear. "Inasmuch as ye have done it to the least of these my brethren, ye have done it unto me." Those who have not done so will go to "eternal punishment, but the righteous into eternal life."

Chapters 26-28 provide the chronicle of Jesus' betrayal, crucifixion and resurrection. They are essentially similar to the narrative by Mark including the desperate cry *"Eli, Eli lema sabachthani."* The major difference in the resurrection story is that an angel of the Lord descended, in full sight of Mary Magdalene and "the other Mary," rolled the stone away from the sepulcher, announced that Jesus had risen, and that they should tell the disciples that Jesus would meet them in Galilee. In addition Jesus showed himself to the women before they had a chance to see the disciples and bring the good news. Some of the "watchmen" who had witnessed this miraculous event subsequently reported it to the Jewish authorities. They bribed them and also gave the stern order to say that while they were sleeping the disciples had come and had removed Jesus' body. In Galilee the apostles did see Jesus who told them "All power is given unto me in heaven and in earth," they should teach all nations and "baptize in the name of the Father, the Son and of the Holy Ghost." He assured them, furthermore, that he would be with them always unto the end of the world.

In summary: Matthew's gospel seems to have been written from the point of view of a Jewish convert because of its marked use of Old Testament rhetoric. It emphasized that Jesus was the Jewish Messiah who had not abolished the Law but by his coming had fulfilled it and the Christian Church which was in the process of separation from rabbinical Judaism had to be embraced quickly lest eternal damnation, on the model of the Old Testament, ensued. What was condemned in the gospel was not the Law *per se* but its elaborations which had led to hypocrisy. The gospel also reveals the ambivalence in regard to the extent the oral law had to be followed. There is no indication throughout the text that Matthew was interested in the conversion of Gentiles. The only sentence where they are referred to as worthy of consideration is in the final commandment after Jesus' resurrection to "make disciples of all the nations."

SAINT LUKE'S JESUS

The author of Luke's gospel is usually regarded as the same person who had written The Acts of the Apostles and he may have been by profession a colleague of mine. Whether or not he was indeed Paul's "beloved physician" cannot be settled conclusively but there are indications in the books that he may have been a medical man who had accompanied Paul on some of his voyages. While Matthew represented, as mentioned, the Jewish element of the new Church, Luke came from the Gentile community. Matthew, imbued with Old Testament fervor, emphasized damnation where the "wailing and grinding of teeth" occurs six times but we find it only once in Luke. His gospel is indeed the "good news" which offers: hope, love, forgiveness and compassion with the poor and downtrodden regardless of national origin.

The date of the composition of the books is unknown. Since *Acts* ends with Paul's house arrest in Rome, and we are left in uncertainty about his future fate, it has been assumed that the books were written shortly before 70 A.D., but this has been contested. In contrast to Matthew, who wrote primarily for a Jewish audience, Luke addressed himself to the Gentile community.

Since there are so many similarities to Mark and Matthew I will limit myself again only to the discrepancies. The first two chapters are unique and contain legends involving an angel's announcement of John the Baptist's birth to the elderly Zacharias and his wife Elisabeth, the angel Gabriel's announcement to Mary of Jesus' conception by the Holy Spirit, the journey from Nazareth to Bethlehem because of the census by Cyrenius, the birth in a stable with shepherds paying homage, Jesus' circumcision on the eighth day, and his teaching at the temple at the tender age of twelve years. Notably absent are: the visit of the wise men, Herod's edict to massacre the innocents in Bethlehem, and the flight to Egypt. Thus, cruelty and fear have been replaced by joy. Jesus humble birth circumstances were to be the medium from which hope could be derived by the lowest segments of society.

Chapter 3 repeats the story of John's preaching on the banks of the Jordan, the baptism of Jesus and, in addition, presents a genealogy of Jesus. In contrast to Matthew who started with Abraham, as the father of the Jews, Luke worked backwards from Joseph having been the son of Heli all the way to Seth who was the son of Adam, who "was the son of God." The genealogy sequence does not agree entirely with that of Matthew, but this is of no particular consequence. The important aspect Luke wanted to get across was that since Adam was the son of God, everybody else was, therefore, also derived to some extent from God, which conformed to Hellenistic tradition. The chapter also contains an interesting snippet which was used by St. Augustine to demonstrate that Christians were entitled to wage war. This has subsequently found its way into St. Thomas of Aquinas' *Summa Theologica* where the concept of "just war" was formulated and has now been used by some authors to support the current "War on Terrorism."

The fact that twenty-first century political decisions, which affect the lives of all of us, are defended by the thoughts of a thirteenth century theologian, who in turn based his opinions on those of a fifth century North African bishop, should dispel all doubt whether the human race is governed by reason and wisdom, or expediency. In view of the importance of the matter I shall give the relevant quotations. St. Thomas wrote in Article 1 of Book II Part II under Question XL *Whether it is Always Sinful To Wage War?* [italics in the original]:

> We proceed to the first article: It seems that it is always sinful to wage war . . . On the contrary, Augustine says in a sermon on the son of the centurion. 'If the Christian Religion forbade war altogether, those who sought salutary advice in the gospel would rather have been counseled to cast aside

their arms, and give up soldiering altogether. On the contrary they were told: 'Do violence to no man; . . . and be content with your pay!' (Luke 3. 14). If he commanded them to be content with their pay, he did not forbid soldiering'.

St. Thomas then lists three conditions which allow "for a war to be just." They are: the authority of a sovereign, rather than of a private individual; a just cause and right intention by the belligerents. It is not my purpose here to question whether or not these conditions are currently met but rather to explore the gospel authority on which all the rest hangs. As repeatedly mentioned, context is everything and when Augustine said "he commanded them" one would immediately assume that the bishop had referred to Jesus. This was not the case because the words came from John the Baptist. After he had called people who came to be baptized "you brood of vipers [3:7]," they asked him what they should do to be saved. The full quote of the relevant section is:

Even tax collectors came to be baptized, and they asked him 'Teacher what should we do?' He said to them, 'Collect no more than the amount prescribed for you.' Soldiers also asked him. 'And we, what should we do?' He said to them, 'Do not extort money from anyone by threats or false accusation, and be satisfied with your wages' [3:12-14].

This is all any of the gospels say about the duties of soldiers and there is no evidence that Jesus had ever addressed the issue of war. His kingdom was not of *this* world and his name is being misused when political issues, apart from paying taxes, were supposedly condoned by him.

Chapter 4 describes the temptations and the working of miracles but also elaborates on the scene in the synagogue of Nazareth. Jesus read from the scroll the prophecy of Isaiah 61:1,2:

The spirit of the Lord is upon me, because he hath anointed me to preach the gospel to the poor; he hath sent me to heal the broken-hearted, to preach deliverance to the captives, and recovering sight to the blind, to set at liberty them that are bruised. To preach the acceptable year of the Lord.

To which he added, "This day is the scripture fulfilled." These verses can be taken as Luke's firm belief of what Jesus' message was all about. At first the audience was simply surprised. Since Luke had given in the genealogy Joseph as Jesus' father he avoided Mark's phrase, "is this not the son of Mary . . ." and the listeners murmured instead, "Is not this Joseph's son?" To which Jesus replied not only that, "No prophet is accepted in his own country," but added that Elijah and Elisha also did not perform miracles indiscriminately. This seeming arrogance of Jesus by putting himself in the same league with the most venerated prophets was too much for the good citizens of Nazareth. They wanted to throw him down a cliff, but he escaped unharmed. In contrast to Mark he is, however, not regarded by family and friends as mentally unbalanced.

Most of the content of chapters 5 and 6 is similar to what has been presented elsewhere except that the Beatitudes in 6:20 begin with, "Blessed are the poor" rather than the "poor in spirit." In 6:29 there is also a difference from Matthew in regard to offering the other cheek. Matthew specifically stated that if the right cheek is struck one should offer the left one also. This was taken by Bible scholars to mean that striking the right cheek requires the use of the back of the striking hand which was regarded as a sign of inferiority. If the struck person then offered the other cheek, equality had been restored. The fact that this automatically assumes that the person who delivers the blow is always right handed was not taken into account by those who endorsed this legalistic stance. Luke avoided this problem and simply stated, "If anyone strikes you on the cheek," the other should also be offered. This simple change endorses humility and indifference to insults rather than pride. As will be shown later this stance is demanded by Stoic doctrine with which Luke, the educated Gentile, was surely familiar with.

Verse 6:31 expresses the Golden Rule in a positive form as, "do unto others . . ." rather than negatively "do not do unto others . . . " The statement is, of course, not original. Not only was it Stoic doctrine but it can even be found in the *Analects of Confucius*. When the Chinese sage was asked, "'Is there any single saying that one can act upon all day and every day?' The Master said, 'Perhaps the saying about consideration: never do unto others what you would not like them to do to you.'" In the Talmud one can find a frequently quoted statement attributed to Hillel (c.70 B.C.- c.10 A.D.). When a heathen came to him and wanted to be accepted as a convert on the condition that he was taught the whole of the Torah while he stood on one foot, the teacher said, "What is hateful to yourself, do not do to your fellow man. That is the whole of the Torah and the remainder is but commentary. Go, learn it." If this were indeed the case and the Jewish people had acted on this principle they would, in all probability, have saved themselves an immeasurable amount of sorrow, which includes the current troubles of the state of Israel. The Talmud story may, however, well be legendary because in Tobit 4:15 we can read, "Do that to no man which thou hatest: drink not wine to make thee drunken; neither let drunkenness go with thee in thy journey."

The book of Tobit is not included in our usual Bibles but is contained in the Apocrypha (Old Testament books which were not regarded as canonical) and several verses from it are important in the current context. The story of the woman (previously discussed in the chapter on Mark) who had lost seven husbands without having produced an offspring, and which provided the challenge of the Saducees to Jesus as to whom she was married to in the resurrection, can be found in Tobit III:7-16. Other aspects from the same chapter are admonitions we are familiar with from Jesus' teachings: to follow righteousness all life long; not to turn the face away from any of the poor, "and the face of God shall not be turned away from thee;" "love thy brethren and do not despise them in thy heart;" give the wages to your workers promptly, rather than delaying; give your bread to the hungry and "of thy garments to them that are naked;" "let not thine eye be envious, when thou givest alms." The essence of all of these statements, which can be summarized as: do good to your fellow human beings, can be found in expanded form in Luke's chapter 6.

In chapter 7 we find the expanded version of the centurion's servant being healed, which has already been commented upon in the chapter on St. Matthew. In Luke's version it is not the centurion himself who comes to ask for help, but instead sent Jewish elders to intercede for him with Jesus on behalf of the sick servant. These elders convinced Jesus that the centurion was a worthy man who, "loves our people, and it is he who built a synagogue for us [7:5]." Thus Luke makes it clear that it wasn't the centurion's profession which led to Jesus' compassion but that he was a good person.

In the same chapter Jesus also raised the son of a widow from the dead, which is not reported by other gospel writers but is similar to one of the miracles performed by Elijah. Otherwise there are no essential differences from the other synoptic gospels up to chapter 10. While the apostles had been sent out to preach the Gospel in chapter 9, which just as in Matthew, had no connection with the rejection Jesus had met with in Nazareth, Luke reports that another 70 (other versions say 72) of the disciples were sent out after the twelve had returned. They received the same instructions which had been mentioned previously and, "He that hears you hears me; and he that despises you despises me; and he that despises me despises Him who sent me." The 70 then returned full of joy over the success of their mission and were told that henceforth they were given, "power to tread on snakes and scorpions, and over all the power of the enemy; and nothing will hurt you." These verses are unique to Luke and remind one somewhat of the inauthentic ending of Mark's gospel. The disciples were then told that they should not rejoice over these worldly powers but rather over the fact that their names are inscribed in heaven.

Verses 21 through 24, which follow the empowerment of the disciples, are also somewhat unusual for Luke. The words are identical with those of Mt. 11:25-30, were apparently interpolated and remind one more of the language found in St. John's gospel. Jesus thanks the Father for having, "handed all things over to me," and that no one, "knows who the Son is, except the Father, or who the Father is except the Son and anyone to whom the Son chooses to reveal him."

Luke continues with Jesus' dialogue with a scribe which led to the parable of the Good Samaritan which is not found in the other gospels. From all of Jesus' parables this is probably the most important one because it clearly broke with Jewish tradition and its separatist attitude. It was this thought which paved the way for Christianity to become a world-wide religion rather than a mere sect of Judaism.

The parable was told in response to the question by a lawyer, "who is my neighbor?" The preceding exchange has already been mentioned in the discussion of Mark's chapter 12. The crucial phrase was, "thou shalt love thy neighbor as thyself." Mark and Matthew also reported this exchange, but only in Luke do we find the obvious next question, "Who is my neighbor?" This was not rhetorical, but a matter of serious concern and involved a fundamental principle. All the laws of Moses, including the commandment to love one's neighbor, were solely directed to the Jewish people. They had no relevance in regard to conduct towards Gentiles. A strict barrier had been erected which was not to be transgressed. Although the Samaritans were to some extent remnants of the former kingdom of Israel, and as such had Yahweh as their God, they had become intermixed with the local Gentile population. They did not adhere to the oral law, worshiped on Mount Gerizim rather than in the Jerusalem temple, and had their own Bible. Thus there was implacable hostility between Jews and Samaritans. One might compare the situation with the split in the Christian Church immediately after the Reformation when Catholics vigorously hated Protestants and vice versa. These members of the "Body of Christ" even delighted in killing each other for what they regarded as heresy.

Jesus had broken a major taboo with this parable. A man who had come from Jerusalem was robbed, beaten, and left for dead on the road to Jericho. He was ignored by a priest as well as by a Levite. It was a Samaritan who did not bypass the distressed individual. He not only bandaged his wounds but took him to an inn, gave the innkeeper some money to take care of him, and if the amount were to have been insufficient to cover the cost, he promised that he would pay the rest upon his return. Jesus then asked the lawyer, "Which one of these three was a neighbor?" When the lawyer answered, "The man who showed him mercy," Jesus replied, "Go and do likewise." With this parable Luke had broken new ground and established the principle which required one to help others in need regardless of their religion, ethnicity or whatever. Neither Mark, Matthew nor John, took that step. It required the physician Luke to do so. Once the fundamental barrier between Jews and Samaritans had been breached, the one between Jews and the rest of the Gentile world could also give way. Sad to say, however, that nearly 2000 years later the parable is still not heeded.

Chapter 11 contains the Lord's Prayer in a somewhat shortened form. In contrast to Matthew's, "Our Father who art in heaven, hallowed be your name . . ." the opening sentence restricts itself simply to, "Father, hallowed be your name." The words, "your will be done on earth as it is in heaven" are also missing. Furthermore, the "daily bread," shows up in the Latin translation as *quotidianum* which indeed means daily, although the Greek word *èpioúsion* is the same as in Matthew's gospel. Since Luke continues with parables which refer to feeding the hungry and giving what is requested, the words have been put into a material context. That this interpretation is not necessarily the only possible one is suggested by Jesus' concluding words, "If you then, who are evil, know how to give good gifts to your children, how much more will the heavenly Father give the Holy Spirit to those who ask him?" This clearly equates bread once again with Spirit.

Verse 23 is puzzling because it is the direct opposite of 9:50 which stated, just as in Matthew's gospel, "He who is not against us is with us." In the current verse the statement reads, "He who is not with me is against me, and whoever does not gather with me scatters." I am making a point of this apparent change of mind because the first part of the sentence has not only been used in the past century by the Nazis but, to my surprise it has also recently become an official statement of American foreign policy when the war on terror was announced. This points out the dangers when sayings directed to an audience of two thousand years ago are used for current political purposes. Muslims and Jews have fallen into the same trap with the sad consequences we find ourselves in today. I believe that verse 23 which actually consists of two separate statements may have been directed by the gospel writer to the enemies of the early Church rather than having been an instruction by Jesus to the disciples. I am strengthened in this assumption because this particular verse does not relate directly to the parables into which it was interpolated. This may be another one of the many instances where Jesus' authority was used in the New Testament to justify current needs.

Verses 27 and 28 are also of interest. A woman called out to Jesus that his mother is blessed for having given birth to him but Jesus replied, "Blessed rather are those who hear the word of God, *and keep it* [emphasis added]." Family relationships are not what counts, doing God's work is important. The chapter concludes with the condemnations of the Jewish ruling classes for their hypocrisy, which are identical with those in Matthew. The content of chapters 12 and 13 is also a duplication of teachings which can be found in Mark and Matthew.

Matthew's wedding feast parable is, however, given a different slant by Luke in chapter 14. It is not a wedding but a supper to which the guests are invited and when they refuse "the poor, the crippled, the blind, and the lame" were to be brought. When this was done and there were still empty places, people were to be collected from, "roads and lanes . . . so that my house shall be filled." On the other hand none of the originally invited guests "will taste my dinner." The meaning is obvious. The Jews to whom the gospel was offered first had refused to hear it now the Gentiles would receive heaven's blessing. But in contrast to Matthew there is no "wailing and gnashing of teeth," they are simply shut out.

Chapters 15 and 16 contain the parables of: the Lost Sheep, the Prodigal Son, the Unjust Steward, and the Rich Man versus Lazarus. The common denominator is that every one of God's children counts, especially if there has been repentance for past behavior and that God's gifts are to be used fruitfully in time. Once one has died all chances for redemption are gone.

Chapter 17 emphasizes forgiveness and faith, provided there is repentance, but also contains the unique story of ten lepers being healed. Only one of them, a Samaritan, thanks God for the miracle, which reinforces the message of Jewish ingratitude. The chapter concludes with the tribulations which will precede the final arrival of the kingdom of God and that perpetual vigilance is required.

Chapters 18 and 19 continue in the same vein. The parable where a hard-headed judge relented when a poor widow kept coming back in her attempt to receive justice emphasized perseverance in the correct course of action. In another parable Jesus told his audience that although riches were likely to be dangerous but, if properly used even a rich and despised "publican," who was the overseer of tax collectors, could be redeemed. Chapter 19 also contains the parable where a nobleman who left the country to be entrusted with a kingship gave each one of his servants some money to conduct business while he was gone. But the citizens of the country sent messengers after him who said that they would not allow him to reign over them if he did return. The rest of the parable is similar to the one previously presented by Matthew. Those servants who had enlarged their gift were rewarded. The one who had not, lost the money he had been given; and those of the people who had not wanted the returned king to reign over them were slain. The message was again clear: make maximal use of the gifts of God, if you do not they will be taken away from you. But there was also added the warning to the Jews: if you stick to your old habits and don't recognize Jesus as the Messiah you will be destroyed upon his return. The chapter concludes with Jesus' entry into Jerusalem and the cleansing of the temple. The latter occurs on the same day of entry and there is, therefore, no mention of the cursed fig tree.

Chapters 20-24 deal with Jesus' teachings in the temple, the theologic challenges by the authorities, the Last Supper, "betrayal" by Judas, trial, crucifixion and resurrection. The account differs only in minor details from Mark and Matthew. I have put the word "betrayal" in quotation marks because it is not the only possible translation for the Greek word *paradídōmi*, or the Latin *tradis* which also means "to surrender," or "to hand over." The words can but do not necessarily imply a treasonable intent by Judas. He might have wanted to force the issue, have Jesus declare himself openly as the Messiah and order a call to arms. With heavenly intervention he would then have succeeded in driving the Romans out of the land. The now common translation with "betrayal," which is consistent throughout the four gospels, was probably intended to further bedevil the Jews.

One sentence of chapter 22:36 has recently been invoked by a prominent American to demonstrate that Jesus was not a pacifist but in favor of what has, centuries later, been called "just war." In *Why We Fight* William Bennett wrote:

Even the story of Gethsemane is not so clear-cut as is often claimed. In the version given of the gospel of Luke, Jesus not only refrains from rebuking Peter but actually urges his apostles to equip themselves with weapons. ("The one who has no sword must sell his cloak to buy one.")

As usual it behooves one to look at the entire context rather than at one sentence from one verse. The words were spoken at the end of the Last Supper after Peter had declared his fidelity. As we are all aware, Jesus had to tell him that before the cock crowed Peter would have denied knowing him three times. Subsequently:

> He said to them. 'When I sent you out without a purse, bag, or sandals, did you lack anything?' They said 'No, not a thing.' He said to them, 'But now, the one who has a purse must take it and likewise a bag. And the one who has no sword must sell his cloak and buy one. For I tell you the scripture must be fulfilled in me. 'And he was counted among the lawless'; and indeed what is written about me is being fulfilled. They said 'Lord, look, here are two swords.' He replied, 'It is enough.'[22:35-38].

This surely puts the situation into a context which is quite different from what Mr. Bennett wanted us to believe. It is also a typical example of what happens when religion is used to serve the state rather than an individual. Jesus' aversion to the use of violence is also attested to by his reaction at the time of the arrest:

> While he was still speaking, suddenly a crowd came, and the one called Judas, one of the twelve, was leading them. He approached Jesus to kiss him but Jesus said to him, 'Judas is it with a kiss that you are betraying the Son of Man?' When those who were around him saw what was coming, they asked, 'Lord, should we strike with the sword?' Then one of them struck the slave of the high priest and cut off his right ear. But Jesus said, 'No more of this!' And he touched his ear and healed him [22:47-51].

It would seem that if one wanted to find justification for war, other sources than the words and deeds of Jesus would need to be used.

The rest of the story is sufficiently similar to the other gospels except for the crucifixion scene. The words, "Father forgive them, they know not what they do" uttered from the cross denote again the spirit of universal compassion which Luke wanted to get across as Jesus' main message. Furthermore, although all gospels are in agreement that two malefactors were crucified with Jesus we find only in Luke the conversation where one of them repented and asked Jesus to remember him when he came into his kingdom. Jesus replied, "Today you will be with me in Paradise." This reinforced the Christian message that genuine repentance, even in the hour of death, is acceptable to God. Jesus' final words, "Father into thy hands I commend my spirit" are also specific for Luke. It is the spirit which counts, never mind what happens to the body!

I also believe that this is why we find, in chapter 24, the story of the two disciples walking to Emmaus and being joined by a stranger whom they only came to recognize later on as the risen Christ. The message is: do not judge by outward appearances, but rather by what the person stands for.

Summarizing one can say that apart from some of the unavoidable polemics which resulted from the time the gospel was written, and may well have been copied from Matthew, the main teachings of Jesus as presented by Luke have universal and immortal significance. They consist of the commandments: to help the sick, the poor, the downtrodden; to humbly serve others regardless of what we now call "race, gender, or creed," rather than dominate them; not to be judgmental in regard to perceived faults of others; to be honest; not to carry a grudge but to forgive; to encourage repentance for misdeeds; to show gratitude for gifts received; to be steadfast in misfortune; to rely on the help of God when treated unjustly; not to answer evil with evil, but to live by the Golden Rule. If we indeed conduct ourselves on a daily basis in this manner the "kingdom of God" will be ours. Finally, what did Jesus, in my opinion, really want us to do when he said at the Last Supper, "This is my body" and "This my blood."? From all the gospel writers only Luke added,

"Do this in remembrance of me." He wanted to be remembered! Surely we can do him this favor when we sit down at the dinner table alone or with our families. We can greet him, thank him for the example he tried to set and renew our intent to follow his teachings the best we can.

THE ACTS OF THE APOSTLES

Inasmuch as the book entitled The Acts of the Apostles is a sequel to Luke's gospel it is presented here to preserve continuity. Although the gospel of John usually follows that of Luke, it is mainly a theologic treatise about Christ and can tell us relatively little about the human being Jesus of Nazareth. The essence of the Jesus story has been presented in the synoptic gospels and we now have to explore the mystery how a dispirited small band of followers created a world religion out of Jesus' death and resurrection.

The scientist may have doubts about the physical resurrection stories as presented in the gospels, but there can be no doubt that Jesus' spirit has remained alive and is still with us two thousand years later. This mystery will never be fully fathomed, apart from a faith which moves mountains, but the circumstances surrounding the development of the early Church are known. Their exploration is not an idle intellectual exercise because they involve the fundamental question of the relationship between Christianity and Judaism. It has become fashionable in certain circles of our society to no longer speak of these two religions in separate terms but amalgamate them under "Judeo-Christian tradition," or "Judeo-Christian heritage." By placing the emphasis on "Judeo-," and thereby Judaism, the terms do not take into proper account the other forces which have shaped the Christian belief system. Since the split between Judaic Christianity and Hellenic Christianity is already apparent in the Acts of the Apostles, this book is an important, but largely neglected, document.

We don't know when Luke wrote The Acts but it is reasonable to assume that he did so soon after Paul's Roman captivity (around

65 A.D.).This seemed to have consisted of house arrest only because the book ends quite abruptly with, "He [Paul] lived there two whole years at his own expense and welcomed all who came to him, proclaiming the kingdom of God [28:30,31]."

In the following pages I am going to present only a few highlights of the book in order to provide some information on the beginning of the early Church, its relationship to Judaism, as well as the struggles between the Jewish and the Hellenistic element within the group of converts. Only when one knows these serious difficulties can one understand some of the more vindictive gospel statements which have been attributed to Jesus. It will be impossible to tease out exactly the words which can be ascribed to the historic Jesus, as the so called "Jesus Seminar" has tried to do, and it will remain up to individual readers of the gospels to decide for themselves what to ascribe to Jesus' actual ministry, and what are later insertions. I am personally well acquainted with how one's name can be "used in vain" and every executive will probably have had the same experience. When persons in subordinate positions wanted to get their views enforced they simply used, what in my situation was, "Dr. Rodin wants this done." I had no idea that intermittently orders were attributed to me which I would never have issued because they were contrary to my belief system. This fact of life must be known and was clearly operative in the works of the gospel writers.

The purpose of The Acts was to provide for Luke's Gentile readership a somewhat idealized essay on the growth and tribulations of the nascent Church rather than an exact history of what all the apostles actually did. Furthermore, Luke followed the practice of the times by putting words in his protagonists or antagonists mouths of which he could not have had personal knowledge. The long discourses are, therefore, Luke's ideas of what might have been said rather than what was "really" said. Nevertheless, he does provide us with a glimpse of the real problems from which we can draw our own conclusions.

The book begins with Jesus having asked the apostles to remain in Jerusalem until they would be baptized with the Holy Spirit. He then ascended to heaven after having told them that the time when the kingdom of heaven would arrive on earth was up to the Father.

They returned from the Mount of Olives, where the event had taken place, and replenished their ranks from eleven to twelve by electing Matthias.

At Pentecost fire from heaven descended upon them in form of "Divided tongues, as of fire, and a tongue rested on each of them [2:3]." The transliteration actually says "tongues-being divided," while some English translations speak of "forked tongues," which has assumed a completely different, and sinister, meaning in our time. The phenomenon was accompanied by a violent rushing sound which drove a whole host of other people into the street. The apostles now found out, to everybody's amazement, that they were able to address the onlookers in the various languages of the Roman Empire. Nevertheless, some of the bystanders were less convinced of this miracle and thought that the ecstatic utterances were simply an expression of the believers having had too much to drink. But Peter, by reciting the history of Jesus' redeeming life and resurrection, was able to convince them otherwise. About three thousand souls were added to the congregation right then and there. Although we may doubt the precise number, it seems apparent that some type of significant event had occurred, which raised the courage of the apostles. Apart from baptism, which assured remission of sins, the Holy Spirit was from then on transmitted by the laying on of hands.

Although the work of the apostles proceeded satisfactorily and many miracles were performed, the Jewish authorities had no use for this new sect. Peter and John were arrested, kept in prison over night and then released with the stern warning not to propagate such subversive doctrines. Peter assured them that this was impossible because he had to follow his conscience, but no further action was taken against him at that time.

The members of the Church practiced a primitive sort of communism and Karl Marx's later dictum, "from everyone according to his abilities to everyone according to his needs" was adhered to. Since everybody who belonged to the congregation firmly believed that the world was about to come to a fiery demise in the immediate future, the parting with their property may have been considerably easier than under normal circumstances. But there were still some, such as Ananias and his wife Sapphira, who hedged their bets and withheld some money in case the Lord's return was delayed. This unbelief was sternly rebuked by Peter. Ananias dropped dead immediately and onlookers were properly terrified. Sapphira also promptly died when she heard about this disaster. "And great fear seized the whole church, and all who heard these things [5:11]."

The carrot of the heavenly kingdom, accompanied by miracles on earth, combined with the stick of eternal damnation worked so well that numerous conversions took place to the great annoyance of the Jewish authorities who again threw the apostles into prison. Their ordeal did not last long and an angel, possibly in form of a secret believer, opened the jail doors for them and they were able to teach again in the temple on the following day. When they were summoned before the High Priest and elders, Peter and some others gave such a spirited defense of their actions that the authorities were "enraged and wanted to kill them [5:33]." The solution was provided by Gamaliel, a Pharisee held in high esteem by everybody, who pronounced words of wisdom. If the behavior of the apostles were to be the work of men it would come to naught anyway, but if it were God's will it could not be opposed. They should be let go and time would reveal the truth. The advice was followed; the apostles rejoiced and kept teaching about Jesus Christ.

But in chapter 6 we get the first inkling that all was not well not only in regard to Jewish authorities but within the Christian community itself. While Peter and the other apostles could continue to teach with impunity, Stephen was stoned to death for preaching the gospel. The reason seems to have been that the Jewish disciples still adhered to Mosaic Law while Gentile converts, like Stephen, may have anticipated the teachings of St. Paul and considered adherence to Jesus' teaching as sufficient. Since Stephen did not mince his words and called the crowd "betrayers and murderers" of "the Righteous One [7:52]," it is hardly surprising that stones started flying through the air.

While a discriminatory attitude by the Jewish Christians toward the Gentile converts was only hinted at in the Stephen episode it was made explicit in a brief comment immediately prior to Stephen having been accused of blasphemy. "Now during those days, when the disciples were increasing in number, the Hellenists complained against the Hebrews, because their widows were being neglected in the daily distribution of food [6:1]." It is, therefore, quite apparent that even in the earliest days Jesus' commandments of equal treatment towards all, let alone love thine enemies, were impossible to adhere to by a larger diverse group of flesh and blood people. The problem was temporarily solved by appointing people to help with the food distribution, of whom Stephen was one. But as noted above he was overly zealous in spreading the word and became the first martyr for the new faith.

A specific point is made that the young Saul, a Pharisee, had not only consented to Stephen's death but was subsequently involved in a house to house search in order to root out such sectarians. All church members, apart from the apostles, were persecuted and imprisoned not only in Jerusalem but throughout Judea and Samaria. Luke gives no explanation why the apostles were exempted from persecution but the vengeance may have been directed towards the "uncircumcised" Gentiles rather than Jews who professed belief in Jesus.

Chapter 9 is the crucial one for the Church. It reports the conversion of Saul while on the road to Damascus in order to destroy the Church in that city. There are three accounts of this pivotal event in Acts: 9:5, 22:7, and 26:14. The story is, of course, exceedingly well known and there are only minor differences between the versions. A bright light appeared and a voice, which identified itself as Jesus, was heard by Saul asking why Saul persecuted him. Saul was struck blind and had to be led by his companions to Damascus where his sight returned after three days through the ministrations of a friend of the Church, and he subsequently became the most ardent apostle. Apart from the fact that this event has been regarded by some of my colleagues as an epileptic seizure, which may or may not have been the case, there is one sentence that struck me as rather interesting. In the King James Version of Acts one finds in 9:5 as well as in 26:14 the words uttered by Jesus, "It is hard for thee to kick against the pricks." When I first read this sentence it occurred to me that a phrase from Euripides had been placed on Jesus' lips. Since Euripides' (480-406 B.C.) play *The Bacchantes,* in which the quote occurs, is highly relevant I shall summarize the content of the tragedy here.

Dionysus (the Roman Bacchus) had come from Asia Minor to Greece in order to establish his worship there. In Thebes he was met by King Pentheus, who had been away from his kingdom for a while, but who had heard, upon his return, about the drunken, frenzied orgies, Bacchanals, the followers of Dionysus were engaged in. Pentheus had no use for this new god from Asia and threw Dionysus into prison. But a god could not be kept in fetters and he confronted Pentheus with this fact in a personal appearance. Nevertheless, Pentheus persisted in his unbelief and ordered his soldiers to go after the frenzied women who were celebrating one of the bacchanals. Dionysus then appeared in disguise to Pentheus as soon as the order had been given; chided him for his unbelief and told him it would be better for him to sacrifice to the god rather than "in a fury kick against the pricks; thou a mortal, he a god." Dionysus also told Pentheus that he would help him spy on the women if he were to disguise himself as one of them. Pentheus followed the advice but came to a bad end. The women, led by his own mother, mistook him for a lion and killed him by tearing apart every one of his limbs.

Although the ending differs, the rest of the story of a new god arriving in distant lands, demanding worship, and punishing the persecutor is certainly consistent with what we read in Acts. We can be reasonably certain that it was not Jesus who quoted Euripides and it may have been either Paul's or Luke's elaboration of the event. It is also likely that at that time the phrase "to kick against the pricks," or against the "goad", as it is sometimes referred to, was a common saying because Aeschylus had used it too. The Greeks and Romans were just as fond of citing their literary heroes as we are in regard to Shakespeare or biblical verses.

After Saul, or Paul as we may call now him, had recovered his sight he was baptized into the faith and became its most zealous advocate. Converts to a cause tend to be even more aggressive in the pursuit of a new-found doctrine than older established members and Paul was no exception to this rule. He started preaching in the synagogues about Christ as the Son of God and since Paul was thoroughly familiar with Jewish ideology he could confound his opponents with the words of scripture. Needless to say this change in behavior deeply annoyed some of his listeners. He was arrested, thrown into prison but smuggled out of town by friends during the night, and went to Jerusalem where, for obvious reasons, he found a mixed reception. Even the apostles didn't trust this sudden change of mind at first, but came to accept it later on. Paul's stay in Jerusalem was limited because of his "speaking boldly in the name of the Lord." He spoke and argued with the Hellenists, but they were attempting to kill him [9:28, 29]." Who these Hellenists were is not made clear, but we might assume that it was the non-Jewish population of the city whom he wanted to convert. The apostles had no use for further trouble and took him first to Caesarea, but since this was still too close for comfort, he was then sent all the way back to Tarsus, Paul's hometown.

The narration subsequently shifts to Peter's activities and the fundamental problem the apostles faced. The question: had Jesus fulfilled the Law and it needed no longer be adhered to, or was the Law still the governing rule of life to which Gentile converts must conform, had to be resolved. At issue were mainly the dietary habits and circumcision. Peter had begun to preach the gospel in various towns of Judea and the fame of his miracles had begun to spread. He was, therefore, invited by a high Gentile official to Caesarea, which presented a considerable problem for Peter. If he declined the invitation this would not only hamper his ministry but might also lead to other repercussions against the Church, while if he accepted he would have to share the meals with the host and his guests. Not only would he have to eat non-kosher food, but the plates themselves would not be ritually clean. Peter's quandary was resolved by a dream which he interpreted as a divine dispensation. He went to Caesarea and his teachings were a great success with the Gentiles whom he then blessed with the Holy Spirit. But his friends in Jerusalem were far from pleased with this turn of events and "the circumcised believers criticized him, saying, 'Why did you go to uncircumcised men and eat with them [11:2-3]?'" Peter was able to convince his brethren of the necessity to meet with Gentiles on their own turf if the gospel was to be taught to all nations and the matter was temporarily shelved.

As a result of this dispensation the Church grew vigorously; Paul was reprieved from his exile in Tarsus, ordered to come to Antioch and to help preach the gospel. But all was not well in Jerusalem. The uneasy truce between the temple authorities and the apostles was shattered by Herod who had "James the brother of John" killed and Peter imprisoned. Peter was again miraculously released, and Herod succumbed soon thereafter to a rather dreadful death.

The narration then reverts back to Paul's ventures. Jointly with Barnabas he traveled through Asia Minor and some of the offshore islands teaching the gospel. The Gentiles were pleased but the Jews less so and there are stories of frequent expulsions from various towns as well as attempts at stoning. As a result of the rapid growth of Gentile converts the question of adherence to the Law, and specifically circumcision, as a requirement for entrance into the kingdom of Heaven became acute. A final decision, which was to determine the future fate of the Church, had to be made. Paul and Barnabas as well as some others were summoned to Jerusalem where Peter rendered the verdict. Gentiles could become full fledged members of the tribe of Israel with all the benefits that this entailed if they abstained: from meats offered to idols, from blood, from things strangled, and from fornication. Since these restrictions were not particularly onerous there was great rejoicing among the Gentile converts and the growth of the Church was now assured. Those Jewish converts who continued to adhere to the Law were reduced to small sects like the Ebionites or the "Jews for Jesus" in our day.

In spite of numerous setbacks and persecutions the Christians, as they were now called, had won their first and decisive battle. From then on adherents of the Jewish religion were condemned to rearguard actions which became increasingly acrimonious as Jews lost some of their previous influence in Rome, especially as a result of the disastrous wars against the Empire in the first and second centuries. While Jews persecuted the Church for the threat it represented to the established religion when they held power, the Christians heartily reciprocated when worldly power had become theirs. The most important loser was, however, Jesus. Although his name appeared on every lip and his message was dispensed at Church services it failed to make a significant impact on everyday behavior. Decent people continued to conduct themselves in a decent manner, while most of those who were more concerned with personal gain, rather than with what benefits others, failed to experience a change of heart.

From the rest of the Book of Acts only a few highlights need to be mentioned. While preaching in Corinth "the Jews made a united attack on Paul, and brought him before the tribunal. They said 'this man is persuading people to worship God in ways that are contrary to the law' [18:12-13]." The Roman governor for Greece at the time was called Gallio in the Book of Acts but his name at birth was Lucius Annaeus Novatus Seneca, and he was the older brother of the famous Stoic philosopher Lucius Annaeus Seneca. The latter's book *On Anger*, which could be read profitably today by politicians, both here and abroad, was dedicated to him. Gallio dismissed the case with the comment that this did not concern Rome. It was the Jews' law that was being questioned and they should settle the affair themselves. When the crowd subsequently beat the ruler of the synagogue, Gallio again refused to intervene. Roman justice, when dispensed by honest people, concerned itself only with criminal conduct and was not interested in sectarian squabbles. I am mentioning this episode only because the influence of Seneca's philosophy on Paul's teaching will be discussed later.

In Acts 20:7-11 we find what is nowadays called a "human interest story." Paul was apparently quite long-winded in his sermons and although he was supposed to leave the next morning he kept preaching until midnight after they had celebrated the Lord's Supper in an upstairs chamber. A young fellow fell asleep, dropped from the third floor to the ground and was given up for dead, but Paul hugged him and restored him to his senses. It is obvious that Paul had ignored Jesus' teaching in regard to prayer, "*Nolite multum loquis*," or colloquially put, "don't talk too much."

Eventually Paul's successes had apparently raised the concerns of the Jewish authorities in Jerusalem, and he was summoned to give a report about his activities. Although he had trepidations and brought a fair amount of money with him from the various congregations, which might have served to assuage hard feelings, he was not well received. Even the required ritual cleansing before entering the temple was of no avail and neither was his declaration that he really was a Pharisee and as such, one of their own. According to 23:10 Paul was about to have suffered the fate of Pentheus at the hands of the mob when the captain of the Roman guard rescued him. Since justice could hardly be obtained in Jerusalem, Paul was sent to the governor in Caesarea for trial. Felix who was procurator at the time, had a Jewish wife and Paul tried valiantly to convert them. This was of no avail because Felix was more interested in money than religion and that was a commodity Paul could not supply him with. Paul had to remain in Caesarea under some sort of house arrest. About two years later Felix was relieved of his job as procurator of Judea by Festus who wanted no trouble with the Jews and, therefore, suggested that a trial be held in Jerusalem. Since this would have amounted to a death sentence, Paul procured his Roman citizenship papers and appealed to be heard by the Emperor who at that time happened to be Nero. Festus then granted Paul a hearing in the presence of King Agrippa. In spite of Paul's best efforts Festus was not impressed and "exclaimed you are out of your mind, Paul. Too much learning is driving you insane [26:24]." But Felix as well as Agrippa, agreed that Paul had not committed a criminal offense against Rome and should be let go. On the other hand this edict could not be enforced because Paul had already appealed to the Emperor, and this is why he had to be sent to Rome. His shipwreck on the way is well known, and we have no information as to what happened to him after his arrival in the capital of the Empire. But from then on the other apostles faded into relative obscurity, and the Christian Church organized itself along the principles laid down in Paul's epistles which are dealt with in the next chapter.

SAINT PAUL'S CHRIST

The change in chapter headings, from Jesus to Christ, is deliberate because Paul did not personally know Jesus, the teacher who had wandered around Roman Palestine. The fundamental element of Paul's life was the experience of the risen Christ on the road to Damascus. In contrast to Jesus' life altering experience, when the Holy Spirit descended gently like a dove, Paul found himself rebuked and blinded by the radiance of God. What the burning bush and its attendant orders were for Moses, the celestial light was for Paul. To understand Paul's thinking we have to keep, in addition to the sudden conversion, one other fundamental fact of his life in mind. He was born of Jewish parents in Tarsus, a Roman free city in the province of Cilicia. He was thus a Jew who grew up in a Gentile environment. In Paul's days Tarsus (modern Terseus, located on the Mediterranean shore of Turkey, in relative proximity to Cyprus) was a cosmopolitan city renowned for commerce and as a center for Hellenistic learning. It had its own university where Greek, and especially Stoic, philosophy was taught. One of its leading men of the time was Athenodorus Cananites (74 B.C. – 7 A.D.). He was born near Tarsus studied under the famed Poseidonius in Rhodes and subsequently lectured in all the major cities of the Mediterranean area. Athenodorus taught the young Octavian (who became Caesar Augustus) initially in Appollonia, then followed him to Rome and remained his life-long friend and advisor. In later years he was allowed by Augustus to return to Tarsus where he remodeled the city constitution along the lines of what has been called *timocracy*. The term has gone out of use and is variously defined nowadays. Among these definitions are: a) love of honor as the ruling principle;

b) honors are bestowed according to property owned; c) honor attached to the ruler becomes an object of contention, and is sought by the ambitious with intrigue, rather than accepted as a trust and obligation. That the last definition may indeed have been appropriate later on can be assumed from Dio's (nicknamed *Chrystosom* - of the Golden mouth, 45-115 A.D.) speech against the Tarsians. In it he told the citizens that:

> philosophers and politicians neglect their duty of telling the people the truth; what is needed is social reform at home, patience with their neighbours abroad, readiness to overlook minor faults in the Roman administration, but determination to fight for matters of importance with all their power [Cambridge Ancient History Vol. XI p.683].

Since Athenodorus was a Stoic the first definition as cited above, combined with aspects of the second, is the most likely to have been incorporated into the constitution he drew up for the city. But like all good intentions, actual practice probably degenerated later to fit the third definition which would have justified Dio's imprecations. None of Athenodorus' writings are extant but we do have the writings of two other famous Stoics from that era. One is the previously mentioned Seneca, who was a contemporary of Paul and lived from 4 B.C. - 65 A.D. The other was Epictetus (c. 60-138 A.D.) of whom more will be said later. Suffice it to say now, that Stoic doctrine embraced all members of society. Seneca came from a highly esteemed family and served for several years as tutor to the adolescent Nero. Although he was able to curb Nero's vicious disposition until about age 18, Lord Acton's dictum "power corrupts and absolute power corrupts absolutely" subsequently came to the fore. While Paul may have been beheaded on Nero's orders, Seneca was commanded to commit suicide, which he did in a truly stoic manner. While Seneca came from nobility, Epictetus was originally a Grecian slave of one of Nero's freedmen who, like his former master, excelled in cruelty. Thus station in life made no difference for Stoic doctrine.

In regard to Tarsus one might also mention that it was the place where Mark Anthony first met Cleopatra who had sailed up from

Egypt to greet him. It is, therefore, quite understandable that Paul was proud of his place of birth as attested to in Acts 21:39. It would have been impossible for young Saul, as he was called at the time, not to have known about Athenodorus, Tarsus' most illustrious citizen, and it seems quite likely that the philosopher might well have served as a model for some of Paul's conduct, especially in regard to his missions to the Gentiles. Paul's easy mingling with non-Jews, in contrast to the circles in Jerusalem, can be traced directly to Tarsus. He had lived in the midst of Gentiles in that cultured city and had probably come to appreciate some of their ways. Whether or not he had received formal instruction in Stoic philosophy or had acquired some of it, as one might say, by osmosis cannot be determined. Regardless of how Paul acquired this information, anyone who reads his epistles, and is familiar with Stoic writings, cannot help but be profoundly impressed by the similarities.

For the other important strain in Paul's character, his Jewishness, he had to thank the previously mentioned Antiochus IV (175-163 B.C.) who is best known for his persecution of the Jews, the placing "of the abomination of desolation" in the Jerusalem temple, and the outbreak of the Maccabean revolt. It has been reported that Antiochus had deliberately sent some Jews to Tarsus in order to stimulate commerce and industry. It appears, however, at least equally likely to me that some of the more industrious and wealthy Jewish citizens, who were part of the Hellenistic faction during the Maccabean wars (which started as a civil war among Jews), were not enamored with the strict theocracy enforced by Judas Maccabeus and later on his brothers. Prudent people may well have taken their families, as well as their money, and moved to greener pastures in order to be as far away as possible from the "Promised Land" and its perennial conflicts.

Be that as it may, the young Saul arrived at some unknown age in Jerusalem where he studied under Gamaliel, who had been mentioned by Luke in The Acts, and joined the Pharisaic belief system. He immersed himself in Jewish scripture and became thoroughly imbued with Old Testament fervor. This manifested itself not only in the initial persecution of Jesus' followers, but even after his conversion in some of the epistles. Thus, there were two conflicting philosophies in his early upbringing: the universalism of Hellenic thought and the tribal Chosenness of Judaism, hemmed in by a Law which was supposed to be followed to the letter. A mental conflict was inevitable, and Paul's subsequent career can be regarded as a continuous attempt to reconcile these two fundamentally different views of life. As such, it was no accident that he became the "Apostle to the Gentiles."

What happened during the conversion experience can, of course, only be guessed at. He was bound to have been immensely troubled not only by the disciples' insistence on the bodily resurrection of Jesus, but also by their willingness to suffer a cruel death, like Stephen, for this belief. The problem Saul was confronted with was Jewish scripture. According to the Law anyone who was "hanged on a tree is cursed of God." The verses 21:22-23 in Deuteronomy are crucial for our understanding of the scandal, the idea of a crucified and resurrected Messiah had created among Jews. They are, therefore, quoted here from the Greek Septuagint, the language Jews and Gentiles were familiar with in Paul's days:

> And if there be sin in anyone, and the judgment of death
> be upon him, and ye hang him on a tree: his body shall not
> remain all night upon the tree, but ye shall by all means bury
> it in that day; for every one that is hanged on a tree is cursed
> of God; and ye shall by no means defile the land, which the
> Lord thy God gives thee for an inheritance.

This was the crux, no pun intended, of the problem. If Jesus had been crucified, hung from the tree, because he had sinned against the Law then it was obvious that God had rejected him. Under those circumstances He would not have raised him from the dead. If He had indeed done so then scripture was wrong. But if the Law was wrong in such a vital point how could the rest of it be trusted? Therefore, the question was: who was right Jesus and the apostles, or the Jews and the Law? Those were the battle lines which allowed no compromise and a decision had to be made. These may well have been the thoughts and doubts which beset Saul on his way to Damascus until he saw literally, as he testified, "the light." We find this spiritual dilemma referred to in its most concise form in the epistle to the Galatians.

Galatians

This epistle was probably written around 54-55 A.D. from Ephesus and in it Paul seriously reproved the churches he had previously founded in Galatia. We don't know when Paul visited the province for the first time because the details of his early life are sketchy and in part conflicting. The closest city of Galatia, Pessinus, was only somewhat over 200 miles, as the crow flies, northwest of Tarsus. It would, therefore, seem likely that Paul had visited Galatia early on in his ministry while he lived again in Tarsus. This was after he had to flee from Caesarea and before Barnabas brought him back to Antioch, the capital of Syria.

The tone of the letter reflects Paul's exasperation over the havoc which was created by the "Judaizers." This was a term which had actually acquired two meanings. In the Gentile communities of the Empire it tended to refer to those Gentiles who followed Jewish law to some extent but did not fully convert. They joined the Jews on the Sabbath in the synagogues, adhered to some of the dietary laws but drew the line on circumcision. For this reason they were the most readily available raw material for conversion to Christianity because it retained the idea of the One God without the onerous restrictions of Jewish Law. These people have also been referred to as "God-fearing," in the literature of the time. In Paul's context, however, the "Judaizers" were Christian Jews who insisted on adherence to the Law of Moses. Thus, from Paul's point of view, his entire effort in Galatia had come to naught and the letter lays out the reasons why the Galatians were wrong and why faith in Christ was the only correct course. Since the letter deals with the heart of the conflict, is mercifully short, and presents the essence of the Christian life, I shall discuss it here in some detail.

There are two versions as to what Paul did after he arrived in Damascus and had received his sight back again. The one from Acts has already been mentioned. The other and probably more trustworthy account comes from Galatians.1:17-19. In these verses Paul stated explicitly that he did not go immediately from Damascus to Jerusalem, but instead went for three years to "Arabia." Although the term has been regarded as referring to Nabatea this seems unlikely. In the context of the Roman Empire, Damascus was at that time an easternmost outpost beyond which stretched the Arabian Desert. The Nabateans lived to the Southeast of the Dead Sea so what would have been the purpose to wander so far away? If he wanted to be alone all he had to do was to head directly east for some nearby oasis, where his tent making skills might have proved useful. From a human point of view a delay between Paul's recovery in Damascus and a visit to Jerusalem seems to be a more likely scenario. Why should he have gone right away into the "lion's den?" He would have had to get his thoughts in order first, and come up with some type of coherent idea as to how the previously mentioned conflicting points of view could be reconciled. This would have required solitude and introspection.

Nevertheless, sooner or later he had to face the apostles in Jerusalem to gain legitimacy for what he now regarded as his mission in life. In contrast to Luke's version in Acts, he stayed only 15 days in Jerusalem and conferred merely with Peter and James, "the Lord's brother." There is also no mention that Paul had already taught in Damascus and that he had been accompanied by Barnabas on his trip to Jerusalem. The visit to the Holy City when he had been accompanied by Barnabas occurs in chapter 2 of Galatians and is dated "fourteen years" after the first one. According to the end of Galatians chapter 1, Paul went after the conference with Peter and James to "the regions of Syria and Cilicia," which were home turf. He is also explicit that, "I was still unknown by sight to the churches in Judea that are in Christ; they only heard it said, 'The one who formerly was persecuting us is now proclaiming the faith he once tried to destroy'[1:21-23]."

In Galatians 1:4 we find the concept that our Lord Jesus Christ "gave himself for our sins, to set us free from this present evil age according to the will of God and Father." The idea that Jesus had died for *our* sins, rather than for *his own* was a concept totally foreign to Jewish thought. On the other hand, death and resurrection of deities had a prominent place in Gentile minds and were regularly re-enacted in various mystery cults. Paul then insisted that his gospel is not of human but divine origin, and he warned the churches in Galatia of the misleading doctrines of others who wanted to "pervert the gospel of Christ." To put it crudely, "I am right and everybody else is wrong." This absolutism, while necessary if one wants to found a new religion, is in the Old Testament spirit rather than Hellenism with its tolerance of other ideas. Paul's anger is also apparent in the statement that anyone who proclaims the false doctrine "let that one be accursed." About 200 years later the Church father Cyprian (200-258) echoed the words with: *salus extra ecclesiam non est*, or as the sentence is now quoted *nulla salus extra ecclesiam*; "there is no salvation apart from the Church."

In chapter 2 Paul discusses the previously mentioned second trip to Jerusalem to acquaint the leaders of the Church, in a private meeting, with the gospel he had been teaching to the Gentiles. Paul contended that he had been entrusted with teaching the gospel to the "uncircumcised," just as Peter had been ordered to teach the gospel to the "circumcised." Peter, James and John agreed, and they only requested of Paul that he should "remember the poor," rather than the other strictures which were mentioned in Acts.

That Paul was not one given to compromise becomes apparent when he took even Peter to task for hypocrisy. When they met in Antioch Peter used to eat with Gentiles but once emissaries arrived from Jerusalem to investigate the situation Peter, as well as Barnabas, and other Jewish Christians segregated themselves again from the Gentile-Christian community. This resulted in a long lecture by Paul to show them the error of their ways which can be found in verses 13- 21.

Paul saw the Law as an "enslavement" from which the Jews had been freed because "we know that a person is justified not by the works of the law but through faith in Jesus Christ [2:16]." This sentence has given rise to much misunderstanding between Jews and Christians because some Jewish writers have abbreviated it to saying that "Jews are justified by works and Christians by faith." But Paul was specific and referred only to the "works of the law" which meant the 613 ordinances which were supposed to govern Jewish life. "Through the law I died to the law, so that I might live to God. I have been crucified with Christ; and it is no longer I who live, but it is Christ who lives in me . . . if justification comes through the law, then Christ died for nothing [2:19-21]." The word *dikaiosúnē* which is usually rendered as "justification" is derived from *díkaios* which means not only "just" but also "righteous." With other words, if righteousness can only be obtained through the Jewish Law, the grace of God is nullified and one can see here Paul's shift from Jewish tribal to Hellenistic universal thinking.

In chapter 3 Paul's anger is in full bloom, and he started out calling his readers "you foolish Galatians! Who has bewitched you?" He went on explaining from scripture that since Abraham had not lived by the Law, but by faith in God, so should they. Moreover he told them that all who rely "on the works of the law are under a curse; for it is written, 'Cursed is everyone who does not observe and obey all the things written in the book of the law' [3:13]."

Paul then went on to explain that the Church is really the inheritor of God's promise to Abraham and that the doctrines of the Jews are no longer relevant. Although the content is theological I shall present the essential quote in full to demonstrate how Paul's legal mind worked:

> Is the law then opposed to the promises of God? Certainly not! For if a law had been given that could make alive, then righteousness would indeed come through the law. But the scripture has imprisoned all things under the power of sin, so that what was promised through faith in Jesus Christ might be given to those who believe.
>
> Now before faith came, we were imprisoned and guarded under the law until faith would be revealed. Therefore the law was our disciplinarian until Christ came so that we might be justified by faith. But now that faith has come, we are no longer subject to a disciplinarian, for in Christ Jesus you are all children of God through faith. As many of you as were baptized into Christ have clothed yourselves with Christ. There is no longer Jew or Greek, there is no longer slave or free, there is no longer male and female; for all of you are one in Christ Jesus. And if you belong to Christ, then you are Abraham's offspring, heirs according to the promise. [3:21-29].

In this passage Paul has made a giant leap over Moses and all of Jewish history. Paul insisted that the Jews were slaves, "But when the fullness of time had come, God had sent his son, born of a woman, born under the law, in order to redeem those who were under the law, so that we might receive adoption as children . . . So you are no longer a slave but a child, and if a child then also an heir, through God [4:3-7]." The point Paul wanted to make, over and over again, was that the previous rules amounted to slavery, but through faith in Jesus Christ one can become a child of God and thereby be freed from the yoke of the Law.

In chapter 4 verses 13-14 point to some type of "infirmity" Paul had suffered from during his original visit with the Galatians. He was grateful that they had not rejected him when his physical condition was such a trial for them at that time, so why would they want to do so now? The actual words are somewhat puzzling. What has been translated as infirmity is literally "through weakness of the flesh" and the Galatians "neither loathed nor despised me, though my condition put you to test." The transliteration of the text reads, "and the trial of you in the flesh of me not you despised nor loathed." The Latin version is also unclear. Paul said that he had previously taught them *per infirmitatem carnis. . . . et tentationem vestram in carne mea non sprevistis, neque repusitis.* The word *per* is confusing because it can mean "during" whatever condition Paul had suffered from, or "by means of," or "because of." The Greek text used *di* for *per,* which as translated above was taken to mean "through," with the implication of "throughout." In the King James Version the verses are translated as, "Ye know how through infirmity of the flesh I preached the gospel unto you at the first. And my temptation which was in my flesh ye despised not, nor rejected." This would suggest that Paul was "tempted, or tested, by the flesh" rather than that the congregation was put to the test. *The New English Bible* takes an idiomatic approach and renders the verses as, "it was bodily illness that originally led to my bringing you the Gospel, and you resisted any temptation to show scorn or disgust at the state of my poor body." It seems that this represents a "sanitized" version of what had actually happened.

I have spent so much space on these verses because not only do they show clearly what happens to translations but also, as a physician, I am naturally interested in what "this weakness of the flesh," which should have aroused disgust, had consisted of. There is only one other reference by Paul to a medical condition he might have suffered from and it is in II Cor.12: 7:

> Therefore to keep me from being too elated, a thorn was given me in the flesh, a messenger of Satan to torment me, to keep me from being elated. Three times I appealed to the Lord about this, that it would leave me, but he said to me 'My grace is sufficient for you, for power is perfected in weakness.'

The "thorn in the flesh" is rendered in Latin as "*stimulus carnis meae angelus satanae, qui me colaphizet . . .*" *Stimulus* had originally not quite the same meaning as in today's English but was used to designate either a goad, spur or incentive. The word *colaphizet* was taken from Greek and means "to be beaten." In the King James Version one reads, "There was given to me a thorn in the flesh, the messenger of Satan to buffet me." *The New English Bible* used poetic license by saying, "I was given a sharp physical pain which came as Satan's messenger to bruise me." We are, therefore left in the dark as to what the condition was Paul had suffered from, but when Galatians and II Corinthians are taken together in their original meaning, the verses do suggest some intermittently recurrent disorder which was rather unpleasant to view and, as mentioned previously, was regarded by some of my colleagues as having been epilepsy.

Let us now make a short detour into contemporary neurology. In the mid 1970s two Boston based neurologists described a clinical personality syndrome which they observed in patients who suffered from epileptic seizures which originated in portions of the temporal lobe. It consisted of: alterations in sexual behavior, excessive religiosity, and a tendency toward an inordinate amount of writing. With my co-workers, I then investigated these claims on a large sample of patients for the specificity of this syndrome. The personality inventory, which was supposed to have demonstrated these traits, was given to epilepsy patients as well as individuals who suffered from other neurologic disorders. It was found that although there were some patients who fit the criteria, the syndrome was neither specific for epilepsy in general nor for temporal lobe seizures. We did find, however, on statistical analysis of the data that four clusters of personality traits could be detected which we termed: 1) Religious-Self-righteous, 2) Hyperemotional-Elated, 3) Hyperemotional-dysphoric and 4) Obsessional-Viscous. The religious-self-righteous cluster is the most interesting in the current context.

The cluster, which means that the answers were correlated with each other to a statistically significant extent, contained the following statements:

> I am very religious in my own way; religion and God are more personal experiences for me than most people; my religious beliefs have undergone major changes; the Bible has special meaning for me which I am beginning to understand; finally I am beginning to understand the true meaning and nature of this world; I have more feeling than most people for the order and purpose of life; I think that I have a special mission in life; often I am the only one to stand up for what is right; I think people would learn a lot from the story of my life; it makes good sense to keep a diary; people should think about the point of many jokes more carefully instead of just laughing about them.

It is, therefore, apparent that a personality constellation of this type does exist and it is quite obvious that if Paul had been given the test he would have answered the bulk of these questions with a resounding yes. One could also argue that Paul clearly exhibited the traits described by the Boston investigators. There is no doubt that he was religious to excess, he wrote a great deal and his lack of sexual interests is testified to by himself in 1Corinthians 7:7. But while this personality structure can be demonstrated in some epilepsy patients, our study found, as mentioned above, no evidence for a statistically significant correlation with the diagnosis of epilepsy or any of its subgroups. These behavioral traits are, therefore, nonspecific and the nature of Paul's "thorn in the flesh" will have to remain speculative because no other information exists apart from the mentioned verses.

After this excursion to contemporary neurology we can return to Paul's attempts to legitimize his ideas on basis of biblical references. Since they are mainly fertile ground for theologians I shall mention only one further example because of its relevance to today's political scene in the Holy Land. In order to re-emphasize the idea that Jews remain slaves, while Christians have been freed, Paul used the story of Abraham's two offspring in Galatians 4:21-31 and I shall let the reader judge the validity of the argument:

> Tell me, you who desire to be subject to the law, will you not listen to the law? For it is written that Abraham had two sons, one by a slave woman and the other by a free woman. One the child of the slave was born according to the flesh; the other, the child of the free woman, was born through the promise. Now this is an allegory, these women are two covenants. One woman, in fact, is Hagar, from Mount Sinai, bearing children for slavery. Now Hagar is Mount Sinai in Arabia and corresponds to the present Jerusalem, for she is in slavery with her children. But the other woman corresponds to the Jerusalem above, she is free, and she is our mother . . . . Now you, my friends, are children of the promise, like Isaac. But just as at that time the child who was born according to the flesh persecuted the child who was born according to the Spirit, so it is now also. But what does scripture say? 'Drive out the slave and her child; for the child of the slave will not share the inheritance with the child of the free woman.' So then friends, we are children, not of the slave but of the free woman.

Paul's reasoning has been endorsed by the Christian Church and vigorously denied by Judaism. Under the name of "supersessionism" it continues to be one of the major bones of contention between the two religions. The reference to the slavery of Jerusalem can be read on two levels. One is Paul's point of having to live under Jewish law and the other is that the Jews were indeed occupied by the Romans and, as such, not a free people.

For those readers who are not thoroughly familiar with the strife in Abraham's family as reported in Genesis Chapters 16 and 21 a few explanations are needed. Sarah, Abraham's legitimate wife, was "barren" and could not conceive. By Canaanite law Abraham's property would have gone to one of his servants. But there was a remedy for this event in those days. The husband could, with the full knowledge and consent of his wife, impregnate one of his servant women and the male offspring would then inherit the property. Hagar gave birth to Ishmael "and Abraham rejoiced." Sarah was less enthused but the Lord consoled her and promised that He would bless her also with a son. The elderly Sarah, who had stopped menstruating, found this rather ridiculous. This is the reason why when her boy was born she named him Isaac, which means laughter. Having her own son and heir now, Sarah grew jealous and did not want to share Abraham's property, upon his demise, with Ishmael. Isaac deserved all of it. When she saw that Ishmael was "making sport" with little Isaac at the time he was weaned, she ordered Abraham to expel the "bondwoman," as mentioned by Paul. In order to keep peace in the family, Abraham had to consent and he sent Hagar and her son out into the desert with only some bread and a water bottle. When they were about to die of thirst and exhaustion Hagar cried to the Lord for help. He showed her not only a well of fresh water but also promised that he would make of Ishmael "a great nation." They survived, Hagar returned to her native Egypt where Ishmael married and in accord with the Lord's promise produced numerous offspring who are today's Arabs. This can all be found in the Bible but Jewish oral tradition went to additional great length which reinforced the illegitimacy of Ishmael and his evil ways.

Thus the entire story has not only religious but also political significance for today's Mideast conflict. As far as ardent Zionists are concerned the Arabs are looked down upon with disdain as offspring of the "bondwoman." The Likud party, as well as some other religious-nationalist parties in Israel's Knesset, would like nothing better then to send the allegorical Hagar out into the desert again with her children plus some bread and a water bottle. The Arab Palestinians, on the other hand, regard the Jewish attitude as racist and want their share of the inheritance as promised by the same God whom both claim as their own. Since Ishmael's name translates into "God hears" the Palestinians hope, pray and fight for deliverance in, what has been called by a British observer during the Mandate period, "the too much promised land." This has now become the title of a book by Aaron David Miller, one of our Middle-East peace negotiators. The book should be read by everyone who is seriously concerned about the future of the Middle East and our involvement in that part of the world.

In chapter 5 Paul reiterated that circumcision not only confers no benefits but actually represents a backsliding which nullifies Christ's sacrifice. As Paul pointed out, if the law of circumcision is accepted then so must be all the other laws of Jewish religion and this was precisely what Jesus had freed his followers from. "For in Christ neither circumcision nor uncircumcision counts for anything: the only thing that counts is faith working through love [5:9]." "Through love become slaves to one another. For the whole law is summed up in a single commandment, 'you shall love your neighbor as yourself' [5:13-14]." But Paul also warned them that love must not be regarded as license to do whatever anyone wanted to do. On the contrary love means living by the Spirit which is unalterably opposed to the desires of the flesh:

> But if you are led by the Spirit, you are not subject to the law. Now the works of the flesh are obvious: fornication, impurity, licentiousness, idolatry, sorcery, enmities, strife, jealousy, anger, quarrels, dissensions, factions, envy, drunkenness, carousing and things like these. I am warning you, as I have warned you before: those who do such things will not inherit the kingdom of God.

> By contrast, the fruit of the Spirit is love, joy, peace, patience, kindness, generosity, faithfulness, gentleness, and self-control . . . and those who belong to Christ Jesus have crucified the flesh with its passions and desires [5:18-26].

These verses, which represent Christian teaching, are important for our time. The word Love is used to justify sexual conduct including its homosexual variety. Sexual activity in any of its forms outside of marriage used to be regarded as "fornication." Although the term has been abandoned by our current society its practice is not only tolerated but regarded as normative.

In chapter 6 Paul reiterated these admonitions and declared "God is not mocked, for you reap whatever you sow. If you sow to your own flesh, you will reap corruption from the flesh, but if you sow to the Spirit, you will reap eternal life from the Spirit [7-8]." The brethren were then admonished to do good to all but especially to those of the "family of faith." Paul then reverted to the problem of circumcision, which is to be avoided, because "new creation is everything! As for those who will follow this rule - peace be upon them, and mercy, and upon the Israel of God [15-16]."

We may wonder why circumcision was such a tremendous bone of contention. The reason is found in Genesis 17. After the birth of Ishmael, the Lord renewed his "covenant" with Abram, whose name was changed to Abraham on that occasion. Before Abram's visit to Egypt, the Lord had merely made a land grant to Abram with no strings attached. But now He demanded that every member of the family and all of his posterity had to be circumcised and that "the uncircumcised man child whose flesh of his foreskin is not circumcised, that soul shall be cut off from his people, he hath broken my covenant." Thus without circumcision there could be no covenant and that is why the old covenant was regarded as null and void by Paul and a new one based on the risen Christ was instituted.

In summary one can say that this letter contains all the ethical values Christians were ordered to adhere to. Most of them were, however, universal among civilized societies, even in Paul's days, as will be shown later. Other specific injunctions refer to the separation from Judaism which was necessary unless Jesus' self-sacrifice were to become meaningless. Since the letter is regarded as one of the earliest documents of Paul's thoughts, it is also important to point out what it did not contain. There was no mention of the "lógos" namely that Christ had always been eternally with the Father; there was no mention of a supernatural or virgin birth, because all Paul said is that Jesus "was born of a woman;" and there was no mention of the Eucharist which has become the hallmark of Christianity. The Galatians were not ordered to have communal meals where the miraculous transformation of bread and wine into the flesh and blood of Jesus was to be celebrated. Furthermore, there is no evidence that the Galatians were asked to share their property. There is likewise no mention made of the *Parousía,* the imminent return of Jesus, with the accompanying judgment of the wicked. This was, however, a prominent feature in the epistle to the Thessalonians.

Thessalonians

Biblical authorities tend to agree that the epistle to the Thessalonians represents the earliest of Paul's letters which have come down to us. But since 1Thes and 2Thes show a different style the authenticity of 2Thes has been questioned. It is assumed that 1Thes was written from Corinth in 50 during Paul's second missionary voyage. I shall relate only those aspects which are crucial to an understanding of Paul's thinking as well as the circumstances in which Paul found himself at the time.

In his earlier attempt to convert the Jews of Thessalonica (today's Salonika in Greece) Paul had failed, but he had found a willing audience among the previously mentioned "God-fearers" and some of the women in high society. When his teachings created a civil disturbance, he was expelled from the city. In Beroae, to where he had fled, he met with a similar fate and then hoped that the sophisticated Athenians might be more amenable to his message. But this hope was unfounded. The Epicurean and Stoic philosophers with whom he tried to debate his ideas were not particularly impressed, "Some said, 'What does this babbler want to say?' Others said, 'he seems to be a proclaimer of foreign divinities' [Acts 17:18]." The word *spermológos* which has been translated as "babbler" was actually used in a derogatory manner to depict people "who made their living by collecting and selling refuse they found in the market places." In the current context the Athenians apparently regarded Paul as someone who had a smattering of knowledge from various schools of thought but brought no new information. Some members of the audience, who were more well meaning, took him to an open forum where Paul taught the gospel of the resurrected Christ. He also tried to convince the listeners that he was only talking about the "unknown god," for whom he had found an altar during his exploration of the city. Paul's success was meager, and that is why he removed himself to Corinth which became a major base.

Aquila and his wife Priscilla were some of the first converts and became Paul's good friends. They, along with other Jews, had apparently been expelled by Claudius, "Because the Jews of Rome caused continuous disturbances at the instigation of Chrestus," as Suetonius tells us in *The Twelve Caesars*. This suggests that there already was at that time serious public discord in Rome between Jews and Christians. At any rate Paul stayed in Aquila's and Priscilla's home and his missionary activities to the Corinthians were conducted from there.

Obviously Paul was concerned how his little flock in Thessalonica had fared, and this is why he wrote the letter. It is rather brief and in the first chapter Paul congratulates the church members for their steadfastness and for spreading the gospel throughout Macedonia and Greece; while they waited for God's son, Jesus, who was "raised from the dead and who rescues us from the wrath that is coming [1:10]."

In the second chapter Paul reiterated that his conduct had shown that he was not preaching to flatter others but to be truthful to the word of God which the Jews prevented him from spreading. He had rather harsh words against them. The phrase "killers of Jesus," which later on became "killers of God," has haunted Jews ever since. The Jews, also, "have constantly been filling up the measure of their sins; but God's wrath has overtaken them at last [2:15-16]." The last words of the quote might lead one to believe that this is a later insertion and refers to the fall of Jerusalem. But the word *pantote* which is translated as "at last" means literally "always," and does not imply a date. Paul also regretted that he could not come and visit with the Thessalonians in person; "Satan" had always prevented him. Nevertheless, the congregation was his hope and joy to which he could point at the coming of the Lord Jesus.

In chapter 3 Paul explains that he had to send Timothy, while they were still at Athens, in order to find out how the congregation was doing. Now that Timothy had reassured him that all was well, Paul expressed his joy and gratitude. He also encouraged the flock to remain steadfast so that they would be found blameless at the time when Jesus would return with all his saints.

Chapter 4 contains admonitions against sexual vice and fraudulent business practices but also the rewards for a quiet and honorable life filled with love towards each other, so that they would be dependent upon no one. Those who had died in Christ should not be mourned because they would be raised again, just as Jesus was. When the angel's trumpet would sound they would be the first to experience the new life in heaven while the then living generation would follow subsequently and be with the Lord forever.

The apocalyptic vision was elaborated further in chapter 5 as to the time of occurrence. The congregation was told that they knew full well that the Lord's coming would be "like a thief in the night." Woe and destruction were going to occur suddenly, but the believers would have nothing to be concerned about because they were the children of light. All that was required of them was to be vigilant, sober, wearing the breastplate of faith and love, as well as the helmet of salvation. The members of the church were to be at peace with one another, encourage the fainthearted, help the weak, and be patient. Furthermore they were not to repay evil with evil but to always seek to do good for each other with grateful rejoicing and prayer. The letter concludes with good wishes and the request that it be read to the congregation.

Thus, apart from Christian virtues, we find two themes in this letter. One is the vigorous condemnation of the Jews who hindered Paul's work and the other is the apocalyptic return of Jesus and the saints, which had been missing in the letter to the Galatians. As mentioned previously, the second letter to the Thessalonians is of dubious origin and cannot be dated. It is rather brief and breaks no new ground.

The rest of the epistles can be dispensed with because they largely reaffirm what has been presented so far. They address themselves to specific circumstances as they existed in the various communities and presented the ground rules for the new Church.

In summary, Paul's character and teaching reveal the conflict between the Old and the New which he tried to overcome by "being all things to all men" as the circumstances required at a given moment. It did not work then, as his fate at the hand of the Jerusalem authorities showed, and does not work now. People want declarative statements where a given person stands. In addition this type of mental attitude can readily lead to "the end justifies the means," which is, of course, a direct violation of what Jesus had stood for. Otherwise Paul's teachings contain everything that we are familiar with in Christian Churches. The centrality is the risen Jesus who is Christ, the Son of God. He will reward the faithful with eternal life and condemn the sinners to punishment. Among the sinners are also those Jews who continue to live "in the flesh" rather than the spirit as proclaimed by Jesus Christ. But since vengeance is up to the Lord in His time, Christians should practice forbearance rather than repay evil with evil. The judgment was up to Christ upon his return which was expected to take place here on earth rather than in heaven. In addition there was a rather misogynist element in Paul's thinking (Cor. 11 and 14; I Tim. 2), which was adopted by the Church.

There are, however, some notable differences from current dogma. For instance there is no suggestion of virgin birth and Mary plays no role at all. Holy services seemed to have been much less formal. The faithful congregated over meals, where the "breaking of bread" and joint partaking of wine was observed in accordance with Jesus' wish at the last supper. A Eucharistic ritual as practiced today is not clearly evident. The meetings were apparently joyful, in anticipation of the Lord's return, but not raucous. Qualified male members presented teachings rather than only the priest or minister. Decorum was preserved but it was not necessary that the entire congregation had to sit in silence. In Paul's time this was required only of women. There was no organized priestly class whose financial support came from the faithful. Since the churches were relatively small, there was no further hierarchy to whose opinions one had to conform. Nevertheless, it was foreshadowed. In essence Paul was the Pope and Timothy, Titus, as well as the others who had founded churches in their communities were the Cardinals. Open debate was probably stifled early on and an authoritarian apodictic spirit of "you do what I say because I say so, in the name of Christ the Lord" became the rule. Since "free spirits" have always existed the way to the expulsion of "heretics" was paved. They in turn did not regard themselves as deviant, which resulted in the steadily increasing denominational splits within "the Body of Christ." Jesus' warning, "Beware of the leaven of the Pharisees and Sadducees" has been thoroughly disregarded, as so many other aspects of his message, while others were added which seem to have little to do with his core teachings.

SAINT JOHN'S CHRIST

Introductory comments

St. Paul had presented a relatively simple theology which mainly required belief in the resurrected Jesus as the way to eternal life for those who follow his ethical teaching. The person of Jesus as portrayed in the gospel of John is, however, so complex that even Albert Schweitzer deliberately omitted it from consideration in his doctoral thesis, *"The Psychiatric Study of Jesus."* One needs to realize, therefore, that John's gospel is not about the human being Jesus of Nazareth, but about Christ the *Lógos,* God incarnate. As such, the gospel is a theological treatise and tends to defy proper understanding unless one is familiar with Hellenistic philosophy which was used by Jewish intellectuals of the time to justify the Jewish and subsequently the Christian religion. Philo, as well as Josephus, went to great length, in their exposition of the Jewish belief system, to stress that the Bible should be interpreted in an allegoric manner. Furthermore, they tried to demonstrate that Abraham and especially Moses had been philosophers similar to Pythagoras as well as Socrates, and that the Jewish doctrine was, therefore, not only older but also superior to all other existing ones. This is what the nascent Church was confronted with, and is the reason why the gospel of John has been regarded by some Bible scholars as the Christian analogue to Philo's writings.

When St. John started his narration with, "In the beginning was the Word [*lógos*], and the Word was with God, and the Word was God," the average person is bound to have difficulty in comprehending the meaning. Even Goethe, in his *Faust*, had a problem with the sentence

> *Geschrieben steht: 'Im Anfang war das Wort!''*
> *Hier stock ich schon! Wer hilft mir weiter fort?*
> *Ich kann das Wort so hoch unmoeglich schaetzen,*
> *Ich musz es anders uebersetzen.*
> *Wenn ich vom Geiste recht erleuchtet bin,*
> *Geschrieben steht im Anfang war der Sinn . . .*

Faust had started to translate the gospel of John but he felt that he could not possibly value the word so highly that it represented the beginning of creation. This is why he then tried to translate *lógos* with *Sinn* (meaning). Nevertheless, even this translation did not meet with his approval and he tried *Kraft* (power or energy), but finally ended up with *Tat* (action, deed).

Goethe's difficulty stemmed from his opinion that John had meant with "In the beginning," the creation of the world. But the use of the term by John reflected the idea that a new era had dawned, and he deliberately used the first words of Genesis to connect the Old Testament with the New. John was not necessarily talking about the creation of the world but the origin of Christian belief; this is why the translation of *lógos* with "word" is not altogether wrong, just incomplete.

One has to be aware that the term *lógos* had undergone a considerable mutation of meanings since Heraclites of Ephesus had introduced the concept in the 6th century B.C.. At first it denoted a "reasoning power" behind the orderly operation of the cosmos. *Lógos* was not considered to have been above the world but immanent in it, and the human soul was part of it. More important in this context is the subsequent Stoic doctrine where *Lógos* was identified with God as the active principle which acts on dead matter. A distinction was made between *Lógos* as *ratio* (reason) and *Lógos* as *oratio* (speech). Philo took over the concept of *Lógos* as speech and expended considerable effort to prove the superiority of the "Word" over everything else, because the Creation resulted from direct commands of God, "And God said . . ." This was necessary because Judaism competed at that time with a variety of mystery cults where the emphasis was on experience of the divine through visual imagery. In addition, since Philo also wanted to stress that Judaism is not merely a religion but a philosophy, the primacy of language had to be established. But for Philo and other Jewish writers the "Word" was not God but an emanation of God. John on the other hand subscribed to the idea that the *Lógos* was eternally pre-existing and identical with God. This is obviously an article of theological faith which is not amenable to empirical proof.

Since John's gospel is the most puzzling of all, it is hardly surprising that countless books have been written about it which attempt to explain how it came about and what its purpose was. A psychological interpretation of the mystic elements, from a "Jungian" point of view, was presented by Sanford, and some other books dealing with this gospel are listed in the bibliography. As far as the date and authorship of the Gospel is concerned, there are divergent opinions without firm agreement among scholars. In general it is assumed that it was written after the three synoptic gospels and their knowledge was expected of the readership. *The Jerome Biblical Commentary* attributes it to the Apostle John, brother of James, and suggests that it was composed in Ephesus. It is assumed that John did not write the gospel himself but that he dictated it over a period of years to Papias, one of his disciples. As a result there are duplications, verses appear out of context, and the chronology differs from the synoptic gospels. Von Wahlde in *The Earliest Version of John's Gospel* has suggested that the gospel can be divided into three different sections which may have been prepared at different times. One section deals with the "signs" (miracles) which Jesus gave, the other with discourses by Jesus and the third with the Passion story. An editor subsequently spliced the various sections together which accounts for the unevenness in the current document.

These are, of course, conjectures and certainty will never be achievable, but what does come through quite clearly from the gospel is that the author came from the Jewish-Christian, rather than Gentile-Christian community and that he was very disappointed by the hostility Jesus and his followers had encountered in Jewish circles. While the word Jew(s) occurs rarely in the synoptic gospels and mainly in regard to events during the Passover week, it occurs nearly fifty times in John and mostly in an uncomplimentary manner. The time frame of the gospel's composition is in dispute but tends to be regarded as between the last third of the first century and the beginning of the first third of the second. It thus coincided with, and paved the way for, the final separation of Christianity from Judaism

As mentioned previously, in contrast to the synoptic gospel writers, who portray Jesus as the promised Messiah, and as the fulfillment of biblical prophecies, John presents us with a divine Jesus who is not only the Son of God but "The Father and I are One." Why John chose to go this route can be debated, but it seems likely that in the political climate of the time a simple assertion of Jesus' resurrection from the grave may not have made the anticipated impact on more intellectually inclined converts, unless it could be clothed in a sophisticated philosophical concept. The other gospels were already full of miracles and teachings to which hardly anything could be added. The goal of the effort seems to have been to provide the theological-philosophical underpinning, which Paul had begun in his epistles. This was especially important inasmuch as the previously anticipated collapse of the world order, the arrival of the kingdom of God, and the triumphant return of the Son of Man, had failed to come about. The expected war between "the sons of light" (Jews) and the "sons of darkness" (Romans) had resulted in defeat and the Roman Empire stood on more solid ground than ever before.

But John had to compete not only for the intellect of people in the Roman Empire but also their passions which were satisfied by the various mystery cults. In these the deities routinely referred to themselves as "I" or "I am" which was followed by a variety of attributes. For instance, Plutarch mentioned in his *Moralia* a statue of Isis in Sais which bore the inscription, "I am all that has been, and is, and shall be and my robe no mortal has yet uncovered." Thus, when John put some of these "megalomanic" words in Jesus' mouth he was merely following the custom of the times and Jesus was, therefore, portrayed in the "I" and "I am" manner. Unless these fundamental points are grasped John's gospel is ununderstandable and the Jesus as portrayed by John would have to be regarded, to put it bluntly, as having suffered from delusions of grandeur. Thus, when reading John's gospel we must always make a conscious effort to discern the allegoric meaning which John put into the mouth of Jesus and not be led astray by the apparent material one.

There is an additional aspect which Elaine Pagels has highlighted in her books, *The Gnostic Gospels,* and *Beyond Belief. The Secret Gospel of Thomas.* The nascent Church was not a coherent organization. It consisted instead of various groups which interpreted the meaning of Jesus' life and death according to their own God given insights. Of these the Gnostics were the most important. The term comes from *gnosis,* i.e., knowledge as imparted through a direct experience of the Divine rather than a belief in what others have related. In the current context the most important doctrinal difference was in regard to the resurrection. The canonical gospels insisted on physical resurrection of the body, while the Gnostics believed in a resurrection of the spirit rather than the body. The battle between these factions will be discussed later but for now it is important to recognize the existence of the Gnostics, because the gospel of John can be viewed as the only officially condoned Gnostic version of Jesus' teachings.

Before proceeding to the main narrative, there are two more points to be made. One deals with the difference between analogy and subsequent dogma, while the other establishes the difference between Judaism and Christianity. Chapter 1 verse 14 states in the King James translation, "And the word was made flesh and dwelt among us (and we beheld his glory, the glory as of the only begotten of the Father,) full of a grace and truth." The fact that a key aspect of the passage had been placed in brackets suggests that it was a later insertion, although the Greek text, available to me, has no brackets. But the main point is that the "of" in the original text "as of the only begotten . . ." has been quietly dropped by the Church later on. The Nicene creed of 325 A.D. which still governs the Catholic Church states . . . Son of God, the only begotten . . ." Yet, St. Jerome had translated the Greek *hós monogenuous* as, "*quasi Unigeniti,*" which clearly points to an analogy rather than established fact. Is this a small point? Yes, of course! But from points like these theologies are constructed and as will be shown later an "i" in a Greek word has led to the split beween the Church of Rome and its Eastern counterpart.

Verse 1:17 defines the difference between Judaism and Christianity. "For the law was given by Moses, but grace and truth came by Jesus Christ." The Greek word *cháris*, which is translated as grace, is derived from "Joy" and, in this context, refers to the loving kindness of God. It is a favor without expectations of return which elicits joy in the recipient. Truth, *alētheia*, refers to the reality underlying an appearance and being concordant with it. With other words Jews are bound to obey God by living within the Law of Moses, while Christians are the joyful recipients of God's spontaneous loving kindness.

The Gospel stories

With these introductions we can proceed to some of the gospel's main aspects. The scene opens on the banks of the Jordan where John the Baptist saw Jesus in the crowd and recognized him as "the lamb of God." It was not Jesus who experienced the descent of the spirit, but John who witnessed the event. There was no baptism of Jesus; it would have been inappropriate since the gospel writer had already identified Jesus in the first verse as the incarnate Word of God. Some of John's disciples then began to follow Jesus among whom were: Peter, Andrew, Philip and Nathaniel. On basis of the Baptist's testimony they accepted Jesus as the Messiah and Jesus confirmed their belief by stating, "you will see heaven opened, and the angels of God ascending and descending upon the Son of Man [1:51]." Thus, there was never any question about Jesus' divinity and, therefore, no temptation by Satan.

In the second chapter we find that Jesus, his mother, and disciples had been invited to a wedding at Cana in Galilee and when they got there Mary found out that there was not enough wine. She told Jesus who replied, "Woman, what concern is this to you and to me? My hour is not yet come [2:4]." This seems to be a rather harsh way of dealing with one's mother and commentators have tried to soften the blow by pointing out that "woman" should really have been translated as "madam." Apparently Mary knew that Jesus would be kindhearted and do something about the situation. Without further prompting he did indeed perform his first miracle of changing water into wine. Its relationship to a common mystery cult of the time will be discussed later. But as has been pointed out by previous authors we need to look beyond the physical water and wine to the allegoric message John wanted to send to his flock. The wine of Judaism had been insufficient; Jesus had then taken ordinary water, i.e., the Gentiles, and produced a better product than what had been available previously. Since this type of allegoric interpretation can be found in various Bible Commentaries I will, with one exception, not discuss them further but merely point to this miracle as an example for a potential meaning which is not immediately apparent.

The family and the disciples then moved to Capernaum where they stayed for a little while, but apparently no further miracles were performed, and there is not even a record of Jesus' teaching in the synagogue. Instead, since Passover was at hand, he went to Jerusalem and the temple. According to John's testimony the cleansing of the temple took place at the beginning of Jesus' ministry and apparently the temple authorities were supposed to have taken it in their stride. The bystanders simply asked Jesus, "What sign can you show us for doing this?" This is clearly not how people would have reacted, when someone came with a "whip of cord [2:15]," overturned the tables of the money changers and drove them out from the temple precincts. Neither is Jesus' answer likely in this context, "Destroy this temple, and in three days I will raise it up [2:19]." Yet nobody objected, apart from wondering what he meant, and he explained later that it was his body which would be resurrected. I am mentioning these details because they illustrate the grandiloquent manner in which the gospel of John is written and that the information should not be taken at face value.

That there seems to have been some undercurrent of anger against Jesus becomes apparent in chapter 3. Nicodemus, an eminent Pharisee, had to visit with him "by night," which might suggest that he may not have wanted to be seen in Jesus' company. He accepted Jesus as a man of God and was then told that, "no one can see the kingdom of God without being born from above [3:3]." Nicodemus balked at the idea of rebirth but Jesus explained that spiritual rebirth was meant. This is followed by a long monologue on Jesus' part where he asserted that God so loved the world, that He gave his only begotten Son and that whoever believed in Jesus, would not perish, but have everlasting life. Whoever did not believe was condemned. The Church's absolutist position which we had previously found in Paul's letters was hereby confirmed and attributed to Jesus. Nevertheless, some of us cannot help but feel that this may well have been a self-serving political statement rather than a reflection of universal truth. Why the one and only loving God of the universe should reject the vast majority of humankind, who serve Him in good conscience under a different name, is a problem the "Judeo-Christian tradition" seems not to have faced up to. While rebirth from above was an incomprehensible concept to Nicodemus, the Pharisee, it would not have even raised an eyebrow in the Greco-Roman community since this was the goal of most mystery cults in the Empire.

We are not told what Nicodemus did with the information because he passed from the scene and Jesus moved on with the disciples to the Jordan where John the Baptist made it clear again that he, John, was not the Messiah. Instead he proclaimed Jesus as the Son of God who had been given all power by the Father and whoever did not believe in him "will not see [eternal] life, but must endure God's wrath [3:36]." This is the recurrent theme which is subsequently repeated with only minor variations throughout the gospel.

In the fourth chapter Jesus returned to Galilee but had to go through Samaria where an exchange with a Samaritan woman occurred at the well of Jacob. Jesus was thirsty, the disciples had gone into town to get provisions, and when Jesus asked the woman to give him some water she was surprised that a Jew would be talking to a Samaritan and especially a woman. It is obvious that the gospel writer used this story only as a frame for the picture he wanted to draw of Jesus and to make further theologic points. It is not likely that a thirsty, weary traveler would have said in reply, when paraphrased into colloquial English, "woman, if you knew to whom you are talking, you would ask me to give you water instead of the other way round." Jesus then used his prophetic gift to tell the woman that she has had five husbands. In answer to where God should be worshiped on Mt. Gerizim, as the Samaritans did, or in

Jerusalem, Jesus explained that it would be irrelevant in the future because God is Spirit and needs to be worshiped, regardless of location, in spirit and in truth; the Messiah is not only on the way but that she was already looking at him.

I shall use this story now not only as the second example to show how seemingly ordinary events can, and have been read in an allegoric manner, but also how theologians proceed on occasion. The woman was drawing water from the well of Jacob. This has been taken to indicate that she was using the "water" provided by the Jewish faith which was, however, no longer adequate. Jesus would give her "living water" from heaven and thereby no one would thirst ever again. But there is one segment of verse 22 ". . . salvation is from the Jews . . ." which seems to be quite incongruous with the rest of the story. Why should Jesus praise the Jews at this point, especially when John had, in general, negative feelings towards them? Since the words "Salvation is from the Jews" have been used for an article by an eminent contemporary theologian Reverend John Neuhaus *(First Things,* November 2001) I shall discuss this phrase somewhat further. The context requires awareness of Jn.4:21-23.

> Jesus said to her, "Woman, believe me, the hour is coming when you will worship the Father neither on this mountain nor in Jerusalem. You worship what you do not know; we worship what we know, *for salvation is from the Jews* [italics added]. But the hour is coming, and is now here, when the true worshipers will worship the Father in spirit and truth, for the Father seeks such as these to worship him. God is spirit, and those who worship him must worship in spirit and in truth."

Jesus seems to chide the woman for her ignorance and the ". . . *we* worship. . . [italics added]," is ambiguous. Does it refer to the Jews knowing how to worship God properly or rather to Jesus and his disciples? which seems more reasonable in the context. But how does the immediately following praise for the Jews fit in?

Father Neuhaus has taken it, in the mentioned article, as a point of departure for fostering more amicable relationships between Jews and Christians. This effort dates back to Vatican II, but has only found a lukewarm reception among most Jewish community and religious leaders. The reason is obvious. The two theologies are basically incompatible. Jews and Christians can meet on a personal level but, their opinions diverge profoundly when it comes to theology. If they are honest with each other, and any genuine dialogue must be based on it, they will have to admit that their views are poles apart. Sweet talk, as was attempted in the mentioned article, is not likely to be reciprocated. In the mentioned article the Reverend wrote:

> To change the metaphor, somewhat, we live in the house of the one people of God only as we live with the Jews of whom Jesus was - and eternally is - one. The second Person of the Holy Trinity, true God and true man, is *Jewish flesh* [italics added]. As is the Eucharistic body we receive, as is the Body of Christ into which we are incorporated by Baptism.

This seems to be putting it rather crassly. Is this really why we partake in the Eucharist or do we believe that this rite will bring us closer to the Spirit of Jesus in whom there is "no Jew or Gentile?" But this is a question each one of us needs to answer for ourselves. The Roman saying, "*de gustibus non est disputandum*," which might be translated as "there's no sense arguing over tastes," applies equally to theology.

Nevertheless, we are still stuck with the phrase "salvation is from the Jews" in the context it appears in John's gospel. It has been suggested that it was meant as a dig by Jesus to show superiority of the Jews over the Samaritans, while Bultmann felt that it was some editorial insert which doesn't belong there. There may be another possibility which resides in the translation. The transliteration of the Greek phrase reads ". . . because salvation *from the Jews* [emphasis added] is." But the word "*sōtēría*" which is translated in all of our Bibles as "salvation" and in Latin as "*salus*," means also in the original Greek "deliverance," "safety," "preservation from danger or destruction." This throws a potentially different light on the phrase. Was it originally meant to indicate that "deliverance from the Jews" is at hand for the despised and oppressed Samaritans via the Messiah, Jesus, whom the woman was already looking at? I don't know. But under these circumstances the first word of verse 23 *Állá*, which is usually translated as "but," might not have been used as an antithesis but instead as an affirmative statement indicating "moreover." The word can have both meanings in the Greek language. I am pointing to this passage only in order to show the problems of translations and to what length theological affirmations can go based on parts of one sentence which do not even fit into the context in which they occur.

It would be repetitious now to continue with a chapter by chapter description of John's gospel, therefore, I shall point out only some highlights and where the narrative departs from the synoptic gospels. The momentous words, of eating Jesus' body and drinking his blood, were not uttered at the Last Supper but instead placed in connection with the miraculous feeding of the five thousand. This miracle is discussed from the point of view of heavenly nourishment. In Moses' time the Lord had sent manna from heaven, but now Jesus himself was the true bread, "the bread of life [6:35,40]," he had "come down from heaven [6:38]" and "Very truly I tell you, unless you eat the flesh of the Son of Man, and drink his blood, you have no life in you. Those who eat of my flesh, and drink my blood, have eternal life; and I will raise them up at the last day [6:53-54]." This point was hammered home for the rest of the chapter to establish the centrality of the Eucharist for Christian worship. On the other hand, it is not surprising to read that a great many would-be followers left Jesus at this point because an implication of cannibalism was too much to accept and an allegorical interpretation eluded these simple people.

In the story of the adulterous woman, whose sins Jesus' forgave, he dismissed her with the words, ". . . from now on do not sin again [8:11]." These words are important in view of some popular interpretations of Christian teaching where forgiveness is emphasized, regardless of repentance and subsequent conduct. Forgiveness is indeed important but unless accompanied by genuine remorse over past behavior and the firm resolve to do better in the future it turns into a sham and has no redeeming quality for the individual.

The rest of the chapter contains typical declamatory statements which were supposed to have been accepted by the audience. They included assertions such as: "I am the light of the world;" "though I bear record of myself, yet my record is true;" "I am not of this world;" "you shall die in your sins, because you don't believe me." But to those who did believe in him he said, "If you continue in my word, you are truly my disciples, and you will know the truth, and the truth will make you free [8:31-32]." When some of the bystanders demurred and said that they were Abraham's children and as such free people Jesus refuted them and said that, "everyone who commits sin, is a slave to sin [8:34]," and only the Son of the Father can free them. When the objection was raised that the father of the Jews was Abraham, Jesus chided them again and told them that if Abraham were their father they would not seek to kill him because Abraham lived by the word of God.

As if these condemnations were not enough, Jesus added, "You are from your father the devil, and you chose to do your father's desires. He was a murderer from the beginning and does not stand in the truth, because there is no truth in him. When he lies, he speaks according to his own nature, for he is a liar and the father of lies [8:44]." This, obviously did not sit well with the audience and they accused him of being a demon possessed Samaritan, which in turn led to the exchange where Jesus assured his listeners, "Very truly, I tell you, whoever keeps my word will never see death [8:51]." Since this seemed apparent nonsense, "The Jews said to him, 'Now we know that you have a demon, Abraham died, and so did the prophets; yet you say, 'Whoever keeps my word, will never taste death.' Are you greater than our father Abraham, who died? The prophets also died. Who do you claim to be'? [8:52-53]." This led to the answer, "Your ancestor Abraham rejoiced that he would see my day [8:56]," as well as, "Very truly, I tell you, before Abraham was, I am [8:58]." These expostulations were clearly intolerable and in true and tried fashion his listeners picked up stones to kill him with, but Jesus escaped unharmed. It is obvious, that if anyone were to make these claims today he would indeed be remanded to a psychiatric facility and would receive a hefty dose of tranquilizers. Even if Jesus himself were to return today, utter these words and thereby create a public disturbance, he would not be spared that fate.

The narration of Jesus' arrest, trial, humiliation, crucifixion and resurrection contains a fair amount of embellishments over the synoptic gospels. Jesus did not remain mute in front of Pilate but entered into a dialogue and told the procurator that "My kingdom is not of this world [18:36]." When Pilate retorted, "So, you are a king? Jesus answered 'You say that I am a king. For this I was I born and for this I came into the world, to testify to the truth. Everyone that belongs to the truth listens to my voice [18:37]."This resulted in Pilate's subsequent immortal question, "What is truth [18:38]?" What indeed? Two thousand years later we are still debating the question in this as well as numerous other political and theological contexts with no agreement in sight.

As related in the synoptic gospels, Pilate didn't want trouble especially on a high holiday and was inclined to release Jesus but the crowd wanted Barabbas, who was referred to in the gospel as a bandit. Pilate was still reluctant to hand Jesus over to the crowd and this is why the soldiers dressed him in a red robe and put a crown of thorns on his head. This was followed by the famous "*Ecce homo*," "Behold the man [19:5]," which is missing in the synoptic gospels. If one visualizes the scene where Pilate parades the humiliated Jesus in front of the crowd he probably might have said: just look at this fellow whom you call your king. He's pathetic; if you want to kill him go ahead but I have no reason to do so. When the Jews yelled back at Pilate that Jesus had offended Jewish law by declaring himself the Son of God which deserved a death sentence, Pilate supposedly "was more afraid than ever [19:8]." He took Jesus back inside and asked him where he was from. When Jesus didn't answer at first, Pilate threatened him with his magisterial powers but Jesus replied calmly that Pilate's power had been given to him from above, but he "who handed me over to you is guilty of a greater sin [19:11]." According to John, Pilate was then again ready to release Jesus but the crowd shouted, "If you release this man you are no friend of Caesar. Everyone who claims to be a king sets himself up against Caesar [19:12]." This was indeed a serious turn of events, as mentioned earlier. Roman historians are unanimous that by that time the Emperor, Tiberius, who had become profoundly paranoid, executed anybody on the smallest of pretexts. Pilate had, therefore, every reason to fear that some of the influential Jews in Rome would blackball him before the Emperor. When it now came to a choice between a poor Galilean's head and his own, the outcome was hardly surprising. What was one more crucifixion after all?

We may now ask the question why the crowd, which had greeted Jesus enthusiastically only a few days earlier, would now so adamantly demand his death. The answer is simple and in total accord with human nature. They felt that they had been duped by an impostor! The Messiah was supposed to lead a successful rebellion against the Romans, return the country to Jewish rule and re-establish David's kingdom forever. That was and still is the job of the Jewish Messiah. His kingdom is to be on this earth and not in some heavenly domain. When Jesus did not conform to that role he had to be done away with and the faster the better. Logic demanded that he was a false Messiah, and he is still today so regarded by the orthodox segment of Judaism. This in turn leads to the inevitable conclusion that the entire Christian religion is built on a sham. This fact has to be firmly understood and is the reason why a theologic dispute between Christians and Jews is fruitless because the fundamental premises differ profoundly.

Although all gospels agree that the crowd demanded Jesus' death from Pilate, it is only in the gospel of John that Jesus carried his own cross (it had been carried for him by Simon of Cyrene in the others), that his mother had stood underneath and that Jesus had ordered "the disciple whom he loved [19:26]," who was also there, that he be henceforth Mary's son and she his mother. Jesus' death was not accompanied by the agonized cry, "My God, My God why hast thou forsaken me?" but by a quiet and dignified, "It has been accomplished [19:30]." The gospel also states that when the soldiers saw that Jesus was already dead they did not break his bones, as was done with the two others who had been crucified with him. Instead one of the soldiers "pierced his side with a spear, and at once blood and water came out [19:34]."

If we were to take this story at face value it would present us with an interesting medical question. Dead bodies don't bleed because there is no blood circulation, so was Jesus really dead at that time? Water can only be released, in an otherwise healthy individual, from two sources either the urinary bladder, or the gall bladder. From some of the pictures of the site of the wound one might expect that the gallbladder may have been pierced and its brownish content might have been taken for blood. Nevertheless, it must be admitted that from a medical point of view death on the cross within a period of six hours was unusual. Victims tended to linger for days, which was the purpose of crucifixion in the first place. An agonizingly slow death was to be endured in full view of others in order to serve as deterrent for would-be violators of Roman law. If people had to be removed from the cross, while still alive, their bones were deliberately smashed which produced death through fat or blood emboli (clots).

The reason why John made a point that Jesus' bones were not crushed was to fulfill scripture. Since Jesus was the supreme sacrifice to the Lord the injunction against breaking the bones of the sacrificial victim as expressed in Exod. 12:46 and Num. 9:12 had to be honored. In addition there was Psalm 33:20 to be considered where the righteous were reassured that, "He [the Lord] keeps all their bones: not one of them shall be broken." In Christian Bibles the reference is in Psalm 34:20. Piercing of the body was also demanded by Jewish scripture. In Zecheriah 12:10 there is a passage which deals with the redemption of the house of David and Jerusalem "and they shall look upon me whom they have pierced and they shall mourn for him . . ." The Septuagint version does not use the word "pierced" but "mocked." These aspects, including the parting of Jesus' clothes by the soldiers are just some others of the many instances where scripture was used by the gospel writers to confirm that Jesus was indeed the Messiah. On the other hand Jews can hardly be faulted when they took exception to what they must have regarded as arbitrary and out of context interpretations of their sacred literature. The gospel writer seemed to assure his audience, however, that he had personally witnessed the events and guarantees the truthfulness of the account in 19:35, "He who saw this has testified so that you also may believe. His testimony is true, and he knows that he tells the truth." Someone with a critical mind might, however, object that since the gospel writer did not specifically give his name, but wrote in the third person, it might have been second hand information.

The resurrection account differs also to some extent. Jesus showed himself first to the apostles in Jerusalem, where he endowed them with the Holy Spirit and the ability to remit sins. The apostle Thomas was not present at the time, but Jesus returned once more and showed the "doubting Thomas" his wounds. In the previously mentioned book *Beyond Belief* the opinion is expressed that this story was specifically directed at the Gnostics. It was intended to affirm the belief in the physical, rather than spiritual resurrection, which was important for the early Church.

Some authors believe that John's gospel had ended with chapter 20 and that the entire chapter 21, which depicts Jesus' appearance to the disciples in Galilee, is a later insertion. The only significant aspect for our understanding of Jesus is that in accordance with the synoptic gospels the disciples and Mary Magdalene had at first not recognized the resurrected Jesus. Mary Magdalene thought that she was talking to the gardener, his followers on the way to Emmaus did not recognize him, and when Jesus appeared to the disciples in Galilee even Peter first regarded him as a stranger. The significance of these statements will be discussed in the context of Jesus' message for our time.

In assessing John's gospel we have to re-emphasize that we should not expect to meet the human being Jesus of Nazareth who gradually came to realize his purpose in life and willingly accepted the consequences; although he still hoped, at Gethsemane, to be spared the cruel death. Instead, we are confronted in John's Christ with the eternally co-existent Son of God who temporarily assumed human form in order to redeem mankind. As such the words ascribed to Jesus contain messages to the disciples who were on a mission to convert the citizens of the Roman Empire to the new religion. In order to do so, several requirements had to be met. The religion had to have a philosophical underpinning and had to be presented as superior to the then existent other belief systems, which included Judaism. This aspect will be discussed in some detail later. For now we can summarize the essence of John's gospel as follows:

1) Jesus is the Son of God, endowed with all His powers and as such, God incarnate.

2) One has to be reborn in God's spirit, as expressed by Jesus' words and actions, to partake of eternal life.

3) Jesus' disciples are to be recognized by the love they have for each other and humanity at large.

4) Unless one "eats my flesh and drinks my blood" one does not have life and will perish. This allegoric statement was then taken by the Church to celebrate the mystery of the Eucharist, as its most distinctive feature.

It is obvious that these are "take it or leave it" statements which have subsequently produced a variety of problems for the nascent Church. The question as to the nature of Jesus led to the previously alluded to battle over an "i" in a Greek word. Was Jesus identical with God, i.e., of the same substance, *homooúsios*, or was he similar in substance to God *homoioúsios*? The *homoioúsios* idea was most prominently championed by Arius, who was ordained bishop of Alexandria in 311. Among others he adhered to the idea that God was unity and, therefore, could not be exclusively incarnated in a single human being. Jesus was created by God, at the beginning of the world, but as the Son he was less than God but more than man.

Inasmuch as this concept did not differ substantially from the idea of demi-gods, which was widely held in the Greco-Roman world, this was regarded as dangerous for the future success of the Church. The council of Nicea, therefore, adopted in 325 the *homooúsios* formula, "eternally one with the father" and "begotten not made," which governs the Catholic Church to this day. But let us not forget that this formulation was arrived at through majority vote. Democracy has its virtues, but it does not always guarantee that wisdom will prevail. On the contrary it serves expediency most of the time. In this instance the purpose, for which Constantine had called the Synod in the first place, was to create political stability in the Empire which was rent apart by religious partisan strife. Arius and his followers were eventually excommunicated as heretics and this became the norm how to deal with sectarians. In the Middle Ages excommunication was not deemed sufficient punishment but was followed in some instances by burning at the stake. Nevertheless, the question as to the "true nature" of Jesus has remained problematic unto this day.

While the point as to the nature of Christ was to some extent adopted for political purposes, eating the flesh and drinking the blood of Jesus, as prerequisite for entrance to everlasting life, may be understood in relation to then existing mystery religions, which will be discussed later. But once Christianity was firmly established it became a powerful political weapon for the priesthood. The Eucharist could be withheld from sinners, even if they were emperors or kings, and their souls would suffer eternal damnation. This was not to be risked lightly in earlier ages when Christian belief dominated all else and when the only skepticism was expressed by Jews, who were, however, relatively powerless at that time. It may be reasonable to assume that the malignant myth that the Jews use human blood, especially Christian, in the preparation of the unleavened bread for Passover originated in an inversion of this Christian article of faith. A charge of cannibalism had in fact been leveled against the Church early on by some of its detractors.

Rebirth in the spirit was a common theme in pagan mystery religions during apostolic times. But the idea that God's spirit can be apprehended directly, without other human intermediaries, led, as has been mentioned, to the various Gnostic factions. These were a considerable danger for the early Church. If anybody, with sufficient diligence, could know God directly what need was there for priests and bishops who alone were supposed to be the guardians of truth? These challenges to authority and hierarchy had to be condemned as heretical.

Since we are now leaving whatever historicity the gospels may claim in regard to Jesus, it is of interest what Josephus had to say about the reign of Pilate. Chapter III, book XVIII of *The Antiquities of the Jews* is headlined, "Sedition of the Jews against Pilate; Concerning Christ, and what befell Paulina and the Jews at Rome." This is the only chapter where Jesus is mentioned. In paragraph 3 of this chapter we find:

> Now there was about this time, Jesus, a wise man, if it
> be lawful to call him a man, for he was a doer of wonderful
> works, - a teacher of such men as receive truth with pleasure.
> He drew over to him both many of the Jews, and many of
> the Gentiles. He was [the] Christ; and when Pilate, at the

suggestion of the principal men amongst us, had condemned him to the cross, those that loved him at the first did not forsake him, for he appeared to them alive again the third day, as the divine prophets had foretold these and ten thousand other wonderful things concerning him; and the tribe of Christians, so named for him, are not extinct to this day.

When one is familiar with Josephus' style and his vigorous polemical attacks against the enemies of the Jewish religion, especially in *Contra Apionem* it seems likely that the words quoted above represent a Christian interpolation and do not belong to the original text. While this paragraph does not help much in finding the "historical" Jesus, the two preceding and the two subsequent ones are of some value. In the first paragraph Josephus relates how Pilate had smuggled Roman military standards, which bore the likeness of Caesar, into Jerusalem and how the Jews of the city were distraught over this event. First they petitioned Pilate to take the offensive standards back to Caesarea, but Pilate was unwilling to do so. When the Jews persisted in their demand Pilate surrounded the crowd with his soldiers and threatened to kill them unless they went home peacefully:

But they threw themselves upon the ground, and laid their necks bare, and take their deaths very willingly, rather than the wisdom of their laws should be transgressed; upon which Pilate was deeply affected with their firm resolution to keep their laws inviolable, and presently commanded the images to be carried from Jerusalem to Caesarea.

This event is followed by one where the Jews objected to temple money being used to finance the construction of an aqueduct which would have brought much needed water to Jerusalem. Again a crowd gathered, "and made a clamor against him, and insisted that he should leave off that design. Some of them also used reproaches and abused the man, as crowds of such people usually do." In this instance Pilate did not show leniency but used his soldiers to teach the unruly mob a lesson and "there were a great number of them slain . . . and others of them ran away wounded; and thus an end was put to this sedition." Paragraphs four and five deal with events in

Rome and will be taken up in the last chapter. For now it is apparent that during Pilate's tour of duty the crowds in Jerusalem were indeed restive and unruly. While "baring" the necks by the devout may well be Josephus' commonly used hyperbole, it does seem that we are dealing with historical events. The stories show that on occasion Pilate was willing to give in to a crowd's demands when only Jewish law was at stake but if it concerned public health, as for instance in the accessibility of water supply, he brooked no dissent and used force. Thus the gospel stories of Pilate's vacillation when confronted with a Jewish mob are not inherently unbelievable. On the other hand a Josephus who is so zealous for the Law as expressed in paragraph 1 of that chapter would hardly have written such a favorable paragraph 3 about Jesus who was brought before Pilate precisely because he had violated the Law. It must be remembered at this point that no historical books the rabbis might have written after the fall of Jerusalem have survived and even the Talmud has undergone excisions and alterations during the Middle Ages.

In conclusion one can state that the gospel of John was a potent weapon in the hands of Christian missionaries of the time who were charged with bringing the good news to the ends of the earth. But being a human document, written for a specific purpose, it also had its weaknesses. An apodictic statement that one can enter into a true relationship with God only "through eating the flesh and drinking the blood of Christ" is open to question. It can neither satisfy the intellect nor can it be verified on experiential grounds as a study of other religions readily discloses. Mystics who did achieve the experience of unity with The All, which we call God, existed and still exist in all civilizations around the globe. The names which are applied to this experience differ, but names are merely symbols in which we try to clothe ineffable direct experience.

Furthermore, the gospel of John, although having borrowed and re-interpreted the notion of *Lógos,* is still in the tradition of the Old Testament. There is the constant division between "Them" and "Us," and although it had become easier to join the "Us," the inherent antipathy against "The Other," who found himself unable to accept dogmatic statements remained. Separation is necessary to create a new religion but cannot bring us to universally accepted truth.

THE APOCALYPSE

The theme of eternal perdition for the vast majority of humankind is elaborated further in the Apocalypse which translates into Revelation. Since authorship, or at least for part of it, has also been ascribed to St. John, I am discussing it here after the gospel of John. The fact that the book is used to produce bestsellers, which proclaim the imminent day of doom, is not as important as that it has become for some evangelical Christians a political action program to be worked towards. The revelation has in recent times been interpreted, that Jesus' return depends upon the ingathering of the dispersed Jews to the Holy Land and construction of the third temple. For this reason some groups are trying to hasten Jesus' second coming by advocating the elimination of the Al Aqsa mosque and the Dome of the Rock so that the temple can be built on the ancient site. Although these visionaries would consent to having the structures removed stone by stone and rebuilt in Arab lands, rather than simply blasting them into oblivion, it is obvious that any attempt of putting this idea into practice would lead to a major upheaval which would not be limited to the Middle East.

It is remarkable that the *Gush Enim* (the Temple Mount Faithful) and evangelical Christians are collaborating in this vision, although a triumphant return of Jesus may not be in the best interest of Jews. Since Jesus has told us explicitly that the time of his return is up to the Lord and known only to God, those who try to apply some of the apocalyptic visions to our time ought to be more conscious of the allegoric aspects of Christianity. For Christians to encourage, and actively engage in, a program which is bound to lead not only to untold suffering, but in no way guarantees the anticipated outcome, is unconscionable. This is why the Apocalypse of St. John is a potentially dangerous book, and why a discussion of this document is essential.

It must now be stated at the outset that the information contained in the Apocalypse cannot be apprehended intellectually because its essence consists of nightmarish symbolic visions which eventually give way to a "heavenly Jerusalem." While the intellect must be held in abeyance, the book also hardly appeals to any of the higher emotions of the average reader. It is geared to instilling crude fear for the disasters which will soon befall this world and bring it to ruin. Although the book is regarded as a Christian text because Jesus is the judge, the tenor is classic Jewish apocalyptic thought with emphasis on tribulations, destruction, revenge and disasters rather than love, mercy and forgiveness. This makes it likely that the author came from the Jewish community rather than the Hellenistic-Christian group.

As mentioned, the author had originally been identified with the St. John of the gospel but this is not warranted. The famed Dionysius, Bishop of Alexandria (c.200-265), pointed out (as quoted by Eusebius) that the Greek language in the Apocalypse, "is inaccurate, and he [the author] uses barbarous idioms and occasional solecisms." Dionysius mentions that these comments should not be taken in a derogatory manner but merely to emphasize that the gospel of John is written in grammatically correct Greek and the two authors can, therefore, not be identical. It seems that the author of Revelation thought in Hebrew-Aramaic which he translated into imperfect Greek. Eusebius assumed that the author, if there was a single one, may have been John the Presbyter who was exiled to the island of Patmos during Domitian's reign of terror. This, however, is speculation and the text suggests that several different documents have been combined at various times.

Although the book contains twenty-nine references to "the Lamb" which hearken back to St. John's gospel, and do not occur in the synoptic gospels, the text is replete with symbolism culled from the Old Testament. McKenzies' *Dictionary of the Bible* gives the references and his article on the Apocalypse, as well as authoritative Bible Commentaries, should be consulted by anyone who wants to read modern political, rather than spiritual, meaning into this ancient vision.

As mentioned, the book consists of separate documents which seem to have originated at different times. The earliest has been dated to Nero's persecutions of the Church because the number of the beast 666 spells "Neron Caesar" when written with the values of the Hebrew characters. When "Nero Caesar" is used it results in 616, which shows up in some of the earliest documents of the second century. The number has also been related to Caligula because the Greek spelling of *Gaios Kaisar* likewise comes to 616. The second document contains the epistles to the Asian churches and the third the visions and persecutions. These segments probably originated towards the end of Domitian's reign (81-96 A.D.), who disliked Jews and Christians with equal impartiality. He reportedly intended to have a huge temple erected in Ephesus which would have contained a colossal statue of himself to which homage was to be paid. For obvious reasons Jews and Christians rebelled, and vigorous persecutions started which ended only after Domitian's death.

The image of the beast that was killed, but whose wound healed, referred to Nero. He had attempted suicide but did not do a good job and his servant, Epaphroditus, had to provide the *coup de grace*. In the vision Nero was resurrected as Domitian who habitually signed himself as "your Lord and God." The image of the beast is his statue which was widely erected across the Empire, and the woman upon whose forehead was written "Babylon the Great, The Mother of Harlots and Abominations of the Earth" was, of course, Rome.

As always we must ask ourselves: what was the purpose for which the book was written? There seems to be little doubt that it was intended to impart strength to the beleaguered churches who found themselves persecuted and to provide the hope that Rome would soon be overthrown with the Christian Church emerging triumphant. There were, however, in the third century already, doubts whether or not the book deserved to be entered into the New Testament canon. Several Church fathers among whom were Caius of Rome, Dionysius of Alexandria, St. Cyril of Jerusalem and Chrysostom rejected its authenticity and even the eminent Eusebius was uncertain. Why it was subsequently retained as canonical, is not quite clear.

The interpretations which have been given to the symbols varied from astrological through mundane and new ones are being invented every day, including 666, as standing, most recently, for the name Ronald Wilson Reagan. Since the book is "visionary" it lends itself to any conjecture one may want to entertain and, as mentioned, is typical for the apocalyptic literature of the time especially Ezekiel, Zechariah, Daniel, Enoch, and Esdras as well as some of the Qumran documents. Some aspects seem to have been lifted practically verbatim. I shall not present the details because Jesus is, for practical purposes, absent; although he is at times referred to as "the lamb" or as the warrior at the head of heavenly hosts and final judge. After Satan and his minions have been finally vanquished the book ends with a description of the heavenly Jerusalem which had the appearance of a very precious jewel. There were twelve gates inscribed with the names of the twelve tribes and the walls had the names of the twelve apostles. Similar to Ezekiel's vision John was ordered to measure the city. The length and width were identical and amounted to fifteen hundred miles, while the walls measured one hundred and forty-four cubits. Since all evil had already been eradicated in previous verses one might wonder why walls and gates were needed but, as mentioned earlier, the book is strictly a theological document, spliced together from several others, and does not lend itself to rational understanding. John then went on to describe in great detail all the precious stones which made up the walls and gates while the street (sic) of the city was "pure gold, transparent as glass [21:21]." The gates of the city were never to be shut and people would "bring into it the glory and the honor of the nations. But nothing unclean will enter it, nor anyone who practices abomination or falsehood, but only those who are written in the Lamb's book [21:26-27]." The most valuable thought of the entire book is that the heavenly Jerusalem did not contain a temple. It was superfluous because the spirit of God and Jesus were immanent in all the people.

Of importance in regard to the search for truth is the concluding chapter 22 where the angel told John "These words are trustworthy and true, for the Lord, the God of the spirits of the prophets, has sent his angel to show his servants what *must soon* [emphasis added] take place [22:6]." Verse 7 reiterates the immediacy of these events. "'See, I am *coming soon* [emphasis added]. Blessed is the one who keeps the words of the prophecy of this book,'" and so does verse 12, "'See, *I am coming soon* [emphasis added]; my reward is with me, to repay everyone's work.'" In verse 16 the speaker is identified; "'It is I, Jesus, who sent my angel with the testimony for the churches. I am the root and descendant of David, the bright morning star.'" In verse 18 John repeats the Deuteronomy (4:2) injunction of Moses not to add or subtract anything from the prophecies which have been uttered here because "God will take away that person's share in the tree of life and in the holy city [22:19]." Although we had been told in chapter 21 that the earth had been completely cleansed from evil this seemed not to have been quite correct, because verse 15 of chapter 22 tells us that a variety of undesirables including "sorcerers, fornicators, murderers, and idolaters" would have to remain outside the city gates. The book ends with the reaffirmation "'*Surely I am coming soon* [emphasis added],'" and the wish that the grace of the Lord Jesus should be with all the saints.

When one reads this document in its entirety, rather than in predigested and edited versions, it is amazing that intelligent people would not only give credence to this book nearly two thousand years later, but actually use it for political purposes. The massive exaggerations and the spirit of hate which this book exudes must have struck people, even in Roman times, as unwarranted. This brings up the question why a document which portrays God and Jesus as bloodthirsty vengeful personalities, was admitted to the official New Testament. I have no definite answer to this question and none is likely to be forthcoming. But the previously mentioned Dionysius of Alexandria, who also confessed that the book surpassed his intellectual abilities, may have left us a clue, "I, however, would not dare reject the book, since many brethren hold it in esteem, but since my intellect cannot judge it properly, I hold that its interpretation is a wondrous mystery." Were these "brethren" frightened by the threat of eternal damnation as mentioned in 22:19, and is that why they retained this unfortunate book? When one considers human nature, and the superstitious fears it can readily succumb to, this seems to be a reasonable explanation.

I have mentioned earlier the book of Esdras as a corollary to John's apocalypse. It consists of two segments and is not in the mainstream Bibles but can be found in the Apocrypha. Esdras 1 deals with Ezra's exile in Babylon and his return to Jerusalem, while Esdras 2 contains the reasons for Israel's rejection; its coming glory; an explanation of human destiny; prophecies of doom and visions of the last days. These two sections were arbitrarily combined and have nothing to do with each other. Esdras 2 is of interest in the current context because it has been dated to about 100 -120 A.D. and is, therefore, contemporaneous with John's apocalypse. The author was Jewish and salvation of the nation of Israel was to be achieved by the Messiah, who was the Son of God. Rome was represented by an eagle. She would be challenged and eventually defeated with all the rest of her allies by a lion, who obviously represented Judah.

The book contains some highly relevant quotes which are reproduced here from *The New English Bible* because it does not exist in the Septuagint. In chapter 7:11 the Lord assured Ezra, "Such is the lot of Israel. *It was for Israel that I made the world* [emphasis added], and when Adam transgressed my decrees the creation came under judgment." I added the emphasis because this is one of many typical examples how some Jewish theologians felt about the purpose of our world.

Esdras' prophecies of doom are preceded by:

> Proclaim to my people the prophecy which I give you to speak, says the Lord; and have them written down, because they are trustworthy and true. Have no fear of plots against you, and do not be troubled by the unbelief of those who oppose you. For everyone who does not believe will die because of his unbelief.

Since this is basically the same wording as in John one is reminded of Pilate's question "What is truth?" which will be discussed in the final chapter. Esdras also tells us that during the calamities which would precede the end of the world "blood shed by the sword, will reach as high as a horse's belly, a man's thigh or a camel's hock," which is basically identical with John's vision. The rest of the disasters are also generic and require no further detail, except that we are clearly told in 16:37:

> The calamities *are here, close at hand, and will not delay* [emphasis added]. When a pregnant woman is in the ninth month, and the moment of her child's birth is drawing near, there will be two or three hours in which her womb will suffer pangs of agony, and then the child will come from the womb without a moment's delay; and in the same way calamities will come on the earth without delay, and the world will groan under the pangs that grip it [16:37-39].

The faithful were exhorted to give up their current lives because all ordinary pursuits would come to naught:

> Listen to my words my people; get ready for battle and when the calamities surround you, be as though you were strangers on earth. The seller must expect to have to run for his life, the buyer to lose what he buys; the merchant must expect to make no profit, the builder never to live in the house he builds. The sower must not expect to reap, nor the pruner to gather the grapes. Those who marry must expect no children; the unmarried must think of themselves as widowed. For all labour is labour in vain. Their fruits will be gathered by foreigners, who will plunder their goods, pull down their houses, and take their children captive [16:40-46]."

The text continues like this for the rest of the book, but the faithful are also reassured that, "Then it will be seen that my chosen people have stood the test like gold in the assayer's fire [16:73]." Thus the messages of John and Esdras are essentially identical except that the ones who were to be saved were believers in Christ, as far as John is concerned, while they were the followers of the Law of Moses for Esdras.

I have singled out Esdras' apocalypse because it can serve as an important warning for what happens when religious visions are taken as a blueprint for political action. The second Jewish revolt in

132 A.D. was inspired by these ideas. Its outcome was even more disastrous for the people and the land than the first one had been. The country was devastated, commerce abolished and henceforth only the most religious Jews would go to live or die there. Large scale Jewish immigration to the "promised land" had to wait until the 20th century. Apart from the Crusader era, Palestine had become a quiet backwater which Jews and Christians visited but didn't want to live in. But now in the 21st century the human being's apparently unlimited capacity for self-delusion reasserts itself again in that part of the world with millennial expectations. A possibly even more terrible outcome than the one Bar-Cochba (son of the star), who was hailed as the Messiah, had brought about, may well be in the offing. It is unfortunate that this chapter of Jewish history does not nearly get the same attention as the destruction of the Temple several decades earlier although it was even more decisive for the peoples' fate and cemented the split between the Jewish and Christian religion. Apocalyptic prophecies had cost the Jews their country and the tragedy of St. John's Apocalypse is that it might well end in a disaster which will not be limited to the Middle East. This is why this book is such a dangerous document.

Let me re-emphasize, therefore, that the book was not written for the dim future; it was an exhortation to the Christian communities of the first and second century to stand fast in the face of persecution. The members were to be vigilant, the Day of Judgment was imminent, the wicked would be punished and the faithful rewarded. This is also the only message Christians can adhere to in our "secular" culture, with the proviso that we may experience the judgment at the time of our personal death, rather than during an imminent cosmic catastrophe.

As far as the coming Antichrist is concerned we have already had several examples during the past two centuries which ranged from Napoleon, through Lenin, Stalin and Hitler. Others will surely come with hopefully equally limited life expectancies. The yearned for Jewish Messiah may also not turn into the blessing the followers of the Lubavitcher Rebbe, who will be discussed in more detail later, expect. He would have to be a scion from the house of David, establish a theocracy in Israel, rebuild the third temple on what Muslims call the Haram al-Sharif (noble sanctuary), conquer vast tracts of land in the Middle East and abolish all other religions apart from Judaism. That the rest of the world would hardly be delighted with this turn of events requires no further comment.

But the Antichrist need not be looked for in a person. More likely it will be an autocratic state which tolerates no dissent and is inimical to all religious thought. God will be declared obsolete and those daring souls who will continue to follow their conscience will be excluded from societal functions and/or hounded to death. This change will not come overnight but gradually step by step so that the citizenry will not get too alarmed. The model for this resides in the reign of terror during the French revolution and subsequently the Nazi era and Communist states. This is the danger Christians are facing and have to be vigilant against lest they wake up one day and find the system in place.

I realize that this assessment of the Apocalypse is too prosaic and will be a deep disappointment to those who firmly believe in the imminent end of the world, and who see New York as the modern Babylon whose measure of sins is full by now. In former years Paris had that reputation and it surely will be bequeathed to other cities in the centuries to come. The same applies to believers of the "rapture" where an angelic "Scottie," of the first Star Trek series, will beam the faithful up to a rendezvous with Jesus, in order to spare them the time of tribulation. In spite of protestations to the contrary on "www.raptureready.com," Paul's 1Thes 4:13-18, which serves for justification of the idea, when read in context, refers to what is commonly called the second coming of Christ, rather than a "pre-tribulation rapture." The biblical text indicates furthermore, that the dead would be raised first and admitted to heaven, before it was the turn for the then living generation. As mentioned earlier the prophecies and epistles were written for people who lived in the first and second century, just as the author of the mentioned webpage is not writing for people who may live two thousand years hence.

While a belief in the "rapture" is certainly less harmful than an attempt to build the third temple on a site which holds some of Islam's holiest shrines it can, nevertheless, lead to false assumptions about daily living. If one is already "saved" one may no longer feel the urge to further redeem one's soul and this can readily lead to arrogance. Let us remember what Jesus said "there is no one good but God alone [Mk. 10:18]." All of us have a long way to go and that is what is meant by being vigilant. Unfortunately the word "vigilant" has become much overused in our country and we are supposed to constantly look out for terrorists who might be lurking behind any and all nooks and crannies. This is what "living by the flesh" means but it would seem, however, to be at least equally important that we watch out for our souls rather than merely our bodies. Furthermore, Christians would be well advised to stay with the words of Jesus as a guide to proper conduct, instead of massaging ancient biblical nightmare visions for any and all potential political meanings.

THE INTELLECTUAL CLIMATE
OF THE FIRST CENTURY.

Jewish ideology

As has been pointed out repeatedly, the early Christians consisted of two groups: Jews who had accepted Jesus as the Messiah and Gentiles who underwent conversion. Although a great many allusions to Old Testament and apocalyptic literature have already been made, it is also essential to point out that Judaism was never monolithic, and different "sects" have always co-existed with more or less animosity between them.

The best information in regard to the most prominent ones comes from Josephus' autobiography. I have previously referred to him but it is helpful to know something about the person as he portrayed himself. He was born Joseph ben Matthias, of Jewish priestly ancestry, around 37 A.D. in Jerusalem, and soon devoted himself to the study of religion. At age sixteen he decided to find out for himself which one of the three sects of Judaism that were prevalent at that time was the most worthy to follow. They were the Pharisees, the Sadducees and the Essenes. By age nineteen after having conducted, what we might call today, a field study he was satisfied that he would fit in best with the Pharisees and he adhered to this ideology for the rest of his life. When he was in his twenty-sixth year he went for the first time to Rome to help secure the release of some priests who were to be tried before Nero. This would put it into 63-64 A.D. and would actually coincide with Paul's stay in Rome.

It was the latter year when the city went up in flames and the first persecution of Christians started.

There are some interesting parallels with what we read about Paul's trials at sea which are recounted in chapters 27 and 28 of the Acts. Paul was not the only prisoner being taken to Rome to be tried before Caesar, but we are not told what crimes they had been accused of. Before the final shipwreck on Malta they were drifting on the Adriatic and eventually they were transported safely by an Alexandrian ship to Puteoli in Italy. Josephus' ship "was [likewise] drowned in the Adriatic Sea." Of the 600 passengers 80, including Josephus, were then picked up by a Cyrenian ship and they disembarked also at Puteoli. These similarities may, of course, be coincidence.

Of greater importance is that Josephus' narration shows that Jews were popular at Nero's court. Nero's wife, Poppaea, who was probably the only person he ever loved and with whom Josephus had dealings, was highly partial to Jewish causes. It may, therefore, not be unreasonable to assume that when Rome was destroyed by fire in 64 A.D. it may have been Poppaea who persuaded her husband to blame the Christians. The latter were becoming a thorn in the side of Jewish circles and a definite hindrance to their proselytizing efforts, which had heretofore achieved considerable success. As an aside I might mention that this assumption is an example what can happen when one follows the course I had laid out in the Introduction. That is: write first, read later. After the book was written and in the process of editing I read in *Judaism and Christianity in First-Century Rome* that Frend had previously proposed this idea in 1965. So much for originality, but a conclusion which was independently arrived at may actually make the suggestion more likely.

Be that as it may, what matters in the present context is that Josephus does provide us in his biography, not only with a detailed description of the belief systems of the Pharisees and Sadducees who represented the establishment in Judea but also of that marginal group the Essenes. Today they are identified mainly with the sect at Qumran who are assumed to have produced the "Dead Sea Scrolls." Yet it is useful to consider what Josephus had to say because he had first hand information and did not have to rely on speculations which result from archeological excavations. Although I have some concerns about Josephus' veracity, especially when he cites numbers or when he found himself under attack, I believe we can trust what he wrote about the Essenes because he had no ax to grind in this respect. It is also interesting to note that the major discussion of Essene philosophy and way of life is found in his *Wars of the Jews*. It is sandwiched between when King Archelaus was deposed, Coponius installed as Roman procurator, and when Pilate used temple money to finance the aqueduct to Jerusalem. This falls, therefore, right into the time of Jesus' life. Pilate was recalled to Rome in 36 A.D. and Josephus was born in the subsequent year. As he said, he personally investigated the various Jewish sects when he was sixteen years old and he is therefore an eye-witness to what Essenism was like in the days of Jesus and the apostles.

Josephus' discussion is extensive and covers the entire chapter 8 of Book 2. While only the highlights will be presented here, the chapter ought to be read *in toto* by anyone who wants to get a better understanding of earliest Christian times. As far as the Essenes were concerned, pleasures were regarded as evil and "conquest over passions a virtue." They did not marry, but chose children from other families and brought them up in their faith. Those who did marry did so only for procreation and not for "lascivious behavior." All property was held in common among rich and poor alike. Stewards were appointed to take care of expenses:

> Oil was regarded a defilement and if one of them be anointed without his own approbation it is wiped off his body .... They have no certain city, but many of them dwell in every city; and if any of their sect come from other places, what they have lies open for them, just as if it were their own .... For which reason they carry nothing with them when they travel into remote parts ... accordingly there is, in every city where they live, one appointed particularly to take care of strangers, and provides garments and other necessaries for them [3-4].

They did not buy or sell and everybody had to ply some craft learned from their elders. As far as daily life was concerned they rose and prayed in the morning, then worked diligently at whatever skill they had learned until "the fifth hour." At that time, they bathed and clothed themselves in white veils. Then they met together "in an apartment of their own, into which it was not permitted to any of another sect to enter. They go into the dining-room, as into a certain holy temple." Bread was brought first then a single plate of food but grace had to be said before tasting any of it. After the meal, grace was said again; thereafter, they worked till evening. "Then they return home to supper, after the same manner; and if there be any strangers there, they sit down with them." There was "no clamor," speech was limited, and silence as well as sobriety reigned. "Their allotted portion of meat and drink is abundantly sufficient for them." They did "nothing on their own free will but that which is approved of by their curators." The exceptions were: to assist those who required help, to show mercy to the needy, and to give food to distressed ones. But they were not allowed to give anything to their kindred. Anger and other passions were restrained. In addition:

> They are eminent for fidelity, and are the ministers of peace; whatsoever they say also is firmer than an oath; but swearing is avoided by them, and they esteem it worse than perjury; for they say, that he who cannot be believed without (swearing by) God, is already condemned. They also take great pains in studying the writing of the ancients, and choose out of them what is most for the advantage of their soul and body [6].

For a newcomer to be admitted to the sect an apprenticeship of at least three years was required. If he was found worthy after that time an oath was administered which included:

> Piety towards God . . . justice towards all men . . . not doing harm to any one either of his own accord, or by the command of others . . . hate the wicked and be assistant to the righteous . . . show fidelity to all men, and especially those in authority . . . will not abuse his authority, nor outshine his subjects either in garments, or any other finery . . . will be a lover of truth . . . reprove those that tell lies . . . [keep] his hands clear from theft and his soul from unlawful gains . .

. neither conceal anything from those of his own sect, nor discover any of the doctrines to others [7].

The punishment for the transgressor was expulsion. Because of the oath he had taken the expelled individual was not allowed to eat food presented to him by others:

> but is forced to eat grass, and to famish his body till he perish; for which reason they receive many of them again when they are at their last gasp, out of compassion . . . thinking the miseries they have endured . . . be a sufficient punishment for the sins they had been guilty of [8].

> They are stricter than other Jews in resting from their labors on the seventh day [9]. They contemn [sic] the miseries of life, and are above pain, by the generosity of their mind. And as for death, if it will be to their glory, they esteem it better than living always [10].

Josephus goes on to recount how during the war against the Romans when Essenes were captured and tortured:

> They smiled in their very pains, and laughed those to scorn who inflicted the torments upon them, and resigned up their souls with great alacrity, as expecting to receive them again . . . . For they believe that bodies are corruptible . . . but the souls are immortal and continue for ever . . . when they are set free from the bonds of the flesh, they then, as released from a long bondage, rejoice and move upwards [10,11].

Josephus subsequently states how the latter idea is similar to that of the Greeks and that some of the Essenes were also gifted in predicting future events and "it is but seldom that they miss in their predictions."

The parallels to the gospels are, of course, impressive. Marriage was approved of only for procreation but not for lust or acquisition of property. Money was held in common. When "the woman" poured oil over Jesus' head shortly before his betrayal, she was reproved by the disciples but permission was given by Jesus. When he sent out the disciples to preach the gospel, they were not allowed to take anything with them, all necessities would be provided, "And into whatsoever city or town ye shall enter, enquire who in it is worthy; and there abide till ye go thence [Mt.10:11]." If they were not received well, they were to shake the dust off their feet and the city would be cursed. Dinner habits mirrored those of the Last Supper. The avoidance of oaths, respect for authority but not claiming privileges for oneself, simplicity in clothing, absence of ostentation, loving truth and reproaching lies, as well as piety and justice are, of course, hallmarks of Jesus' teaching and conduct. He also followed the command of not divulging the doctrines to others. This is why he spoke in parables which had to be explained to the disciples. The primacy of the soul over the body was, of course, the hallmark of Jesus' teachings and so was abstention from violence, as exemplified by his behavior at Gethsemane.

There is, however, a major difference; the Essenes, as described in the literature, took the Sabbath and other aspects of the Law seriously, while Jesus adapted them to the needs of the moment, which would have shocked the Elders of that group. It is likely, however, that even the Essenes were not monolithic but contained a spectrum which ranged from the most orthodox, as represented in the monastic Qumran society, to a more liberal group, which lived in cities and towns. The latter probably held some but not all of the views of this sect and this may have been the group Jesus sent the disciples to as a base for their missionary activities in the various towns they visited. He also had a joyous soul, early on in his career, and did not mind mingling over dinner with "sinners and publicans." This was bound to have outraged the righteous, including Essenes, because the dietary laws and ordinances were thereby flouted. Josephus' description fails to mention, however, the apocalyptic aspects which were so prominent in Jesus' belief system, as well as in that of the Qumran community.

As stated earlier the apocalyptic parts of the gospels are mainly based on the book of Daniel, but there also were several other documents of this type extant at that time. Apart from lesser known records the most important one for the topic under consideration is *The Book of Enoch*. The authorship of the various scrolls which were combined in this document has been assumed to extend over a period from pre-Maccabean times to the immediate pre-Christian era. The books consist of dream visions and parables but also contain chapters "On the course of the heavenly Luminaries" which are symbolic as well as astronomical. I am mentioning this specifically because an astronomic explanation for some of the visions in St. John's apocalypse has also been put forward.

In Enoch's visions, which abound with symbolisms, the righteous are rewarded, the sinners condemned and the judgment would be carried out by the "Son of Man," also referred to as "The Elect," who sits at the side of the ancient "Head of Days." The Son of Man:

> hath righteousness, With whom dwelleth righteousness, And who revealeth all the treasures of that which is hidden . . . . And he shall put down the countenance of the strong, And shall fill them with shame. And darkness shall be their dwelling, and worms shall be their beds, Because they do not extol the name of the Lord of Spirits . . . . The Son of Man was named in the presence of the Lord of Spirits . . . . Yeah, before the sun and the signs were created, before the stars of heaven were made, his name was named before the Lord of Spirits. He shall be a staff to the righteous whereon to stay themselves and not fall, and he shall be a light to the Gentiles, and the hope of those who are troubled of heart. All who dwell on earth shall fall down and worship before him, and will praise and celebrate with song the Lord of Spirits. [46-48] . . . . And he sat on the throne of his glory, and the sum of judgment was given to the Son of Man, and he caused the sinners to pass away and be destroyed from off the face of the earth, And those who have led the world astray. With chains shall they be bound, and in their assemblage-place of destruction shall they be imprisoned . . . . For that Son of Man has appeared, And has seated himself on the throne of his glory, And all evil shall pass away before his face, And the word of that Son of Man shall go forth and be strong before the Lord of the Spirits. [69:27-29]

Even if Jesus had not identified himself personally with the Son of Man, his disciples would have surely done so after the resurrection. It is this context in which the puzzling words "Before Abraham was I Am [Jn. 8:58]," as well as many other aspects especially of John's gospel, should be seen.

The imprecations showered by Jesus on the religious authorities can also be found in Enoch. The difference being that they were generic for all sinners and not directed against one group only:

Woe to those, who build unrighteousness and oppression . . . .
Woe to those, who build their houses with sin. . . . .
Woe to you, ye rich, for ye have trusted in your riches . . . .
Woe to you, who fulminate anathemas which cannot be
    reversed . . . .
Woe to you, lying witnesses . . . .
Woe to you sinners, for ye persecute the righteous [94-95]

Apart from legends we know nothing about Jesus' life before he began his ministry. It would, therefore, not be unreasonable to assume that he might have spent a considerable period of time with the Essenes from whom he could have received his extensive biblical information. Since he was endowed with an independent spirit, he may subsequently have rebelled against the strict rules of the sect, joined first John the Baptist and subsequently struck out on his own. A life with the Essenes would also explain why Jesus had not married since the majority of the members of this sect were celibate. Thus the occasionally expressed current notion that Jesus was a Pharisee and as such may have been married, because the title of rabbi had required it, is not likely to be the best explanation for Jesus' conduct.

There is an additional possible Essene connection of Jesus which has to do with his ancestry. On the one hand Messianic hopes had to be fulfilled by a descendent of David, which Joseph was to have been, but on the other, conception was supposed to have occurred in a supernatural manner due to action of the Holy Spirit. We don't know whether or not the virgin birth aspect was a late insert for theological reasons but doubts about Jesus' paternity had been raised early on by detractors. In Albert Schweitzer's *The Psychiatric Study of Jesus* there is a footnote which refers to an allegation that Jesus was the illegitimate child of a Roman soldier by name of Panthere. This idea had existed in the Jewish community for a long time and the Roman philosopher Celsus, who had little use for Judaism or Christianity, gave it wide circulation in his book, *"The True Word."* The book no longer exists, but Origen felt obliged to write an extensive refutation, *Contra Celsum* in 248 A.D.. Since he quoted key passages from *The True Word*, Celsus' thoughts survived in part, just as Josephus provided us in *Contra Apionem*, which has been discussed in *The Moses Legacy*, with Manetho's opinions on the origin of Judaism. Celsus' book features what a Jew might have said to a Christian in regard to the improbability of the gospel stories. The relevant passage for the current context states "when she [Mary] was pregnant she was turned out of doors by the carpenter to whom she had been betrothed, as having been guilty of adultery, and that she bore a child to a certain soldier named Panthera." Origen took issue with this statement and emphasized that only supernatural birth was appropriate for the Savior of the world.

When I first read the comment by Schweitzer and *Contra Celsum* I felt that, while Jesus' birth may well have been illegitimate because of the ambiguity of Matthew's gospel and several hints in that of John, "adultery" by Mary was unlikely because under those circumstances Joseph would have had little reason to maintain the relationship. On the other hand if she had been a victim of rape by a Roman soldier, human kindness would have dictated his subsequent reported conduct.

Let us now consider what Galilee was like around the time of Mary's conception. Although we do not know the precise year when Jesus was born all authorities agree that it fell at some point between 7 B.C. and 8 A.D. In Matthew's account Herod the Great was still alive and he died in 4 B.C.. In Luke's version, Jesus was born at the time of the census under the Roman governor Quirinius which took place in 8 A.D. Josephus tells us in *The Antiquities of the Jews,* how Herod suppressed frequent uprisings against his rule, which was regarded as illegitimate by the faithful and that after Herod's death riots had broken out all over Palestine, including Galilee. The Roman governor of Syria, Publicus Quinctilius Varus, had to send the legions, supported by Arabian auxiliaries, to quell it. We don't know the precise date of these events but Varus was governor of Syria from 2 B.C. to at least 1 A.D.. After he had returned to Rome he had spent "a few years" as a private citizen but in A.D. 7 he was sent to Germany, where he committed suicide in A.D. 9 after he had suffered a disastrous defeat against Armininius in the *Teutoburg* forest.

During the Jewish revolt, after Herod's death, the capital of Galilee, Sepphoris, which was located only a few miles from Nazareth, was conquered, looted and burned to the ground. As such, this was a violent time and marauding soldiers may well have taken their liberties on young women as they always did in war time. The fate of Viennese girls and women in 1945, of which I have personal knowledge, was described in *War & Mayhem*.

If Joseph and Mary had indeed lived in Nazareth it would have made sense that Joseph would have taken his pregnant wife with him on the journey to Bethlehem. They would have been away from a major war zone and potential gossip as well as ostracism in Nazareth might have been avoided. David Friedrich Strauss pointed out in his *Life of Jesus* that the census which was the ostensible reason for the journey to Bethlehem did not require the presence of his betrothed and that in view of the lowly status women held at that time it was quite unusual for her to have made the journey for that reason. If Joseph and Mary had indeed fled Galilee, this could also explain a delayed return until the situation there had become more settled.

But I was not the only one to whom the rape theory had occurred as I found out later when I came across Emil Jung's, "*Die Herkunft Jesu Im Lichte freier Forschung,*" The ancestry of Jesus in the light of free thought; which was published in 1922. Bolstered by excerpts from the Talmud he concluded that the soldier mentioned by Celsus, Panthera, was probably a centurion who had raped the adolescent Mary. The rest of the circumstances Jung adduced, to support his theory, are rather convoluted and need not be repeated.

More recently the New Testament Scholar Gerd Lüdemann has published *Virgin Birth? The Real Story of Mary and her Son Jesus*. Although the book covers the same ground as Jung's, but without references to the Talmud, it reaches the same basic conclusion and was originally published in German. Lüdemann was apparently unaware of Jung's work because it is not listed in the fairly extensive bibliography. What strikes a more scientifically inclined reader is the absolutism which permeates both of these publications. No one knows "The Real Story" regarding the historical circumstances of Jesus' birth, life and death and as such all conclusions based on currently available literature need to be tentative and represent the personal faith of the author.

Nevertheless, the possibility of rape cannot be excluded because it would explain, as mentioned above, some aspects of gospel reports. In this connection we might also recall Josephus' comment that the Essenes took in boys who for some reason could not be properly cared for. If Jesus had indeed been placed under Essene tutorship this might account for the "lost years," and his education in the Torah. It would, furthermore, explain his conflicted relationship to "fatherhood" as suggested by his emphasis on "the Father in heaven" and "Call no one your father on earth for you have one Father; the one in heaven (Mt. 23:9)." These are obviously speculations because firm data are non-existent. One may now ask, why bring up ancient gossip? The reason is that Celsus' *True Word* with Origen's reply exists on the Internet and Lüdemann's book is also readily available. An even more important reason is for us to recognize that it does not matter what we were, but what we have become. What really counts in our lives are not the circumstances of our birth, but what we do with the cards we have been dealt with. The parable of the "five talents," as mentioned in Matthew's chapter 25, also comes to mind in this respect.

While the Jesus connection with the Essene community is now widely accepted in scholarly circles, I had not been aware of purported relations with Buddhist communities until this book was in its essence finished and undergoing editorial review. Holger Kersten's, *Jesus lived in India* attempted to provide a scholarly link by postulating the following events. The flight to Egypt, as reported by Matthew, lasted for several years, sufficiently long for Jesus to come to know about the "therapeutae." This group of people lived a monastic life and was organized essentially on Buddhist principles. They resided mainly in the areas of the Nile delta and their habits, as well as means of subsistence, have been described by Philo in a chapter, *On the Contemplative Life*. According to Kersten this prolonged stay in Egypt was followed by a brief sojourn in Palestine with the temple visit at age 12, where Jesus astounded the authorities with his erudition. He then made his way to India where he stayed until age 30. When he returned to Palestine he reconnected with Essenes and embarked on the mission all of us are familiar with.

Although he was crucified, he did not die on the cross, because Nicodemus and Joseph of Arimathea, who were secret followers of Jesus' teachings, had previously made arrangements for the comatose Jesus to be rapidly removed from the cross and taken to Joseph's nearby new tomb. The coma had been induced by the "sour wine" that had been given to him for his thirst while hanging on the cross, and which had been laced with a soporific of the opium family. In the tomb he was tightly wrapped with healing herbs in what is now known as the "Shroud of Turin." After Jesus had recovered to some extent he was taken by the conspirators to a safe location, for full restoration of health. Since life in Palestine was no longer possible, Jesus went to Damascus where he met and converted St. Paul. Subsequently he gradually continued on his way east along the "Silk road" while bringing the gospel to the inhabitants of Syria and what are now Iraq, Iran, and Afghanistan to eventually end up in Kashmir where he died peacefully at a ripe old age. He was known in these regions as *Yuz Asaf* and his tomb is in the center of Srinagar, Kashmir's capital.

One may regard this scenario as highly fanciful, but the book has been translated into 15 languages and because of detailed documentation, including analysis of the "bloodstains" on the shroud and medical facts dealing with crucifixions, it has attracted a wide readership. Kersten also gave the "lost sheep of the House of Israel" new meaning by pointing out that the ten tribes who had been forcibly removed from Israel to Assyria had gradually made their way along the same presumed route and that there are remnants of Jewish names and customs in these countries. As a result of my "scientific" method of coming to conclusions first on basis only on what is available in the New Testament I had been unaware of this theory but some aspects of Kersten's conclusions did agree with what has been presented in the main body of this book. A major defect is, however, that he relied for the crucifixion aspects entirely on the gospel of John. This is crucial because the induced coma theory requires drug administration and in the synoptic gospels Jesus refused any type of drink, although he was thirsty.

Kersten failed to mention this fact but did draw attention to the title on the cross above Jesus' head which has usually been interpreted as Jesus of Nazareth, King of the Jews. The Latin version was: *Jesus Nazarenus Rex Iudeorum* which has given rise to the well known INRI on pictures of the crucifixion. The Greek New Testament has the first part as "*o nazōraíos;*" where "*o*" refers to the definitive article "the." A footnote in the Greek New Testament to the words, "of Nazareth" states: "Gk. the Nazorean." Kersten correctly pointed to an ambiguity in regard to the Greek and Latin terms. They do not necessarily refer to Nazareth, the village in Galilee, but could have pointed to Jesus as a member of the Nazarenes or Nazirites, a group of people well known in biblical times.

They are referred to in Numbers 2-21 where Moses issued orders in regard to a vow taken to serve the Lord. The salient excerpts from the Socino Chumash translation are:

> When either a man or woman shall clearly utter a vow, the vow of a Nazirite, to consecrate himself unto the Lord, he shall abstain from wine and strong drink: he shall drink no vinegar of wine, or vinegar of strong drink, neither shall he drink any liquor of grapes, nor eat fresh grapes or dried. . . . . All the days of his vow of Naziriteship there shall no razor come upon his head; until the days be fulfilled, in which he consecrated himself unto the LORD, he shall be holy, he shall let the locks of the hair of his head grow long. . . . [2-5].

In general this vow was temporary, as suggested above but there are two Old Testament examples of life long Naziriteship. One was Samson and the other Samuel. John the Baptist fits this role in the New Testament. The interesting aspect is that all three synoptic gospels have Jesus take this vow, which clarifies the meaning of his words after the Last Supper: "Truly I tell you, I will never drink of the fruit of the vine until the day I drink it new in the kingdom of God

[Mk. 14:25]." With these words Jesus had taken the Nazirite vow and was no longer just Jesus of Nazareth, but "Jesus the Nazirite" who had from that moment on devoted his life completely to the service of the Lord.

As mentioned the synoptic gospels agree that Jesus took this vow on that occasion, but this passage, just as Jesus' baptism, does not appear in the gospel of John. It would have been inappropriate because, for John, Jesus always was throughout his earthly life, God incarnate. There is one other possibly relevant observation in the gospel of Matthew. We are not told where Joseph and Mary had lived prior to their voyage to Bethlehem and their sojourn in Egypt. Instead Mt. verses 2:22-23 state:

> And after being warned in a dream he went away to the district of Galilee. There he made his home in a town called Nazareth, so that what had been spoken through the prophets might be fulfilled, 'he will be called a Nazorean.'

In contrast to John the Baptist who had been described in the gospels as a Nazirite from birth, Jesus became one after the Last Supper. This explains also the rift between the followers of the Baptist and those of Jesus because the latter freely imbibed in the "fruit of the vine," and did not adhere to some of the other Nazirite obligations either. Nazirites were not favorites of the establishment because they freely spoke the truth, as they saw it, and what happens under those circumstances is well known, with the fate of John the Baptist the most obvious example. Throughout the Greek New Testament we find *nazōrean* or *nazōraíos* for what is being translated as "Jesus of Nazareth." When the place name Nazareth occurs, it is rendered as *nazarét*,

In conclusion we have to recognize that Jesus lived in violent times. The Jewish authorities, who were regarded as Roman toadies, were confronted with several sects which did not approve of their religious conduct. Other zealots (patriots, freedom fighters) tried to shake off Roman occupation, with inevitable reprisals from the Romans. We know from the Qumran scrolls that an imminent end of the existing world order and the establishment of a messianic kingdom were widely expected. The looming apocalypse was not

Jesus' fantasy but a firmly held belief by a significant portion of the Jewish people of the time and this is the context in which his reported words and actions, as well as his execution, need to be viewed.

The Greco-Roman milieu- Hellenism

The concept of Hellenism is of utmost importance because it has shaped "Western Civilization" via Christianity to this day. We can give it a birth year and birth place: 324 B.C., Susa in Persia. In 333 Alexander of Macedon, the Great, had decisively defeated the forces of Darius III. and after incorporating the country into his Empire took his troops eventually all the way to Pakistan, where they finally revolted and forced him to give up further conquests. He returned to Persia and in the mentioned year arranged for a massive wedding feast where he, his generals, and the troops married the cream of the crop of Persian ladies. This symbolic act was to cement the relationship between East and West so that the best of both cultures could become common property. The individual marriages were not blessed with success but the principle survived and we are still beneficiaries, although we don't want to admit the contribution the East has made to our thinking. This origin of Western civilization had actually been foreshadowed by the myth of *Europa*. She was a Phoenician princess whom Zeus fell in love with and by transforming himself into a bull he brought her to Crete where the first "European" civilization appeared before it spread to mainland Greece.

Philosophy

By the time of Jesus the old anthropomorphic images of the gods of the Greco-Roman world as depicted by Homer, Hesiod and the great Greek tragedians were no longer taken seriously by the intelligentsia. Zeus, the father of gods and men, had become an abstract notion and the name which was applied to the all-embracing Deity was no longer important. Aeschylus had already paved the way in the fifth century B.C.. In Agamemnon he has the Chorus say "Zeus, whoever he might be, if it pleases him to be called upon by that name I shall do so." Lest one be put off by the postulate of subordinate gods let us remember that only names have changed. We simply call them angels now. In the Catholic Church the Saints also fulfill some of the functions which had been previously performed by the minor divinities.

As far as Hellenistic philosophy is concerned there were, apart from the Cynics, two major competing opinions in the first century. These were represented by the Stoics and the Epicureans. The latter are nowadays wrongly regarded as having simply pursued the pleasures of life. "Eat and drink, because tomorrow we die," tends to be the sum and substance in today's popular mind. But this is incorrect. Epicurus, for whom his school was named, lived during the second half of the fourth century B.C. and had rather frugal habits. His meals consisted of bread and water but on feast days he allowed himself a slice of cheese in addition. Although he firmly believed that pleasure was the supreme good it was to be derived from shunning whatever leads to physical or mental pain. Thus, gluttony and other excesses, which by the way included sexual intercourse, were not to be indulged in. Mental pleasure was a boon because it allowed one to contemplate pleasant aspects of life even when in pain. The goal of life was the achievement of mental tranquility regardless of circumstances. Inasmuch as he was plagued by ill health throughout most of his life he was fully acquainted with physical suffering, which he bore with great patience.

Like Democritus before him, Epicurus was an "atomist." In this view the world consisted of a forever changing combination of atoms, which were insensate by themselves. Since the body dissolves into its atoms at time of death, there could be neither heaven nor hell and the fear of death was, therefore, groundless. There was no life apart from the body and religion was a superstition to be shunned. The laws of nature were to be studied, but different theories about natural phenomena should be tolerated rather than a single one to be exhorted over others. The gods existed, but only for their own pleasure and did not concern themselves with the affairs of men. It is easy to see why some adherents of this philosophy could readily abandon the loftier notions and concentrate instead on what we now call "the pursuit of happiness" by any and all means. Furthermore their battle against religion, which the Epicureans fought with vigor, rather than the forbearance of their teacher, inevitably brought them in conflict with society. These were the immoralities against which the Stoics thundered.

The founder of that school was Zeno of *Citium* (Cyprus) who was contemporaneous with Epicur, but while the latter taught in his garden, Zeno preferred the public *Stoa* from which the name of the followers was derived.

Seneca

The two best known Stoics of the first century A.D. are Seneca and Epictetus. Since Seneca lived at the same time as Paul and his writings bear a great deal of similarity to some of Paul's epistles it has been assumed that the two not only knew of each other but even exchanged letters. Berry has recently published a book on these letters which he had found in the Austrian National Library and he translated them from Latin into English. Unfortunately Berry does not mention even in a single line that these letters have always been regarded as inauthentic forgeries dating from the early Middle Ages. Sevenster had previously discussed these letters in detail and had pointed out not only the similarities but also the differences between Seneca's and Paul's thoughts. These differences obviously relate to the fundamental importance of Christ for Paul which cannot be found in Seneca. Nevertheless, the ethical principles, which ought to guide one's life, are for practical purposes identical.

Although Seneca (4 B.C. - 65 A.D.) was one of the foremost proponents of Stoic thought in his time, being human his personal life did not necessarily always conform to these principles. As a result of court intrigues he fell out of favor and was banished by Claudius to Corsica in 41 A.D.. Eight years later Claudius married Agrippina, who did her level best to bring her son Nero to the throne. She intended to give him the best possible education and had Seneca recalled from exile to become tutor to the 11 year old boy. Initially Nero showed signs that he might become a benign ruler but after he became emperor at age 18 his well known vicious nature came to the fore. Seneca thought that he could still influence the teenager and wrote a lengthy letter entitled *De Clementia*, which has been translated as On Clemency or On Mercy.

In it he congratulated Nero for his good nature which supposedly had manifested itself by a remark when Nero was asked to sign a death warrant, "I wish I had never learned to write." As is well known he soon lost his scruples. Seneca also admonished Nero in this letter to avoid the wanton cruelty of his predecessors, because it would ruin him as well as the citizenry whose shepherd he was supposed to be. But one really can't blame the teacher for the pupil not having absorbed the lessons because Aristotle had done no better with Alexander. Although he is called the Great nowadays he was a disaster for his contemporaries including some of his friends.

The fact that Seneca valued his position at Nero's court, in disregard of the Stoic principles he proclaimed in his letters and essays, is attested to by a letter he wrote to the Senate to exculpate Nero for the murder of his mother Agrippina. Seneca was obviously aware of the truth but he also knew which side the bread was buttered on. To his credit is the manner of his death. Sixty five A.D. was a bad year not only for Christians, but for anyone who raised the slightest doubt about Nero's character. Real and imagined conspiracies abounded and Seneca was one of its victims. When he was told that a death sentence had been issued he requested tablets to write his will on, but this was not granted. According to Tacitus (*Annals* 15.62) he then told his grieving friends, "Where are your maxims of philosophy, or the preparation of so many year's study against evils to come? Who knew not Nero's cruelty? After a mother's and a brother's murder, nothing remains but to add the destruction of a guardian and a tutor." Seneca then embraced his wife, retired and cut his wrists. Since the blood flowed too slowly because of age and meager diet, he "also severed the veins of his legs and knees." His wife had intended to join him in death but she was rescued on Nero's orders, and her wounds were bandaged.

In the following paragraphs I shall give a few examples of Seneca's writings to show the similarity to New Testament ideas as well as their relevance for today. "Blessed are the merciful for they will receive mercy [Mt. 5:7]" is given a philosophical underpinning in the mentioned essay *On Clemency*. Seneca introduced the topic with:

I have resolved to write on mercy, Nero, my emperor,
I would serve the function of a mirror and display you to
yourself as one within reach of the greatest of pleasures. The
true fruit of right deeds is, to be sure, in the doing, and no
reward outside themselves is worthy of the virtues.

The translation used here is that by Moses Hadas, which differs
in minor idiomatic details from that of Cooper and Procopé for
instance. Had Nero been able to take Seneca's suggestions to heart,
his fate would have been far different from what it turned out to
have been. Here are some examples of why a prince, and not only a
prince, should be merciful:

In all men, as I remarked, mercy is a natural quality, but
it especially becomes monarchs, for in them it has greater
scope for salvation and ampler opportunity to show its
effect. How petty the mischief private cruelty can work! But
when princes are savage it is war . . . . Mercy will make
whatever house she enters happy and serene, but she is more
admirable in the palace in the degree that she is rarer . . . .
Now the distinguishing marks of a high spirit are composure
and serenity and a lofty disregard of insult and injury, to
be peaceful and calm, looking down from above at injuries
and affronts [1:5] . . . . Gentleness enhances the security of
kings, because while frequent punishment does crush the
hatred of a few, it provokes hatred of all . . . . The will to
harsh measures must subside before harsh measures do . . . .
Parents and children, relatives and friends step into the place
of individuals who are put to death [1:8] . . . . Fear should
leave a residue of security, and hold out a larger prospect of
hope than of menace; otherwise, if the docile man is in equal
jeopardy with the activist, he will gaily rush into danger,
indifferent to preserving a life no longer his [1:12].

If we substitute the word governments or politicians, for
monarchs, palaces or kings, we find the truth especially of the last
sentences re-enacted in our time in the unfortunate Israeli-Palestinian
conflict.

St. Paul's views on the Law leading to sin are expressed by Seneca as:

> You will observe, furthermore, that sins frequently punished are sins frequently committed . . . . Children did not venture on the ultimate enormity [parricide] when the law did not envisage such a crime . . . . Parricide thus began when a law was passed about it; the penalty pointed the way to crime . . . . In a state where men are seldom punished innocence becomes the rule and is encouraged as a public good [1:23].

One might add parenthetically that the Ten Commandments did not forbid cannibalism, for instance, because it had been unthinkable. For Seneca and the Stoics, the goal for the human being was to strive for mental tranquility. For instance in a letter to Paulinus, a supervisor of Rome's grain supply, he wrote in regard to "The Shortness of Life" that the search for physical pleasures is undesirable because they cannot last:

> It is this mood which has made kings weep over their power; the extent of their might gave them no pleasure, its inevitable ending terrified them . . . . Anything that comes by chance is unstable, and the higher it rises the more it is liable to fall. But what must inevitably fall can give no one pleasure; therefore the life of those who acquire with toil what takes greater toil to hold must not only be very short but also very miserable . . . . New preoccupations take the place of old, one hope leads to another, one ambition arouses another.

These sentiments are also typical for Buddhist thought and the relationship between these two systems will be discussed later. Seneca, therefore, advised Paulinus to retire from public life, now that he was old enough to do so and instead devote himself to serene contemplation because "it is better to know the balance sheet of one's life than the public grain supply."

In an essay written for the police commissioner, Serenus, he pointed out:

Anything carried to excess is wrong [9] . . . . Nature . . . knowing that man was born to sorrow she invented habit as an anodyne to calamity, thus reducing extreme hardship to the level of the ordinary. If adversity kept the force of its first shock permanently, no one could bear it . . . . Man must therefore habituate himself to his condition, complain of it as little as possible, and grasp whatever good lies within his reach. No situation is so harsh that a dispassionate mind cannot find some consolation in it [10] . . . . If he [a person] lives as if he were on loan to himself, and is ready to return the whole sum cheerfully . . . he will not quarrel with Fortune . . . . If nature should reclaim what she had previously entrusted to us, we too shall say to her: 'Take back the spirit, better than when you gave it to me' . . . . What hardship is there in returning whence you came? A man will live ill if he does not know how to die well . . . . Know, then, that every station in life is subject to change, and whatever has befallen anybody can befall you as well [11].

That our lives are on loan and that our spirit will be recalled are facts of life for stoics. That we should return our soul in better condition than we had received it surely brings to mind the gospel parables of the master who had gone away and had entrusted his servants with his property. The next quotes, from the same chapter, will strike a responsive chord in the hearts of Muslims:

A man who engages in many activities often puts himself in the power of Fortune; it is safest never to tempt her too often but always to bear her in mind and take nothing for granted on her security. 'I will sail, if nothing happens,' is the proper style, or 'I shall become praetor if no obstacles arise,' 'This negotiation will prove satisfactory if nothing interferes.' This is the basis for our assertion that nothing befalls the sage contrary to his expectations. We exempt him from the mistakes of mankind, not from their accidents. For him no more than for other men do all things turn out as he wished; they do not turn out as he thought, and his first thought was that something might oppose his plans [13].

This is why Muslims usually end their sentences of hopeful expectations with *In sha'allah*, God willing. It is not blind fatalism but the recognition of a higher power which may have different plans. Seneca and the Stoics called it at times Fortune, or Fate but the message is the same: If you want to live a serene life expect the unexpected and do not be distressed when it occurs.

In regard to God, Seneca had this to say in his letter (41) to his friend Lucilius:

> It is a fine and salutary course if, as you write, you are persevering in your pursuit of a good mentality; it is stupid to pray for it when you can obtain it by your own efforts. We do not need to lift our hands to heaven or beg the sexton for nearer access to the idol's ear, as if he could hear us more clearly; *god is near you, with you, inside you* [emphasis added]. Yes Lucilius, *there is a holy spirit abiding within us* [emphasis added] who observes our good deeds and bad and watches over us. He treats us as we treat him. No man is good without god. Could any man rise above Fortune without his help? It is he that imparts good and upstanding counsel. In every man 'indwells a god, what god we know not'

The quote comes from Virgil's Aeneid 8.352. For Paul this "unknown god" was Christ and his fruitless efforts to convince the Athenians of this idea have already been mentioned earlier. Seneca continued with the explanations of the divine:

> A soul which is of superior stature and well governed, which deflates the imposing by passing it by and laughs at all our fears and prayers, *is* [emphasis in the original] impelled by a celestial force. So great a thing cannot stand without a buttress of divinity. Its larger portion therefore abides at its source. Just as the rays of the sun do indeed warm the earth, but remain at the source of their radiation, so a great and holy soul is lowered to earth to give us nearer knowledge of the divine; but though it is in intercourse with us, it cleaves to its source; it is tied to it, it looks toward it, it seeks to rejoin it, and its concern with our affairs is superior and detached.

In this way "The Father and I are one," is not a delusion of grandeur, if Jesus had indeed said it, but the expression of a noble soul who "is in this world but not of this world."

In letter 47 which deals with the treatment of slaves we find the golden rule, "The essence of my teaching is this: Treat your inferior as you would wish your superior to treat you . . . . Treat your slave with compassion, even with courtesy; admit him to your conversation, your planning, your society."

Seneca expressed the relationship of the body to the soul, in this manner in letter 65:

> All these questions, provided they are not minced and fragmented into futile hair splitting, uplift the soul and make it light when it is weighed down by a heavy load and eager to return to whence it sprang. For body is a weight upon the soul and its punishment; under its pressure the soul is squeezed and trussed until philosophy comes to its support by prescribing contemplation of nature as a refreshment and directs it away from the earthy to the divine. This is the soul's liberation, this its enlargement; in the process it obtains release from the custody which restrains it and recovers its heavenly energy . . . . The wise man and the devotee of wisdom is indeed attached to his body, but in his better part he is elsewhere; his thoughts are directed to lofty matters. He is bound, as it were, by a military oath, and regards his life span as his term of enlistment. He is disciplined neither to love life nor hate it; he puts up with mortality, though he knows there is a fuller kind of existence . . . . Contempt of body is unqualified freedom . . . . What is death? Either end or transition. I do not fear ceasing to be, for it is the same as not having begun to be; nor am I afraid of transition, for no alternative state can be so limiting.

Seneca accepted our inability to predict what a life of the soul without a body would be like and did not engage in unprovable speculations. The Christian hope of a resurrected body would probably have been met with a faint smile because evidence is lacking. Since death is not to be feared he had no problem with suicide. If life for a valid reason, rather than a frivolous one, becomes unbearable, nature has given us the freedom to end it. "Living is not the good, but living well." "Dying early or late is of no relevance, dying well or ill is." "A prolonged life is not necessarily better, a prolonged death is necessarily worse." Those were the maxims to be adhered to. Just as life had to be honorable, so had to be death. If life cannot be lived with honor either on account of external force or due to illness which has robbed the person of one's intellectual abilities, "Eternal law has never been more generous than in affording us so many exits from life to one entry." The freedom of choice is ours and, "It is a great man who not only orders his own death but contrives it [letter 70]."

Let's face it, is this not what Jesus did? He knew perfectly well that if he did not recant before Caiphas that he would be killed and it didn't matter whether the Jews or the Romans did it. His was a divine suicide by forcing others to kill him so that his mission could succeed. The example was followed by the Christian martyrs, who could simply have offered token sacrifices at the public altars, while keeping their private thoughts secret. That they did not do so is to their credit. But this behavior was completely ununderstandable to Antoninus, the Roman proconsul of the province of Asia. According to Gibbon he exclaimed in frustration, 'Unhappy men! If you are thus weary of your lives, is it so difficult for you to find ropes and precipices?' [Vol.1 Chapter 16]. He simply couldn't grasp the concept of the divine suicide. Neither could the Nazis, in more recent times, when they were confronted with the behavior of some of Jehovah's Witnesses. All the Witnesses had to do was to sign on the dotted line that they no longer adhered to the tenets of this sect and they could have gone free. Some did not and were either incarcerated or beheaded for their belief.

In view of Paul's dealings with Seneca's brother Gallio, it is of interest to briefly review the essay "On Anger" which was addressed to him. It is quite extensive and consists of three books, which shows the importance Seneca attributed to this unhealthy emotion. Although I shall present only some highlights it will immediately become apparent how topical this essay is. The quotes come from Cooper and Procopé, and they show that Seneca concerned himself mainly with lingering resentment which turned to hate, rather than the sudden surge of anger most of us intermittently experience:

> Now look at its consequences and the losses which it occasions. No plague has cost the human race more. You will see slaughter, poisoning, charge and sordid counter-charge in the law-courts, devastation of cities, the ruin of whole nations, persons of princely rank for sale at public auction, buildings set alight and the fire spreading beyond the city walls, huge tracts of territory glowing in flames that the enemy kindled [1:2,1].

What accounts for it?

> Anger is 'a burning desire to avenge a wrong' or, according to Posidonius, 'a burning desire to punish him by whom you think yourself to have been unfairly harmed' [1:2,3]. There is no need to chastise in anger if error and crime are to be repressed. Anger is a misdemeanour of the soul and one ought not to correct wrong-doing while doing wrong oneself [1:16,1]. Reason gives time to either side, and then demands a further adjournment to give itself room to tease out the truth: anger is in a hurry. Reason wishes to pass a fair judgment: anger wishes the judgment which it has already passed to seem fair [1:18,1].

> If we wish our judgment to be fair in all things, we must start from the conviction that no one of us is faultless. For here is where indignation most arises - 'I haven't done anything wrong,' 'I haven't done a thing!' On the contrary you won't *admit* [emphasis in the original] anything! We grow indignant at any rebuke or punishment, while at that very moment doing the wrong of adding insolence and obstinacy to our misdeeds [2:28,1].

A subsequent sentence "Other people's faults are before our eyes, our own lie over our shoulders [2:28,8]," surely recalls, "the mote in your brother's eye and the beam in your own [Mt.7:3]." The following sentences cannot fail to bring to mind the World Trade Center disaster and its result our "War on Terrorism."

'How is it, then, that wrongs by enemies provoke us?' Because we did not anticipate them, or certainly not on that scale. This is a result of excessive self-love. We consider that we ought not to be harmed, even by enemies. Each of us has within him the mentality of a monarch; he would like *carte blanche* for himself but not for any opposition. So it is either arrogance or ignorance of the facts that makes us prone to anger [2:31,3].

'But there is pleasure in anger - paying back pain is sweet.' Not in the slightest! The case is not like that of favors, where it is honorable to reward service with service. Not so with wrongs. In the one case, it is shameful to be outdone; in the other to outdo. 'Retribution' - an inhuman word and what is more, accepted as right - is not very different from wrongdoing, except in the order of events. He who pays back pain with pain is doing wrong; it is only that he is more readily excused for it [2:32,1].

Two thousand years later we are still practicing "retribution" and regard ourselves as virtuous in its pursuit. Seneca followed up with what would be an example of "turning the other cheek":

Marcus Cato was once struck in the public baths by some fool who did not know who he was - would anyone have ill treated that man if he had known? Afterwards the man apologized and Cato said 'I don't remember being struck,' thinking it better to ignore than to punish. 'You mean, after such effrontery, he escaped scot-free? More than that he came to know Cato. The mark of a great mind is to look down on injuries received [2:32,2-3].

What is the cure for anger?

The greatest remedy for anger is postponement, which allows its initial heat to abate and the darkness that oppresses the mind to subside or thin out [3:12,4]. Fight with yourself.

If you wish to conquer anger, it cannot conquer you [3:13,1]. The mark of true greatness is not to feel the blow, to be like the mighty beast looking round slowly at the baying of the hounds, like the huge rock as the waves dash in vain against it . . . . The wrong done has a definite limit, but quite how far anger will take me is uncertain [3:25,3-4]. 'I cannot endure it. It is hard to submit to wrong.' Untrue! Anyone can put up with wrong done to him, if he can put up with his own anger. Besides, what you are now doing is to put up with them both [3:26,1].

Seneca then exhorted us to make allowances, to be forgiving and magnanimous. He summed up his opinions with:

So this gruesome aggressive affection contains nothing of value. On the contrary it contains every evil, the sword and the flames. Trampling shame underfoot, staining its hands with slaughter, scattering the limbs of its children, it leaves nothing free of crime. Without any thought for glory or fear of infamy, it stands beyond all correction once it has hardened from anger to hatred [3:41,3].

Nothing will help more than a meditation on our mortality. Each of us should say to himself and to others: 'What joy is there in acting as though we were born to live for ever, declaring our anger and squandering our momentary span of life? What joy is there in turning the days which could be spent in honest pleasure to the pain and torture of others? These things cannot survive the waste, we have no time to lose [3:42,2].

It would seem that Gallio, or Novatus as he was called, took his brother's advice to heart. When the Jews pestered him he didn't enter into their squabbles. They were below his dignity. How many innocent lives in Palestine, Afghanistan and Iraq might have been saved had Seneca's, or Jesus', words taken preference over revenge? How many more innocents will have to die needlessly by continuing on the course we are on? It is not that we haven't been told what to do, we simply don't want to because hate, greed and opportunism come so much easier than forgiveness.

Epictetus

Apart from the Emperor Marcus Aurelius (121-180 A.D.), the other Stoic philosopher best remembered today, Epictetus, lived at the time the gospels were written (c. 60-138 A.D.) I have mentioned some aspects of his life and teachings in *The Moses Legacy* but they bear repeating and expansion because they provide an excellent insight into the Gentile intellectual milieu the followers of Jesus were confronted with and, in part, came from.

Epictetus' most important teaching was, "Of the things which are in our Power, and not in our Power." The essential aspects are: there is "the will" and what has been translated as "appearances" of the external world. We are only free in our will and it is our duty to make proper use of the appearances the world confronts us with. The will is internal and God given. Appearances are externals over which we have no control except to make the best use of them in conformance with reason and honor. We have no influence over the conduct of others, even if it is harmful to ourselves, therefore it is not our concern. What matters is our own attitude to misfortune and to understand that certain features of life such as illness, injuries, or death are part of life and unavoidable. But we need not complain or lament over the cruel fate which nature has dished out to us. What we ought to do is adopt the attitude that those things are externals, not in our power to change, and to cultivate instead the only aspect God has given us, which *is* in our power and nobody else's, our free will.

In the chapter on "How a man should proceed from the principle of God being the father of all men" Epictetus explains:

> If a man should be able to assent to this doctrine as he aught, that we are all sprung from God in an especial manner, and that God is the father of both men and of gods, I suppose that he would never have any ignoble or mean thoughts about himself . . . Yet we do not do so; but since these two things are mingled in the generation of man, body in common with the animals, and reason and intelligence in common with the gods, many incline to this kinship, which is miserable; and some few to that which is divine and happy. Since then

it is of necessity that every man uses everything according to the opinion which he has about it, those, the few, who think that they are formed for fidelity and modesty and a sure use of appearances have no mean or ignoble thoughts about themselves; but with the many it is quite the contrary. Through the kinship with the flesh some of us become like wolves . . . some like lions; but the greater part of us become foxes and other worse animals. For what else is a slanderer and a malignant man than a fox, or some other wretched animal [I:3].

On the other hand man's freedom has limits because even Zeus is limited by *Moros*, the son of Erebus (night), which is fate or necessity:

But what says Zeus? 'Epictetus, if it were possible, I would have made both your little body and your little property free and not exposed to hindrance. But now don't be ignorant of this: this body is not yours, but it is clay finely tempered. And since I was not able to do for you what I have mentioned, I have given you a small portion of us, this faculty of pursuing an object and avoiding it, and the faculty of desire and aversion, and, in a word, the faculty of using the appearance of things; and if you will take care of this faculty and consider it your only possession, you will never be hindered, never meet with impediments; you will not lament, you will not blame, you will not flatter any person . . . . Be content with them and pray to the gods' [I:1].

Rabbi Kushner in his book *When Bad Things Happen to Good People* has expressed the same thought but without giving credit to the Greeks. Therefore, regardless of occasion, Epictetus teaches that if a man always maintains his proper character he will be mentally free, even as a slave. On the other hand, a "free-man" can be, and frequently is, a slave because he is chained by his passions and desires. The New Testament uses the word "sin" but the meaning is the same:

Have you not often heard that you ought to remove entirely desire, apply aversion to those things only which are within your power, that you ought to give up everything, body, property, fame, books, tumult, power, private station? for whatever way you turn, you are a slave, you are subjected, you are hindered, you are compelled, you are entirely in the power of others [IV:4].

This sounds, of course, familiar not only to Christians but also Buddhists. All one has to do is to substitute the word "mind" for "will," as is apparent in Epictetus' discussion of good and evil:

Where is the good? In the will. Where is the evil? In the will. Where is neither of them? In those things which are independent of the will . . . . What do we admire? Externals. About what things are we busy? Externals. And have we any doubt then why we fear or why we are anxious? . . . . Then we say "Lord God, how shall I not be anxious?" Fool, have you not hands, did not God make them for you? Sit down now and pray that your nose may not run. Wipe yourself rather and do not blame him . . . . Has he not given to you endurance? Has he not given you magnanimity? . . . . When you have such hands, do you still look for one who shall wipe your nose? . . . . And what is the divine law? To keep a man's own, not to claim that which belongs to others, but to use what is given, and when it is not given, not to desire it; and when a thing is taken away, to give it up readily and immediately, and to be thankful for the time that a man has had the use of it [II:16].

But, it will be argued, is death not the ultimate evil?:

When death appears an evil, we ought to have this rule in readiness, that it is fit to avoid evil things, and that death is a necessary thing. For what shall I do, and where shall I escape it? . . . . I cannot escape from death. Shall I not escape from the fear of death, but shall I die lamenting and trembling? For the origin of perturbation is this, to wish for something, and that this should not happen [I: 27; IV: 7].

In the chapter on "How from the fact that we are akin to God a man may proceed to the consequences" Epictetus said, "If the things are true which are said by the philosophers about the kinship between God and man, what else remains for men to do then what Socrates did?" We are not to identify with our separate little places of birth but:

> He then who has observed with intelligence the administration of the world, and has learned that the greatest and supreme and the most comprehensive community is that which is composed of men and God, and that from God have descended the seeds not only to my father and grandfather, but to all beings which are generated on the earth and are produced, and particularly to rational beings - for these only are by their nature formed to have communion with God, beings by means of reason conjoined with Him - why should not such a man call himself a citizen of the world, why not a son of God, and why should he be afraid of anything which happens among men? . . . to have God for your maker and father and guardian shall not this release us from sorrows and fears?
>
> But a man may say,'Whence shall I get bread to eat when I have nothing?'
>
> And how do slaves and runaways, on what do they rely when they leave their masters? Do they rely on their lands, or slaves, or their vessels of silver? They rely on nothing but themselves and food does not fail them [I:9].

Are these not the same ideas as "Therefore I tell you, do not worry about your life, what you will eat or drink, or about your body, what you will wear . . ." which we find in Mt. 6:25 as well as Lk. 12:22? The evidence is, therefore, quite compelling that the ethical teachings of Jesus conform fully to those expounded by the Stoics, and this may have been of considerable help to the apostles in gaining converts from the gentile community.

But when I used the words "ethical teachings" I limited myself to rules for everyday conduct among people and do not imply that the religious speculations on the nature of God and the soul were also similar. All Christianity and Stoicism have in common in that respect are: the existence of God as our father, the superiority of the soul over the body, and its desire to return to its maker.

Buddha

I have previously mentioned that the ethical aspects of Jesus' teachings also bear close resemblance to those of Siddartha Gautama. He is better known as the "Enlightened One," the Buddha. In contrast to Christ, "the Anointed," which has become a title uniquely reserved for Jesus and is unattainable by anyone else, there have been and continue to be several Buddhas. As a matter of fact Buddhahood, namely permanent complete enlightenment, is the goal of Gautama's disciples. Just as I have made a distinction between Jesus the person who lived and taught in a historical period and who became the Christ, I shall now make the same distinction between Siddartha Gautama, the person who lived and taught in northern India (c.563-483 B.C.), and the religion, Buddhism, which was established after his death.

The most concise description of Gautama's principles is contained in *The Teaching of Buddha.* For my acquaintance with this book I am indebted to my Japanese colleagues who had invited me in the 1970's for a two-week lecture tour to their country. My hosts were exceedingly gracious and in the larger cities I spent the nights in international luxury hotels. There was, however, one night in a smaller town near Shizuoka, the home of Japan's National Epilepsy Center, where I was quartered in a typical Japanese style hotel. In the drawer of the night stand, where one usually finds a Bible, there was instead the mentioned book in Japanese and English. I began reading and the thought immediately arose, "I have to have this book." Since I had not seen it previously in other hotels and my visit to the country was coming to an end I intended to keep it. But the very next thought was, "you don't start your acquaintance with Buddha by stealing," and I put the book back in the drawer. Next morning while going to the breakfast area, I passed the gift shop of the hotel and there was the coveted book in the window display case. I bought it for the nominal price of one dollar and have treasured it ever since.

As with all important teachers of humanity, Gautama's life has been embellished by legends and miracles but he would have only smiled at them as being quite unnecessary. His words, and the *Dharma* (teaching) which employed parables for illustration, were all that counted. When the fundamental truth about the human condition was grasped, and the way he outlined it was followed, Buddhahood (Enlightenment) would be achieved. The *Dharma* was based on the law of causation, the supremacy of the mind over externals, and specific rules of conduct which can be adopted by anyone. The admirable simplicity of Gautama's teaching can be summarized in a) the Fourfold Noble Truth and b) the Eightfold Noble Path.

Ad a) 1) Life is suffering. 2) The cause of suffering is the desires of the physical body and the illusions we hold about the world around us. 3) If desire, which lies at the root of all suffering, is removed suffering will cease. 4) In order to reach this state the eightfold noble path has to be followed.

Ad b) The path consists of: right view, right thought, right speech, right conduct, right livelihood, right effort, right mindfulness, right concentration.

These were the thoughts Gautama arrived at in his quest to understand how a person can be relieved of the sufferings of this world and prevent rebirth which would only lead to continuation of suffering in a different form. It is the supreme irony of the human condition that we always want what we think we do not have. Jews, Christians and Muslims believe that life on this earth is limited to one birth and one death. Death, therefore, becomes an evil and life has to be prolonged, if not here then in heaven. Hindus and Buddhists, on the other hand, believe that life goes on forever and one's soul is reincarnated into another body depending upon one's conduct during life. Karma is the accumulation of all one's thoughts, passions and deeds. The goal of life is to gain gradually, through numerous cycles of birth and death, sufficient good karma to be reborn into more desirable circumstances. If the individual is, however, driven by passions which prevent an ascent from the material into the spiritual sphere, one will be reborn into that shape which most conforms to the passions harbored. Thus both ascent and descent are possible and there is no permanent hell. What the Greeks called Fate, is Karma and for that you yourself and nobody else is responsible. Everything depends, therefore, on the will of the individual and the ability to control one's mental faculties.

The idea of reincarnation reached Greece via Pythagoras and was endorsed by Plato as well as Virgil. Jews and Christians rejected the idea but under those circumstances they had to embrace the concept of heaven and hell to redress potential injustice. An evil person who had prospered on earth would be punished in the afterlife and vice versa. But since rebirth, even as a sage, still involves suffering, on account of illness for instance, Gautama's insight was that rebirth can be avoided altogether because it likewise depends on desire. Nevertheless, extinction of desire does not necessarily mean nothingness but rather a state where there is "no thing." The intellect itself, when uncontaminated by forms and appearances, is a pure, shining light in which the individual ought to remain especially at the time of physical death. Thus Nirvana, which means extinction, is not necessarily the extinction of consciousness but only that of passions, appearances and false ideas.

It may now be objected that suffering is too harsh a word for the human condition because, fortunately, most of us truly suffer only for limited periods of time. But the Sanskrit word *duhkha*, which is usually translated as suffering, has additional meanings. The Dalai Lama has recognized the limitation the word "suffering" imposes on our thoughts and has, therefore, suggested that *duhkha* be rendered as "unsatisfactoriness." This is indeed an excellent way to describe the condition we find ourselves in most of the time. We surely frequently want things to be better than they are at any given moment.

This gets us to the next problem. A life free from all desire is impossible and it is, therefore, better to think of "craving," rather than "desire." We can distinguish between, "wouldn't it be nice to have," "I'd like to have" and "I have to have." The first step can be contemplated in relative serenity while the third one demands action and can enslave the person. It is this step which needs to be avoided and can be achieved by following Gautama's noble path. Buddhism is usually accused of being a pessimistic philosophy because it tends to disregard the beauty life can offer. For my private purposes I have, therefore, modified Gautama's first fundamental truth from "life is *duhkha*" to "life contains a great deal of *duhkha*." This is experientially realistic, allows one to appreciate the beauty of life without necessarily becoming overly attached to one of its aspects and thereby minimizing *duhkha*. When disasters happen, as they will in everybody's life, the Eightfold Noble Path can ensure that they are properly dealt with.

Right view is to understand, and accept the four-fold noble truth of *duhkha,* to accept the law of cause and effect and not to be deceived by appearances and desires.

Right thought follows from the insight that everything in this world is transient. Wherever we look, including at our own mental processes, we see constant flux. Some things change faster, others slower, but as Heraclites allegedly has formulated it "you never step into the same river twice." Right thought also includes the decision to persevere on the path. Since everything is transient it is foolish to form an attachment to anything. If we do so we will suffer when the object of attachment is taken from us. Therefore, everything is to be regarded as on loan, and, as the stoics have phrased it, needs to be returned cheerfully. An attitude of this type does not come easily for the human being but this difficulty does not make the concept less valuable. Furthermore, right thought also demands the realization that we live in a world of phenomena which our mind interprets to its liking and, therefore, forms false opinions. It is not "sin" which renders us unhappy but the erroneous ideas we hold about ourselves, others, and the world at large. The major failing is "Greed!" This English word has no particular meaning but the German equivalent, "*Habgier,*" carries within itself the definition: a voracious craving to possess. This craving is truly protean in its manifestations. It usually attaches itself to material values but can also involve idealistic ones, such as the quest for fame and honor regardless of harm to others.

Right speech means that we should limit our conversations to the exchange of "amiable and thoughtful words." We should not lie, exaggerate, or use deceptive speech, should avoid idle chatter, gossip and slander.

Right conduct means not to steal, not to murder, not to commit adultery, not to gamble, not to act in anger, or indulge in other unhealthy practices.

Right livelihood refers to choosing a profession which does not harm others or bring shame upon the individual. While a soldier's life in the service of one's country would be condoned, that of a Mafioso would not.

Right effort is required in order to do one's best in one's tasks, including the pursuit of the path, at all times.

Right mindfulness is a more difficult concept. It refers to keeping the teachings constantly in the forefront of one's mind. When the mind is not fully concentrated on a given task at hand it should not be allowed to wander and run on what one may call "automatic pilot." This is, of course, what happens to most of us. When we are driving, for instance, we tend to have music on. Some of us talk on the cell phone, even send text messages and the mind roams over various and sundry topics. This is why Nietzsche was correct when he wrote, "it is wrong to say 'I think,' one should say 'it thinks.' " These uncontrolled ruminations of the mind over past injuries or future hopes are unhealthy. They detract from a life that should be oriented towards the present moment. Parenthetically one might add that this was the reason why the Pharisees imposed the 613 regulations on the lives of observant Jews. Each act of daily life was to be performed as a service to God which would lead to holiness of the person and the nation. That most people are not cut out for such rigor has inevitably led to ritual and to hypocrisy. Nevertheless, it was intended to be the Jewish analogue to right mindfulness or, as the Hindu *Baghavad Gita* has called it, "Krishna consciousness."

Gautama did not concern himself with theologic ideas and the panoply of Indian gods. Just as Jesus can be understood as liberating his followers from a burdensome Law, which had assumed unmanageable proportions, Gautama's goal was to free his disciples from the multitude of gods and their rituals. He did not deny their existence; they were simply of no concern. Liberation was not to come from the outside, but it was to be achieved by diligently following the *Dharma*. The kingdom of God is truly within us.

Right concentration seems to be obvious but is also one of the most difficult tasks to master. Without training most of us are unable to concentrate on a given object or idea for more than about 20 or 30 seconds before another thought intrudes. If one were to think that this number is too low I would suggest that you take a minute and concentrate exclusively on the tip of a pencil for instance. It is a wholesome exercise to find out how unruly one's mind really is. Since control of one's own mind is the goal of Gautama's teaching, training in concentration is essential.

The *Dharma* is rational and does not require faith in miracles. Peace of mind, if not nirvana, can be achieved by one's own efforts. There is no "them and us" and there is nobody who can be blamed for failure. There is not a single saying reported by Gautama which might correspond to the "woes" which we find even in the New Testament. Even when people follow the wrong path and end up in hellish circumstances gradual ascent, albeit over eons, is possible. Furthermore, the situation where Jesus was supposed to have advised his disciples to shake the dust off their feet if they were not treated hospitably was dealt with differently by the Indian sage.

When Ananda, his favorite disciple, returned from a fruitless attempt to beg for provisions, he complained to the master saying, "This is a terrible village, the people here don't respect us, they give us no food and they insult us in addition. Let us move to a different village, where people are friendlier." The sage replied, "And if the same thing happens to you there, what will you do?" "Well, we'll just move on again," Ananda said. This went on in this vein until Gautama said, "Since this can happen anywhere, is it not better to stay here until the abuse ceases?" This can be regarded as turning the other cheek.

As a summary of Gautama's teaching it may be best to quote excerpts from his last advice to his disciples:

> Make of yourself a light. Rely upon yourself; do not depend on anyone else . . . . Consider your body; think of its impurity; knowing that both its pain and its delights are alike causes of suffering, how can you indulge in its desires? Consider your soul; think of its transience; how can you fall into delusion about it and cherish pride and selfishness

knowing that they must all end in inevitable suffering? Consider all substances . . . are they not all aggregates that sooner or later will break apart and be scattered?

The point of the teachings is to control your own mind. Keep your mind from greed, and you will keep your body right, your mind pure and your words faithful. Always thinking on the transience of your life, you will be able to resist greed and anger, and will be able to avoid all evils.

A man's mind may make him a Buddha, or it may make him a beast. Misled by error, one becomes a demon; enlightened one becomes a Buddha. Therefore control your mind and do not let it deviate from the right path. Under my teachings, you should respect each other and refrain from disputes; you should not, like water and oil repel each other, but should, like milk and water, mingle together . . . .

If you neglect them [the teachings], it means that you have never really met me. It means that you are far from me, even if you are actually with me; but if you accept and practice my teachings, then you are very near to me; even though you are far away . . . . The demon of worldly desires is always seeking chances to deceive the mind. If a viper lives in your room and you wish to have a peaceful sleep you must first chase it out. You must break the bonds of worldly passions and drive them away as you would a viper. You must positively protect your own mind.

My disciples, my last moment has come, but do not forget that death is only the vanishing of the physical body. The body was born from parents and was nourished by food; just as inevitable are sickness and death. But the true Buddha is not a human body: - it is Enlightenment. A human body must vanish, but the Wisdom of Enlightenment will exist forever in the truth of the *Dharma*, and in the practice of the *Dharma*. He who sees merely my body does not truly see me. Only he who accepts my teaching truly sees me.

After my death, the *Dharma* will be your teacher. Follow the *Dharma* and you will be true to me.

During the last forty five years of my life, I have withheld nothing from my teaching. There is no secret teaching, no hidden meaning; everything has been taught openly and clearly. My dear disciples, this is the end. In a moment I shall be passing into Nirvana. This is my instruction.

Although the master had told his disciples not to dispute with each other this was beyond their ability and when Buddhism was created from *Dharma* the admirable simplicity was lost. Legends as well as sects arose and a complex system of rituals evolved. The *Dhammapada*, which is the Pali version of the *Dharma* shows in its commentary that even seemingly simple words became replete with elaborations. For instance one finds that in the *dhamma* there are thirty-seven factors conducive to enlightenment; there are seven kinds of learners who go through threefold training and so on. Nevertheless, the principle that control of the mind must be maintained under all circumstances has remained constant. For daily living the centerpieces are "Right Mindfulness" and "Right Concentration."

Siegmund Feniger, who was of Jewish ancestry, left Germany in 1936 for Sri Lanka and having had previous exposure to Buddhism entered the Hermitage on Dodanduwa Island where he received the name Nyanaponika Thera. Prior to leaving Nazi Germany he had sent his mother to Vienna and when Austria was annexed he was able to bring her to Sri Lanka where she likewise converted to Buddhism. As Nyanaponika Thera he has written several books but the one which impressed me most was, *The Heart of Buddhist Meditation* because it can serve not only as a teaching manual, but also because it brought to mind neurophysiologic principles. Since my goal is not to present a cookbook with recipes for "Instant Zen," I shall limit myself to only a few aspects which can be practiced in daily life.

The first fundamental aspect of right mindfulness is called "bare attention." By this is meant that we should learn to look at the world around us in a scientific detached manner without immediately forming a judgment, and subsequent ruminations, about what our senses tell us. For instance: One is stuck in traffic. The usual reaction is annoyance, restlessness, fear of missing one's appointments and so on. Right mindfulness would dictate to simply regard the event as a fact. Instead of worrying about the consequences one might study the car ahead in every detail: size, shape, color, age, make and what not. Under theses circumstances detachment is reached and the normal negative emotions will be subdued.

You my now ask what does this have to do with neurophysiology? Everything! Any sensation regardless of its nature elicits two electrical responses in the brain. One is called the primary response which is limited to the area responsible for the perception, the other is the secondary response which is more wide-spread and involves a great many different structures. It is this secondary response which becomes conditioned throughout our lives. This is why when we see a rose we think of smell and when confronted with a bear in the woods experience fear. The interesting aspect is that this secondary response, which ordinarily has become automatic, and results in specific behavior, can nevertheless be changed. A rat, for instance, which has been trained to react to one set of stimuli in a given manner, can be fooled into an inappropriate behavioral reaction when the secondary response is experimentally manipulated. The brain is a machine, which learns "the good" just as readily as "the bad," and the difference is only what it has been taught through numerous secondary and tertiary responses to regard as such when a new event takes place. In the course of our lives we have stored an inordinate number of conditioned secondary responses in our brains, which may be quite inappropriate to changed circumstances. These have to be unlearned for spiritual progress to proceed. Bare attention is the key and brings to mind Jesus' command, "do not judge, do not condemn."

The second aspect of right mindfulness to be discussed is "clear comprehension of purpose." While bare attention deals with sensation, purpose deals with action. The Buddhist is encouraged to consider before even the simplest action what its intended purpose is. We are not concerned here with such concepts as the purpose of life, or that of the universe but only with what one wants to accomplish at any given moment. Once you have consciously defined the goal of your intended action you are to consider the next step namely "clear comprehension of suitability [of means]." With other words: once you defined the purpose is it really worth while and are the means you intend to use indeed the best ones to achieve it? By following these simple precepts we can not only get rid of ingrained prejudices and thereby faulty thought patterns but also become mentally healthier individuals. It is staggering to contemplate how much evil could be averted if politicians were to use these rules in their decision making. The current wars are the most recent examples of evils which could have been avoided had "clear comprehension of suitability [of means]" be practiced.

The eighth noble truth "right concentration" has already been dealt with but also has additional ramifications which require further discussion. These are perhaps best exemplified in the *Tibetan Book of the Dead*, which deals with the interval-between physical death and rebirth, the *Bardo* state. As mentioned previously, the goal of Buddhism is to prevent rebirth and the book tells the dying person how this can be accomplished.

While scientists can have serious reservations about the occurrence of reincarnation there are very valuable aspects for the living and the dying individual in this book. The most important part is the description of what the person is going to experience during the process of dying. The individual is admonished over and over again that the phantasmagoria of demons, wrathful and peaceful deities, are not external events. They arise from his own consciousness and are therefore not to be feared nor should attention be paid to them. Instead the person should direct his total effort, with supreme concentration on the primordial light "which is thine own consciousness." Only if he can abide in the light will liberation be achieved. How does the Catholic Requiem Mass start out? *"Requiem aeternam dona eis, Domine, et lux perpetua luceat eis."* "Grant them everlasting rest, Oh Lord, and may the eternal light shine upon them." While the Christian asks God for this act of mercy, the Buddhist is supposed to achieve the same result by will power, which has been trained to utmost concentration. Nevertheless, even the Tibetans seemed to have realized that some assistance might be helpful and the dying person is, therefore, also admonished to pray to his tutelary deity for strength in his resolve. Although this reintroduced the notion of God, so to say by the back door, I have a feeling that Gautama would not have objected too strenuously when it is limited to an extreme circumstance as death surely is for the average person.

From the foregoing it is apparent that there are close parallels between Gautama's teaching, the Stoics and Jesus' words. How this similarity came about can, as has been mentioned earlier, be debated but it is known that Buddhist missionaries first went west before they directed their steps towards Tibet, China and Japan. Even before Alexander had opened up India to the West there were contacts, which intensified subsequently and reached new heights under King Asoka who reigned from 268-232 B.C. After a series of wars he converted to Buddhism and sent missionaries to Syria, Egypt, Anatolia, Greece and Macedonia. While these contacts could undoubtedly have had some influence on religious thoughts of the mentioned regions, including on the Essenes in Judea, I am not adverse to the idea of the Holy Spirit having had a share. At certain times certain ideas seem, so to say, hang in the air. They are then grasped by different individuals in different civilizations and adapted to their local circumstances. While I have given in the fore-going a Christian perspective on Gautama and his teachings a Buddhist one can be found in *Going Home. Jesus and Buddha as Brothers*. A more detailed exposition of Jesus' teachings and its similarity to the Baghavad Gita was published in two volumes by Paramahansa Yogananda, who is also the widely known author of *The Autobiography of a Yogi,* under the title: *The Second Coming of Christ. The Resurrection of the Christ within you. A revelatory commentary on the original teachings of Jesus.*

Mystery Cults

A pure ethic appeals to the intellect but most people tend to need and expect more from a religion. This is where the various mystery cults of the Roman Empire come in, and why their relationship to evolving Christianity has to be discussed. Unfortunately we have far too little information on their rites but, as mentioned earlier, without a profound life transforming experience words will just remain words and the soul may not be touched. Marvin Meyer in *The Ancient Mysteries* provides an overview of the various cults through translations from original sources. Since some of them are by necessity Christian in origin one has to sift through polemic to the potential meaning. Nevertheless, the common goal of all the cults was the initiation of the individual into a higher realm of consciousness through "rebirth." The rites were kept secret because pearls were not to be thrown before swine. We have an indication, however, from Plotinus of what the Attic mysteries, also called Eleusian, were supposed to accomplish. Although he lived in the third rather than first or second century A.D. the experience he related is timeless and independent of intellect or culture:

> There were not two; beholder was one with beheld; it was not a vision compassed but a unity apprehended. The man formed by this mingling with the Supreme must - if he only remember - carry this image impressed upon him: he is become unity, nothing within him or without inducing any diversity; no movement now, no passion, no outlooking desire, once this ascent is achieved; reasoning is in abeyance and all Intellection and even, to dare the word, the very self; caught away, filled with God he has in perfect stillness attained isolation; all the being calmed . . . utterly resting he has become very rest . . . he is like one who having penetrated the inner sanctuary, leaves the temple images behind him . . . for There his converse was not with image, not with trace, but with the very Truth in the view of which all the rest is but of secondary concern . . . .

> There is thus converse in virtue of which the essential man outgrows Being, becomes identical with the Transcendent of Being. The self thus lifted, we are in the likeness of the Supreme; if from the heightened self we pass still higher - image to archetype - we have won the Term of all our journeying. Fallen back again we awaken the virtue within until we know ourselves all order once more; once more we are lightened of the burden and move by virtue within towards Intellectual-Principle and through the Wisdom in That to the Supreme.

> This is the life of gods and of the godlike and blessed among men, liberation from the alien that besets us here, a life taking no pleasure in the things of the earth, the passing of solitary into solitary.

This is about as close as the mystical union with the All can be expressed in words. It is totally independent of cultures and only the names differ which are applied to the experience: Nirvana, Zen, the Tao, God, Allah, etc., Hindus referred to it as the recognition of *Tat Tvam Asi,* Thou art That; there is no differentiation only unity of the cosmos. As Plutarch stated, the names which people give to the sun and the moon vary between languages but the heavenly bodies are the same everywhere.

The mystic experience is what the human being longs for, and it has been achieved by some noble souls in all cultures and at all times but it is ephemeral. It is reported that Plotinus achieved this state four times during his lifetime. One cannot abide in it and once returned to the world of phenomena the individual is on his own again. What to do afterwards becomes the problem. Some go on to found religions but in the telling and retelling the experience, which is intrinsically holy, it gets watered down, and conflicts with the existing culture become inevitable. Under those circumstances what was holy becomes mired in political power struggles, unless the person devotes himself to a monastic or philosophic life. This kingdom is truly not of this world and if we try to bring it down to the level of the masses with missionary zeal, we introduce confusion and strife. Plotinus was not a Christian, as a matter of fact he had no use for Christian dogma, yet to deny him his experience of God would do violence to a saintly life. At his moment of death he is reported to have said, "Now I shall endeavor to make that which is divine in me rise up to that which is divine in the universe." A further exposition of mystic experiences throughout the ages can be found in William James', *The Variety of Religious Experience* and the previously mentioned book by Dr. Bucke.

Mithraism

While Judaism's fortunes were clearly in decline in the Roman Empire, not least on account of the lost wars, the cult of Mithra was in ascendance until it was eclipsed by Christianity as a result of Constantine's edicts. Apart from numerous sectarian rivalries within the Christian community, Mithraism presented one of the most serious challenges to the nascent Church because it was widespread and enjoyed imperial favor. The origin of the cult is shrouded in mystery and so are its main tenets. Our information is limited and comes mainly from statuary displays of what is being called *tauroctony*, the slaying of the bull, and accompanying symbols. David Ulansey has published an interesting short book on *The Origins of the Mithriac Mysteries,* which also provides additional sources and is well worth reading.

It is generally agreed that originally there were Persian influences but the cult's main distribution throughout the Roman Empire started from St. Paul's home town, Tarsus. During the last century B.C., while Rome was preoccupied with civil wars, Cilician pirates roamed the eastern Mediterranean and created havoc among the various islands. These were, however, not pirates on the model of Blackbeard, but they could be regarded as the ancient equivalent of the Vikings, who instead of sacking England concentrated on property in Greece and Italy. To be one of these pirates was a noble enterprise and in their forays they even reached Ostia and Rome. Pompey destroyed their fleets but the cult of Mithra, to whom these pirates adhered, persisted from then on in the Empire where the military spread it far and wide.

The key aspect seems to have been that Mithra who had originally been in a father-son relationship with Helios, the sun god, was subsequently amalgamated into one. As *sol invictus*, the invincible sun, he was the ruler of the universe in charge of the stars, the constellations, the planets, and the earth, which he moved in accordance with his will. Initiates into the cult had to ascend through seven steps or ranks. These were Raven, Bridegroom, Soldier, Lion, Persian, Courier of the Sun and Father. The goal was to bring about the transformation and salvation of the individual. The initiates had to undergo several ordeals and tests of courage. They were also "baptized," by washing with water, and they received a "seal" on their foreheads. This, of course, immediately brings "the mark of the beast" from St. John's Apocalypse to mind. The blood of the slain bull was the life giving force and, in the depictions, grain sprouted from the wound as well as the tail of the sacrificed animal. Thus blood, wine, and bread provided the redeeming qualities. Some of the similarities to Christian belief, especially the ceremonial meal, were apparently of a magnitude that the early Church fathers regarded the cult as a perversion of Christianity brought about by Satan.

As mentioned, there is practically no independent written information on the cult except for inscriptions on monuments, the Mithrae, and one sample of liturgy from an Egyptian papyrus. It describes how the initiate should conduct himself on his ascent from earth to the ether, the stars and planets until he comes face to face with Helios whom he is to address with:

> Oh Lord be greeted, full of might, king of highest power, Helios, Lord of heaven and earth, God of gods, powerful is your breath, mighty is your power, Lord if it pleases you announce me to the highest God who has created you as well as me: a human being is N.N, son of N.N. delivered from a mortal mother and the living source of the seed, who has today been newly born through thee who has been called from many thousands to immortality, desires in this hour to adore you to the extent it is humanly possible.

The translation from the German text by Dieterich in *Eine Mithrasliturgie* is my own and the complete English language liturgy can be found in Meyer's *Ancient Mysteries*. All I wanted to show here is the similarity of the language used by priests regardless of the specific religion. Ulansey's book presents not only a summary of what is known about Mithraism, but also an intriguing theory which explains the *tauroctony* in an astronomic-astrologic context based on the precession of the equinoxes. It is well worth reading but a discussion would lead us too far afield. Another useful book by Clauss is listed in the bibliography. A limitation of the cult was that it emphasized martial qualities and as such did not admit women. This may have proved fatal because women tend to be more attracted to new religions than men and by excluding half of humanity the growth potential was seriously curtailed.

Dionysus

Another mystery cult which should be briefly mentioned because of its relevance was that of Dionysus. Although the frenetic Bacchic orgies, as described by Euripides, had in general become somewhat more civilized they could still create a scandal in Rome during the second century B.C. as reported by Livy. The identification with the god's powers was to be achieved by the consummation of his flesh and blood. The sacrificial meat was originally eaten raw and blood was symbolized by wine.

Pausanias the Greek traveler of the second century A.D. reported a miracle which was to have taken place at a festival of Dionysus at Elis. The priests had brought empty jars into the sanctuary of the god and on the next morning they were found to be filled with wine. The similarity to St. John's story of Jesus' first miracle is of interest because the changing of water into wine was not reported by the other evangelists. Furthermore, only John had made such a distinct point that, "Those who eat my flesh and drink my blood have eternal life, and I will raise them up on the last day, for my flesh is true food and my blood is true drink. Those who eat my flesh and drink my blood abide in me, and I in them [6:55-56]." While the other evangelists had placed the Eucharist in the context of the Last Supper and were content to report that on this solemn occasion bread and wine had become Jesus' body and blood, John used language as might have been found in a Dionysian or Mithraic liturgy. Further information on Greco-Roman mystery cults has been collected by Frazier in his *Golden Bough*, while Rahner has ably demonstrated how the Church fathers incorporated Greek myths into Christian mystery literature.

Egypt's Influence

The extent to which ancient Egyptian thoughts had been incorporated in the Bible, especially Proverbs and Psalms, has already been documented in *The Moses Legacy*. But to understand its influence on Christianity, Egyptian ideas about the cosmos and man's relationship to it, need to be discussed. This is especially important because the biblical writers, as well as those who composed the Talmud, and the historians Philo and Josephus present a thoroughly biased view. For instance the fact that certain gods in the Egyptian pantheon were pictured with animal heads on human bodies was ridiculed by Hebrew and Jewish writers because animals were regarded as clearly inferior. In their view, animals were created to serve the human race and could be dealt with in any way one wanted; that they could be in a way co-equal in the cosmic sheme was clearly blasphemy. But this need not be the correct opinion.

Thomas Mann, in his book *Joseph und seine Brüder,* narrated a conversation between young Joseph and a wise Egyptian which deals exactly with this point. While Joseph ridiculed these images, the Egyptian explained that only by combining animal and human qualities can one achieve an inkling of the Divine. Those Jewish writers, who even today, criticize the Egyptian religion as polytheistic and absurd, because some animals were even elevated to the status of a divinity, have failed to consider the symbolic, allegoric aspects. It was not the specific animal per se, be it crocodile or cat, as extreme examples, which were admired but the qualities they represent. For the crocodile it was its power to fiercely devour whatever it wants, against which humans are helpless; and for the cat its supreme solipsism who uses humans for its benefit, rather than providing dog-like devotion.

I have previously discussed the fundamental thoughts behind the Egyptian religion in two articles on my website under the titles of "Our Need for Maat" (August 1, 2007), and "Counter-Religion" (September 1, 2007). They were based on the book by Breasted and that of Jan Assmann which are listed in the bibliography and I shall, therefore, relate only the most salient points here.

The pre-existent God, Atum (the All, the not yet existent) did not create the world through biblical executive fiat, but the universe, so to say, unfolded in analogy to a seed. In this view God was not external but immanent in all aspects of the terrestrial and cosmic world. From *Atum* came *Shuh,* the wind and life. But inasmuch as life without direction is meaningless, he had a twin sister, *Tefnut,* who equaled *Maat*:

> Then said Atum: Tefnut is my living daughter,
> She is joined with her brother Shu.
> Life is his name,
> Maat is her name.
> I live conjoined with the pair of my children,
> Together with my twins,
> By being in the Middle of Them,

The one on my back, the other on my front.
Life sleeps with my daughter Maat,
One in me. One all around me.
I have raised myself between them,
While their arms enfolded me.

Maat was the regulating force which prevented the cosmos, and with it humanity, to fall into chaos, *Isfet*, which was its natural condition. For this reason *Maat*—as the principle of order, truth and justice—had to be re-established by the human race on a daily basis and this required effort. The King, Pharaoh, as Son of God was the mediator between heaven and earth. It was his duty to uphold *Maat* and thereby provide harmony between celestial and terrestrial forces by appropriate sacrifices. The duty of the common people was to also practice *Maat* in daily living within the family unit and society.

Living in accordance with Maat required from everyone, high or low, what Assmann had called: communicative and active solidarity. Communicative solidarity consisted of: the person to listen to another's complaint or viewpoint; to speak calmly in a polite manner and to keep silent when silence was called for. Active solidarity demanded that injustices had to be corrected. To turn a "deaf ear" or a "blind eye" to a person in need was a sin against Maat. But the overarching sin was greed, as the root of all evil. These principles were regarded as self-evident and transmitted as such within the family unit which was held in high esteem. Thus, *Maat* can be viewed as a positive feedback system. The people here on earth, foremost the king as their representative, live in accordance with *Maat* which is also offered in form of liturgy to the gods who in turn see to it that cosmic order is maintained which reflects itself in well-being on earth. Or as the Egyptians put it, "the deed returns to the doer;" analogous to our saying: "What goes around comes around." When *Maat* rules society no law books and lawyers to interpret them are needed, because everybody has a conscience and for trespasses specific punishments could be fixed. Death sentences were rare; beatings or cutting off body parts were preferred because they were visible reminders of wrong-doing and thereby acted as deterrents. Assmann pointed out that this vertical scheme of solidarity with interaction from top to bottom and from bottom to the top was in contrast to the horizontal connectedness which is supposed to exist in a democracy where all citizens are equal. The limits of this "horizontal" solidarity in our democracy can be observed on a daily basis and instead of *Maat*; *Isfet* is beginning to rule the roost. Conscience has largely disappeared in our society and has supposedly been replaced by laws, but in fact there is no law, only lawyers who interpret it and the one who has, in civil or criminal affairs, the most persuasive tongue will win. In Congress the rule of law is further compromised by special interest groups and the members of the House or Senate who get the most money from a given special interest group will pay the piper with their vote.

The ancient Egyptians would have regarded this state of affairs as absurd. Vertical connectedness was derived from nature where nothing could grow unless the soil is watered from above and the rising plant is nourished by the sun. Since human beings were part of nature a biblical type discrimination against animals was unthinkable, as has been explained above.

Maat was represented as a winged goddess crowned by an ostrich feather, which played a prominent role during the judgment of the deceased's soul. The latter had two aspects. One was the Ka, essentially the person's "Doppelgänger" during life, which resided thereafter in his mummified body and effigy in the tomb. The other was the Ba, which was located in the individual's heart. During the Final Judgment, in presence of Osiris, it was weighed against the feather of Maat. If the scales did not balance the heart was devoured by a hideous monster. If they did the Ba entered heaven as a bird, but contact with the Ka was maintained because the Ba returned from its daytime celestial abode to its Ka at night.

Although this might strike one as idle fancy, the deeper meaning was the preservation of the continuity of life even beyond physical death. It was, therefore, the duty of the son to keep the father's tomb in order. In this way connectedness extended beyond the limited time span the individual spends on earth and lasted for generations. The Egyptians were, therefore, not "obsessed with death," as is sometimes stated, but with a long, if not eternal, life on earth as well as in heaven. Since the Ka and the Ba were both aspects of the soul

I have often wondered whether the Muslim's Holy Shrine the Ka'b (Arabic spelling, meaning cube), or Kaaba in English, might not have a deeper symbolic meaning as: the Soul of heaven and earth.

There was, however, a break with tradition during the reign of the heretical Pharaoh Akhenaten (c. 1353-1336 B.C.), who was subsequently expunged from the realm of the living by erasing his name from all the monuments. He established an exclusive monotheism with Aten (the sun) as the sole god, and made him co-regent with a personal cartouche. Aten was a jealous god who tolerated no others and iconoclastic fury swept the land thereafter. Aten was the King of Egypt and his son Akhenaten was the executor of his father's will. Maat was henceforth no longer the reciprocal relationship that had heretofore existed but was exercised by Akhenaten in an autocratic manner, against which there was no recourse. It is small wonder that Isfet ensued and that Akhenaten's successor, the boy Tutankhaten became Tutankhamen within the first few years of his reign.

All of this may strike the modern reader as quaint and rather irrelevant. Nevertheless it is not. Aten had the properties ascribed to Yahweh, and Moses' role as the authoritarian executor of Yahweh's will was similar to that of Akhenaten. Only the visual representation of the sun disk, the rays of which ended in human hands holding the ankh, symbol of life, was abandoned. In addition some of Akhenaten's words are echoed in the gospels. In the great hymn to Aten, we can read: "There is no other that knoweth thee save thy son Ikhnaton [alternative spelling for Akhenaten]. Thou hast made him wise in thy designs and thy might." In word for word identical passages Matthew and Luke have Jesus say: "All things have been handed over to me by my Father . . . and no one knows the Father except the Son." The Last Judgment, with Jesus taking the place of Osiris, is a fundamental aspect of the Christian religion.

On a secular level the statue of Maat, shorn of wings and blindfolded, but holding her scales, still adorns our Court Houses as the symbol of justice, A replica of an Egyptian obelisk, which in ancient times symbolized a ray of the sun god Ra, stands as a monument to our first President, George Washington, in the center of our capital. The "all-seeing eye," surrounded by celestial light on top of a pyramid, can be found on the obverse of the Great Seal of the United States. It is reproduced on the back of our one dollar bill. As such the heritage of ancient Egypt is still with us, except that we have, by and large, forgotten the meaning of the symbols.

But let us return to the time of Jesus and its gods. In the chapter on Saint John's Christ I have mentioned Josephus' discourse on Pilate and that there was a paragraph on Isis. Her cult had spread from Egypt to Rome and the goddess had become merged with most of the other female deities who existed in the Empire. She ruled the upper and lower world and was revered as Queen of Heaven. Plutarch wrote that she represented the female principle of Nature; her names were countless; she strove for good and eschewed evil. Jointly with her husband Osiris and their son Horus they were the first trinity. Her image with little Horus sitting on her lap became the model for subsequent depictions of Mary with the Christ-child. She was revered as the Mother of God, a title which the Church likewise transferred to Mary in the fourth century. It is probably no coincidence that the closure of the last Isis temple occurred in close chronologic proximity to the official elevation of Mary into the Christian pantheon. Mankind has always needed not only the image of a heavenly father but also that of a devoted kindly mother who can be appealed to. Even the biblical Jews presented sacrifices to Ashera, which was just another name for the Babylonian Ishtar. The Catholic Church recognized this human need and responded accordingly.

While the idea behind Isis worship was noble, her priests, being human, were fallible as the paragraph by Josephus indicates. It described a sex scandal in Rome which led to the closure of the temple of Isis and expulsion of her devotees. A Roman of high society had pined after the favors of a virtuous married lady who refused to grant him his desires. A servant of the lady then contrived a stratagem where she would bribe the priests of Isis to let the lover spend a night in Isis' temple where he would appear to Lady Paulina disguised as the god Anubis. The priests agreed, Decius Mundus had his tryst, and Paulina was delighted to have been so honored by the god. All would have been well had Decius had good sense and not bragged about how he had enjoyed the lady's favors. To mate with a god was honorable but a night of pleasure with a mortal was clearly something else. Paulina was forgiven by her husband and society, Mundus was banished, but on Tiberius' orders the temple of Isis was demolished and her statue thrown into the Tiber. Thus sex scandals in religions are nothing new either. The Isis cult survived in the rest of the Empire and returned to Rome a little while later.

But in the synopsis of the chapter Josephus also said that he would relate a disaster which befell the Jews in Rome at about the same time. It is dealt with in the last paragraph. Since the story highlights the religious-political scene of the time I shall quote the essence here:

> There was a man who was a Jew, but had been driven away from his own country by an accusation laid against him *for transgressing their laws* [emphasis added], and by the fear he was under of punishment for the same; but in all respects a wicked man: - he then living at Rome, professed to instruct men in the wisdom of the laws of Moses. He procured also three other men, entirely of the same character as himself, to be his partners. These men persuaded Fulvia, a woman of great dignity, and one that had embraced the Jewish religion, to send purple and gold to the temple at Jerusalem; and when they had gotten them, they employed them for their own uses, and spent the money themselves . . . .Whereupon Tiberius, who had been informed of the thing by Saturninus, the husband of Fulvia, who desired inquiry might be made about it, ordered all the Jews to be banished out of Rome; at which time the consuls enlisted four thousand men out of them, and sent them to the island Sardinia; but punished a greater number of them, who were unwilling to become soldiers, on account of keeping the laws of their forefathers. Thus were these Jews banished out of the city by the wickedness of four men.

This paragraph is obviously important in relation to the fate of Jesus as well as that of Paul. Apparently the Jewish authorities, having been deprived of political power in Jerusalem brooked no open dissent from the Law. If Jesus had a relatively large group of followers, turning him over to the Romans for crucifixion would indeed have been the best strategy. The more so, since Josephus had reported in the same chapter that Pilate could be intimidated by an unruly mob, as mentioned earlier. The behavior of Paul, as reported in The Acts, also makes good sense because he surely would have shared the fate of James the Just had he not appealed to be heard by the Emperor. As a citizen of Tarsus which was under direct Roman rather than Jewish jurisdiction, this was his privilege and had to be honored. This little vignette also points out that Jews, if they did not engage in criminal behavior, had less to fear from Rome than from their own brothers. It shows, furthermore, that banishment of Jews from a given city or country was not invented by the Christian Church. Expulsions of Jews from Rome recurred periodically, but they soon returned when the regime changed.

Egypt had become a Roman province in 30 B.C and Alexandria was the intellectual capital of the Empire. It is reported that St. Mark had gone to Egypt to spread the gospel and some of the most influential members of the early Church hailed from Alexandria. It is, therefore no coincidence that the Christian Church borrowed extensively from Egyptian lore.

In summary one can conclude that the simple message of Jesus, in order to be heard and spread, had to be formatted into the existing religious sentiments of the time. Since Jews, by and large, refused to join the Church, Jesus' followers had to be recruited from the Gentile population of the Empire. In this respect the Church Fathers did an admirable job. In regard to Jesus' ethical message there was no problem because it coincided to some extent with Stoic and Platonic philosophy. But while the philosophers were a small elite group the Church could popularize the ideas and make them the norm. The frequently barbaric rites of the mystery cults could be elevated and purified by the *Mysterium Christi*, the transubstantiation. What was good and noble was retained while aspects which were regarded as harmful, especially the pronounced sexual concomitants, were discarded. We have to be grateful to the Church for her attempt to civilize the masses, but unfortunately as with all human enterprises, this ideal was never achieved. The subsequent power struggles of the

Church with internal as well as external enemies, which were many, showed that Jesus' message can be followed only by individuals and may get lost in institutions.

This is especially true when the persecuted achieve worldly power and the tables can be turned on the former persecutors. The desire for revenge is powerful, and in spite of Jesus' commandments, neither the early adherents of the Christian religion nor their later followers could resist this temptation. Eusebius tells us that after the Edict of Milan in 313, which guaranteed freedom of religion to all, including Christians, the mob went on a rampage against the former rulers and their followers in the eastern part of the Empire. This is understandable but the sad aspect is that Eusebius and some of the subsequent Church fathers condoned and glorified the vengeance. This proves again that, for the most part, the human race is quite immune to betterment and only names tend to change, as well as the excuses, under which the same passions are acted out. We can't blame Jesus for this failure. The fault lies in human nature. Apart from a few notable exceptions we simply find ourselves unable, or at times unwilling, to live up to his high ideals.

WHAT IS TRUTH?

In John 18:37 we read:

> Pilate asked him "So you are a king?" Jesus answered, "You say that I am a king. For this I was born and for this I came into the world, to testify to the truth. Everyone who belongs to the truth listens to my voice." Pilate asked him, "What is truth?"
>
> After he had said this, he went out to the Jews again and said, "I find no case against him."

Pilate's question has lingered through the ages and we can debate endlessly why he walked away without waiting for an answer, or what Jesus might have replied. The question is fundamental and deserves an answer because at this time in world history our society is about to drown in an ocean of half-truths and outright lies. So, how do we get at truth and specifically that of the gospel narratives?

At this point it is necessary to be clear about what we mean with the word truth. We live at present in an intellectual climate which takes pride in a degree of cynicism and whenever I mention to others the name of my website, thinktruth.com, I frequently receive the reply, "there is no truth, it's all opinion," with the unspoken thought that all are equally valid. This attitude needs to be examined and the difference between cynicism which is harmful, and skepticism which is helpful, clarified.

The cynic declares, "This is balderdash, I don't believe it," and is done with it. Intellectual laziness and/or pride prevent him from further inquiry and he shuts himself off from meaningful dialogue. The skeptic on the other hand says, "I don't believe what you just told me but if you can give me some proof for your assertion, I will examine it and if what you are saying can be verified I may agree with you." This is the level rational human beings should conduct their affairs on controversial matters.

The key word here is "level" because it is important for the understanding of the topic. Just as there are degrees of freedom, there are levels of truth. The first point to realize is that "Truth" is an abstract noun and as such a symbol for an underlying thought. The Truth by itself is not a fact, but occurs within a sentence which expresses a given person's opinion on a given subject. That sentence may or may or not be truthful. "Absolute truth" is a topic which philosophers argue about but no agreement will be achievable. As a physician I shall not engage in these discussions because they are not in my area of expertise. I am limiting myself instead, deliberately at this point, to that level of truth which exists in human interactions.

Here we can deal with what may be called empirical truth which is dictated by the common function of our central nervous systems where a house can be distinguished from a rosebush and when somebody refers to the one as the other he is either deluded or is deliberately trying to deceive me. In practical day to day matters the physician, for instance, is concerned with the veracity of his patient. Statements about compliance with a given medication regimen can be verified by objective means. This is the level of truth which is important in our everyday lives. Telling the truth can then be qualified with the statement, "to the best of my knowledge." This leaves open the possibility of human error but still allows for the legal demand, "to tell the truth, the whole truth and nothing but the truth."

All of this is obvious, but when it comes to spiritual truth we are dealing with a completely different level. Since it is a personal revealed experience it cannot be objectively verified by anyone else and needs to be taken on faith. But before discussing this aspect let me relate a personal event which deals directly with what the human being regards as knowledge. I have previously reported it in the medical literature as "The Reality of Death Experiences: A Personal Perspective," but inasmuch as the insight gained at that time was fundamental for the question at hand I shall recount it again here.

In 1953 during my training in neurology, neurophysiology and psychiatry at the Mayo Clinic a routine chest X ray revealed a "lesion in the right upper lobe of the lung," which was regarded by the radiologist as "probably metastatic." This created a profound mental problem. We had been married not quite two years, our daughter was less than one year old and metastatic cancer was in those days a death sentence. It was obvious that this lesion had to be removed and examined histologically to determine its nature. As I lay down on the operating table I prayed that if the lesion were to be indeed metastatic I would be allowed to die on the table because I did not want to face a slow lingering death for several months thereafter and at the same time being a burden to my young family. The next thing I remember was a sensation of tremendous bliss with the knowledge: it was a metastasis, I am dead, I am free, I can sin no more. The point to emphasize is that this was not an opinion or belief but knowledge; just as I know right now that I am sitting here typing these words onto the keyboard. But when I opened my eyes, experienced the postoperative pain, and saw my wife, Martha, leaning over the bedrail I said, "Let me die, let me die." The idea that the blissful experience had not been the end, but that I was condemned to a future life of pain and suffering was too much to bear. Martha was obviously shocked because she was grateful that I had survived the operation and couldn't understand why I wanted to die.

This was a once in a lifetime experience which I regarded as sacred and, therefore, discussed it only with Martha. But in the late 1970s a flurry of books appeared in regard to Near Death Experiences (NDEs) with or without associated Out-of-Body Experiences (OOBEs) which intimated that these were evidence for an afterlife. I agreed that the experience by itself was real for the person who had undergone it, but the conclusion that it constituted proof for life after death was unwarranted. This is why I published the mentioned paper in 1980.

I had obviously given the matter a great deal of thought in the interval and had come to the conclusion that subjective reality can differ profoundly from objective reality as seen by a bystander. For Martha, I had been in dreadful shape on that day in Rochester.

She saw her husband in a hospital bed with tubes in various places including the throat, ashen gray with labored breathing, but I had never been better off in my whole life than the moment(s) before awareness of this world had returned. This is why I differentiated in the mentioned paper subjective reality, which is limited to one person, shared subjective reality which governs our conduct in society and objective reality as can be ascertained by scientific experiments.

It can now be argued that even objective reality does not exist because all of our reality requires an observer, the subject, as the Upanishads had stated thousands of years ago, and was subsequently put in modern language by Schopenhauer in his *Die Welt als Wille und Vorstellung,* which might rendered as: The world as Will and Representation; although the word *Vorstellung* has additional meanings. Among them are for instance: imagination, idea, concept, appearance and even theatrical performance.

In retrospect I now believe that the 1953 experience was what ancient Indian sages have described as: *sat, cit, ananda*; namely: being, knowledge, bliss! The experience was real but the interpretation, "It was a metastasis; I am dead" was conditioned by the specific circumstances with concomitant expectations and inaccurate. I had experienced supernatural bliss but was not dead! The implications of this fact for our outlook on life are, of course, considerable. The event could be regarded as a gift of *cháris* because it has permanently removed all fear of death but it also points out that the thoughts associated with even the strongest conviction of truth may be in error.

Thus, the subjective feeling of knowledge as truth, regardless whether or not it is "objectively" verifiable, is related to the intensity of a given sensory experience. Since the intensity can vary, we can then regard a given event in relationship to truth as: maybe, probably, or certain. This manifests itself in interpersonal relationships as trust or faith which we place into a given person or information from books, lectures, etc. Faith is inborn in every human being and only subsequently modified by life experiences. Let me illustrate this statement by two examples: one from the Bible and the other from a personal event.

The biblical story of the original sin has, of course, been debated for thousands of years, but there is an important psychological element that bears discussion. Adam had received God's instruction that he could eat from the fruit of every tree in paradise except for the "tree of knowledge of good and evil" and the tree of life. Some modern writers have omitted "the good and evil" qualification and tell us that God had intended to deprive human beings of all aspects of knowledge. According to that opinion the snake was, therefore, the true benefactor of the human race because it allowed for scientific discoveries. This interpretation is, of course, incorrect and one could even argue that Adam was already engaged in the rudiments of scientific investigations when he "named" the animals, which is the first step towards classifications.

The Bible does not tell us whether God had only instructed Adam in regard to the danger that particular tree posed and if Eve had received the information second hand from Adam. At any rate the ordinance was accepted without question as a simple fact. The idea of doubt had not yet existed. This required the intrusion of another party, which in the biblical context was the snake; the tempter. When Eve was asked why she wouldn't want to eat what that tree had to offer, she cited God's demand but embellished it with the statement that they were not even allowed to touch it, which was not part of the original commandment. When the snake then told Eve that they would not die "in the day thereof," after eating and on the contrary they would be like God knowing good and evil; faith was eroded and doubt took its place. We know the rest: Eve believed the snake, took a bite and when Adam came back from his expedition she told him what she had done. Since nothing untoward had happened and the "fruit was good to the taste," Adam also helped himself and then disaster struck.

The story is obviously legend, but it contains apart from the creation of doubt by others two more noteworthy aspects: in regard to the biblical God's absolute knowledge and the nature of the lie. If the biblical God had been "all knowing and all powerful" he would have been aware that Adam and Eve were destined to eat from that tree and under those circumstances the punishment was clearly uncalled for because God had been responsible for that foreordained outcome. Furthermore, He had to ask Adam where he hid and whether he had eaten from the forbidden tree. For an all-knowing God the question in regard to eating would not only have been rhetorical but a possible incitement to lying which would have aggravated the situation. The biblical writer seemed not to have been concerned about these inconsistencies and repeated God's "rhetorical" question in the Cain and Able story, where Cain did lie.

I shall postpone discussing the problem of free will until later; for now we need to deal with the nature of the Lie? Did the snake lie and if so to what extent, by what means? The statement that their eyes would be opened, that they would be like God knowing good and evil and that they would not die in the day "thereof," which could be taken to mean immediately, was also correct. The lie which was the most vicious, the most effective and, therefore, the still most widely used one, consisted of withholding information which would have influenced the choice. They became like God only in one aspect, moral judgment and with its inappropriate use the human race has created a tremendous amount of grief for itself. All the other aspects of the Divinity have remained a matter of faith and provide a most fertile field for arguments by theologians.

Let us replay the scene in our skeptical day and age. Assuming that good natured, believing Eve had done what was disapproved of and then told Adam about it. By that time the tempter would already have disappeared and it was strictly a matter between these two people. Adam had at that point several options. The most reasonable one would have been to ask Eve what she knew about that creature and by what authority the snake could contradict God. Since Eve wouldn't have had an answer, Adam's next rational statement would have been: Look, this is potentially serious, let's find God and ask Him what we should do now. He didn't do so, but we can't blame him because mankind was in its infancy while we had in the meantime an opportunity to learn.

I am bringing up these particulars because the original sin is re-enacted in all our lives at some point or another and baptism doesn't wash it away. It can be defined as: the impulsive act for a perceived gain in knowing disregard of an existing order to the contrary. It was also the first incitement towards greed. They had everything they needed, but when the prospect of even supposedly better things was dangled before them, they jumped at the opportunity in total ignorance of the potential consequences. When one looks at the human race today, especially as it manifests itself in American society, one is impressed that for the most part it represents the stage of puberty with uncontrolled, and at times uncontrollable, hormonal rages and impetuosity. There are some individuals who have reached maturity but these do not yet occupy center stage and, therefore, lack the necessary impact.

For our society which is obsessed with sensual and sexual gratification it is important to realize that the word "sin" need not only have the theological meaning of willful disobedience against God's command for which punishment will be meted out. In the New Testament the Greek word *hamartía*, which is translated as "sin" stood for "missing the mark." As such it had the broader meaning of missing one's purpose, direction, or goal in life. This ought to make us pause and think about what we really ought to be doing.

After this biblical detour, let me relate why I know that faith is still innate in human beings. In the beginning of December 1957 I took my specialty Board Examination in Psychiatry and Neurology. Inasmuch as it was held at New York's Columbia-Presbyterian Hospital I thought we might use the occasion to stay with Martha's mother for a few days and give her the opportunity to enjoy her grandchildren. Our daughter, Krista, was five years old at the time while Peter was one month shy of his third birthday. After the exam Martha and I took the children on a tour of midtown Manhattan which included a visit to Macy's Santa Claus. The line was short and when it was our turn little Peter ran up to that man hugged him and cried out "My Santa Claus!" It was an unforgettable demonstration of childhood faith and innocence of which his older more world-wise sister deprived him some time later on.

Faith, however, is never lost because it is the root from which our "free will" arises. The Greek word for faith in the New Testament is *pístis* and by analogy one might relate it to the English word "piston." It is the driving force of the engine, which provides the "will" with direction and meaning. In the U.S. we hear a great deal about "faith-based" institutions or organizations. The term has thereby become limited to religious aspects. Yet, all of our actions are faith-based. We simply don't call it faith, but use the word "trust" instead and without it society could not function. If we define faith ontologically as 'the firm unquestioned expectation that what is hoped for will come to pass,' we can conclude that even what is regarded as the ultimate loss of faith, suicide, is actually still faith-based. The seriously despondent person hopes to escape from an apparently unendurable situation. But since none of us know what real physical death is like, this hope is not based on facts.

While faith in "something" is never lost, it can give way to skepticism or even cynicism, especially in regard to religious dogma. It is then redirected into the secular arena where pet ideas are pursued with equal vigor. It is obvious that this faith/trust also can be misplaced. This pertains not only to individuals who may disappoint us on occasion, but more importantly charismatic leaders can create havoc by promoting a particular secular political faith. This was amply demonstrated in the past century and is still apparent in this one.

In catechism class religious faith was defined for us as: "*Etwas fest für wahr halten,*" "to firmly regard something as true." In contrast to common experiential truth, this level of truth is intrapersonal. To this one might add in the religious sphere "revealed truth," which is not only an intense subjective experience but knowledge experienced as truth reaches the level of certainty. For the person who has had a spiritual revelation, as Jesus, St. Paul and others, it was such an intense experience that it could not be doubted; but it could also not be shared. It could only be incompletely described because it involved either merely a feeling, or a vision, which did not lend itself to faithful verbal reproduction. Inasmuch as our nervous systems are at present so constituted that we are not able to receive this type of experience in a routine manner and since it occurs extremely rarely, even in gifted individuals, the cynic regards himself as justified by declaring it as nonsense and writing it off as a delusion.

While it is true that religious and/or political faith can readily be based on a delusion, i.e., false impression, this does not mean that the belief in a world beyond this one, which our sense receptors commonly allow us to perceive, is always a product of false information. There is, however as mentioned, a fine line between the emotions of a spiritual experience which are genuine and their subsequent interpretation. The latter can be prone to error as has been shown above in the personal 1953 event.

In the previous chapter I have mentioned the *Tibetan Book of the Dead* and shall return to it again later but in the present context the cover page of the Evans-Wentz translation paperback edition, which I bought in 1962, is the relevant aspect. It depicts the peak of the mythical Mount Meru, the center of Tibetan cosmology, as formed of overlapping slabs. While reflecting on this picture the thought came that if this mountain is also a symbol of truth, then the slabs are not formed of granite but are reflecting crystals where the viewer always sees his own picture albeit in various distortions. This is our reality upon which we base our actions.

What a person sees and experiences is, therefore, conditioned by events in his past and as such the search for esoteric truth, the one which is experienced outside of our normal sensory channels, must proceed carefully and cautiously. As noted previously, Zodhiates' dictionary also mentioned "unveiled reality" as one of the translations for *aletheia*. This reminded me of Schiller's poem, "The Veiled Image of Sais," which deals with a young man who went to Sais in Egypt full of yearning for truth and secret wisdom. While he was walking with a guide in the gardens they came upon an enormous veiled statue. When the young man asked his mentor what was hidden behind the veil he was told: "the Truth!" "What" cried the youngster, "but this is precisely what I came here for and this is what one wants to hide from me?" "You have to discuss this with the goddess," his companion replied, "No mortal lifts this veil until I do so myself" she says" and "whosoever does so with profane and sacrilegious hands shall see - the Truth." "Strange words" the student said, "and you have never lifted it?" "Absolutely not and haven't even been tempted to do so" was the reply. "I don't understand it, this is such a thin veil," "but a law" the guide interrupted, "easy for the hand, but of enormous weight on conscience." Unable to sleep the student stole away at night to visit the statue. Although afraid he cried "I want to see it" and removed the veil. "What did he see?" Schiller continues, "I know it not. Unconscious he was found the following morning and whatever he had seen he never spoke of." Whenever he was pressed to answer he merely repeated, "Woe to him who approaches truth with guilt she will never be pleasant."

The original story came from Plutarch and the inscription on the statue of Isis, "I am all that has been, and is, and shall be, and my robe no mortal has yet uncovered," has been previously mentioned in the chapter on St. John's gospel. The lesson is that esoteric truth is not to be trifled with. The human being cannot handle a flash flood, it must come in small doses with sufficient intervals for it to be correctly apprehended and I shall return to this aspect later. For now let us stay with "gospel truth."

The first serious attempt to separate historical from legendary material in the gospels was made by David Friedrich Strauss in 1835 with his book *Das Leben Jesu*. It created a massive uproar in theological circles and cost him appointments to universities. Strauss was only 27 years old when he wrote the book and youthful ardor was manifest. In 1865 he tried to soften it somewhat by an even longer tome but added no new information. The idea to extend historical criticism beyond secular literature and portions of the Old Testament to the New had taken root and Ernest Renan published his *La vie de Jesus* in 1864. He followed the path Strauss had laid, but with Gallic élan. The common feature of all these publications by a number of authors was that the image and teachings of Jesus had become overlaid with legends of miracles and supernatural powers. These had become dogma and an extraordinary, charismatic, human being had been turned into God, which was regarded as an error.

Strauss used the German word *Mythus* for Christianity which when translated into the English "myth" loses its meaning because the English word is akin to falsehood, lie. Although the word had retained its Greek meaning in the German language, in the sense of legends and ancient sacred history, some "free thinkers" have used Strauss' writings to assert that the gospels are based on a lie. Nietzsche, of whom more will be said later, was the most prominent proponent of this idea but he failed to make the above mentioned distinction between objective and subjective reality in regard to intrapsychic events.

Theologians have subsequently written a plethora of books on the "historical" Jesus. But no new light has been shed because the basic documents, on which all opinions are based, have remained the same and we are, therefore, dealing only with different interpretations of the gospel material. It is true that the Qumran scrolls have added information on the apocalyptic aspects of Jewish thought in the 1st century, and the Nag Hammadi scrolls have brought forth information about Gnostic ideas, which had been banned by the Church, but they have failed to produce reliable information on the person of Jesus of Nazareth. Unless new authentic scrolls were to be found which deal with Jesus the person, and which can be reliably dated to the reign of Tiberius, the truth about the historical Jesus will remain a matter of conjecture.

Some modern religious writers have tried to separate the pre-Easter "historical" Jesus from the post-Easter resurrected Christ with its concomitant theology. But this is possible only to a limited extent because the resurrection is the basis of the faith and without it nobody would have written the gospels. As has been shown, whatever account of Jesus, the person, one wants to write it will always be subjective and influenced by the goal the author has in mind. Thus, the search for the "authentic" Jesus is not very fruitful. For example Paula Fredriksen's, *"From Jesus to Christ. The Origins of the New Testament Images of Jesus,"* can be seen as a modern sequel to Strauss and Renan. It is a valuable depiction of the development of the gospels but after one has read it one wonders why Jesus should have any relevance for us today. The same applies also to efforts by Bultmann, for instance, to "demythologize" Jesus. A philosophical discussion of this topic between Karl Jaspers and Rudolf Bultmann was published under the title: *Myth & Christianity. An inquiry into the possibility of religion without myth.*

Another attempt to find the historical kernel of Jesus by concentrating solely on his words, as reported in the gospels, was made by the so-called Jesus Seminar. Its participants consisted of 76 eminent professors from North American and European religious colleges who devised a rigorous scientific protocol where the words attributed to Jesus by the gospel writers could be graded for presumed authenticity. Each gospel, including that of Thomas, was examined and a color code was assigned to every one of Jesus' sentences. A colloquial way to define the words for authenticity as proposed by one member was: red for "That's Jesus!," pink for "Sure sounds like Jesus," grey "Well, maybe," and black for "There's been some mistake." A vote was cast by each fellow of the seminar and a probability score was assigned to each color: greater than 75 percent for red, between 51 and 75 percent to pink, between 26 and 50 percent for grey, and 25 percent or less for black. When the scores were tallied it was found that of the more than 1500 passages only 90 had received a red or pink score, and only 10 were unequivocally placed into the red column! I have a feeling that even the members of the Seminar may have been surprised at the outcome of this academic exercise in the search for truth.

How should we interpret this result? The Jesus Seminar refrained from presenting conclusions because a consensus would obviously not have been achievable and they simply published their efforts in, *"The Five Gospels. What Did Jesus Really Say? The Search for the Authentic Words of Jesus."* Since one is dealing with opinions and theology, the problem is inherently unsolvable because all judgments are inevitably influenced by the background of the individual who renders the verdict.

As mentioned in the chapter on Saint John's Christ, the Council of Nicea in 325 ended the epoch of helter-skelter growth for the followers of Jesus and established the Catholic i.e., Universal Church for all time. The creed was fixed and the Gnostics relegated to obscurity. But the fundamental question as to what the New Testament really stood for has never been fully resolved by the Church. For the Gnostics the critical problem was not only the physical versus spiritual resurrection of Jesus, as has been mentioned in the chapter on St. John, but also the fact that the Jewish vengeful, jealous, Yahweh, who had to "magnify himself," bore no relationship to the loving Father of Jesus. The Gnostics could not agree with the idea that a loving God would have created a world so full of misery and concluded that the creator god was only a demiurge, namely a subordinate one who manufactures things, rather than the higher God of the All. This is not the place to discuss the details of Gnosticism because they have been presented not only in the previously mentioned books by Pagels, but also in Stephan A. Hoeller's, *"Gnosticism. New Light on the Ancient Tradition of Inner Knowing,"* and *"The Nag Hammadi Library"* in English, as edited by James M. Robinson. There are, however two points to be made. One is the "Knowledge" of the Gnostics and the other the relationship to the established Church.

As discussed above, on basis of personal experience I can grant the Gnostics the validity, reality, of their subjective insights but that does not mean that these experiences are the final word on the Truth. In regard to Gnosticism's relationship to the Church we have to realize that the latter found herself in a difficult position. Accommodations with Judaism had to be made early on because Christians would have lacked legitimacy within the Empire. Judaism was an established and accepted religion while initially Christians were regarded as a sect of Judaism. The Jewish Wars of the first and second centuries cemented the split between the two religions and since Christianity embraced women, did not require circumcision and abolished the dietary laws, it had far greater growth potential than Judaism. But the problem the Gnostics had laid their finger on did not go away simply by excommunication of its adherents. The ideas of Orthodox Judaism and Christianity are incompatible. The divinity of Jesus is the stumbling block for one and the cornerstone for the other.

To understand the quandary, in regard to Judaism, the Christian Churches still find themselves in, we have to fully realize and accept that the New Testament was woven from two major and separate strands. These were Judaism and Hellenism and whoever tries to give precedence of the one over the other violates the whole and thereby truth. Yet Jewish and Hellenistic ideas have always been in conflict with each other. Judaism as practiced in Jesus' time was defined in the post-exilic period. It has been ascribed to Ezra and was isolationist in nature. Upon the return from Babylon some of the congregation had intermarried with the local population and since this was a cardinal sin Nehemiah, the governor, and Ezra, the priest, were profoundly disturbed. In Ezra 9 we read:

> And when these things [sacrifices] were finished, the
> princes drew near to me saying, The people of Israel, and the

priests and the Levites, have not separated themselves from
the people of the lands in their abominations . . . . For they
have taken of their daughters for themselves and their sons;
and the holy seed has passed among the nations of the lands,
and the hand of the ruler has been first in this transgression.
And when I heard this thing, I rent my garments, and
trembled, and plucked some of the hairs of my head, and of
my beard, and sat down mourning [9:1-3].

Chapter 10 provided the remedy:

So when Ezra had prayed, and when he had confessed,
weeping and praying before the house of God, a very great
assembly of Israel came together to him, men and women and
youths; for the people wept, and wept aloud. And Sechenias
the son of Jeel, of the sons of Elam, answered and said to
Esdras, We have broken covenant with our God, and have
taken strange wives of the nations of the land . . . . Now
then let us make a covenant with our God to put away all
the wives, and their offspring, as thou shalt advise: arise and
alarm them, with the commands of our God; and let be done
according to the law. Rise up, for the matter is upon thee; and
we are with thee: be strong and do [10:1-4].

The message was clear: Israel had been punished with the
destruction of Jerusalem and the exile of its people because of
transgressions against the Law. This would never be allowed to
happen again in the future. Strict separation from the other inhabitants
of the land had to be enforced, regardless of the cost to individuals.
Marriages were dissolved, wives and children were expelled. This
intolerance led subsequently to the Maccabean wars, internecine
strife within the community, and in turn, to Roman occupation as
reported by Josephus, and summarized in *Whither Zionism?*

While Jews jealously guarded the uniqueness of their God and
the separation from Gentiles, the Hellenistic world pursued a directly
opposite course. A religious-political program as depicted above
would have been regarded not only as cruel but chauvinistic and
deluded. Colloquially expressed, the Gentile population of Palestine
may well have said, "Who do these guys think they are?" For non-

Jews all foreign gods were equal and were readily appropriated from other cultures. Even the members of the various mystery cults did not practice exclusiveness but participated joyously in festivals devoted to other gods. This greatly concerned Paul, the Pharisee, because some of the new converts failed to see a reason why they should no longer share festivals and sacrificial meals with friends and relatives who had not converted. Exclusiveness, rather than inclusiveness, was foreign to the Hellenistic spirit. Paul tried to bridge this gap but was unsuccessful, especially as far as Jews were concerned. They correctly saw him, and the propagation of his message, as a serious danger to their religion and the heretofore successful proselytizing efforts. His attempt to be "all things to all people [1 Cor. 9:22]," might have worked in the Gentile world but could not in Jerusalem where he was about to share the fate of Jesus, Stephen, and James the Just.

As such, the gospels are a mixture of Jewish and Hellenistic ideas and this has practical political consequences. At this time it is no longer polite in the U.S. to talk about Christian values because Jews would be offended. This sentiment has given rise to the term Judeo-Christian "heritage," "values," or "traditions." As mentioned earlier, and in *The Moses Legacy*, I regard this amalgamation as a mistake. The term gained currency in America prior to and during WWII as a result of Hitler's persecution of Jews and was intended to promote Christian-Jewish solidarity. The motive was political rather than religious-theological. The term may have been useful at the time but it should not be perpetuated because it can lead to wrong conclusions. Christians thereby deny their Hellenistic heritage and those Jews who take their faith seriously cannot accept the term either. As mentioned in *The Moses Legacy* one Jewish author, Stephen Feldman, has even branded it as an "anti-Semitic lie" in his book, *Please don't wish me a Merry Christmas*. There can be no understanding between people of different religions unless we are totally honest with each other and not only stress the similarities but also don't shy away from the fundamental differences. Except for members of some small splinter groups, the Jewish people will continue to resist efforts for their conversion. A crucified Messiah could not be accepted two thousand years ago and there is no reason to do so now. But if the Church were to give up the resurrection story what would be left of the faith? This is the dilemma both the Christian and the Jewish religions face when they talk about the Judeo-Christian heritage. Something has to give: it's either Moses' Law or Jesus.

It may now be argued that we share the Ten Commandments. Do we really? The preamble in Exodus 20:2, which tends to be ignored, defines who is talking. "I am the Lord *thy* [emphasis added] God, who brought thee out of the land of Egypt, out of the house of bondage." This identifies Him as a local deity for a specific nation. Christians like to start with number 3, "Thou shalt have no other gods before me," and feel secure in the belief that Jesus as one person of the indissoluble Trinity is thereby acceptable. For Jews as well as Muslims this assumption is invalid and cannot be condoned. The worship of Jesus as God falls under idol worship and blasphemy which are expressly forbidden in commandments 2 and 3. The commandments 5-10, starting with honoring one's parents and ending with the admonition not to covet, are common property of all civilizations and neither specific for Judaism nor Christianity. The only other specific commandment is number 4 to keep the Sabbath holy. This one has been adopted by Christians as well as Muslims, albeit on different days.

The Catholic Church, in which I grew up, realized at that time the essential philosophic difference between the Old Testament and the New. We had no contact during religion classes with the Old Testament because that was the preserve of the heretical Protestants of whom there were few in Austria. Recently I found in my library the *Gebet- und Gesangbuch für die katholische Jugend der Erzdiözese Wien* (Prayer and Songbook for the Catholic youth of the Archdiocese of Vienna), which was to guide the student's life. When I read it I was vastly impressed with the difference between the "Old Testament," which I had read later in life, and the "New". There is no reference to "enemy" or "hate" in that little book and when Moses is mentioned at all, it is in the context of liberation from bondage, gratitude and blessedness. The centerpiece is Jesus: his example of having given his life for us out of pure love; how to endure suffering, and the help he provides to those who follow his teachings in their daily lives. In addition the child is exposed to a healthy dose of, what has been called in this country, "Catholic guilt" for the sins committed in everyday life. These include: being sassy, not paying enough attention to parents and teachers, lying, stealing, cheating, being lazy, not praying twice a day and not going regularly to Mass and confession. While excessive guilt is to be deplored so is its absence which we find so abundantly in our current day and age. The feeling of guilt for one's trespass can trigger remorse and the intent of acting better in the future. Yet, the words "conscience" and "shame" are hardly heard any more in popular culture.

Since Vatican II the Catholic Church has made efforts to atone for past persecutions of Jews but the difference between Catholic and Protestant countries is still noticeable. While hotel rooms in the U.S. tend to provide weary travelers with a Bible in their night tables, in Catholic countries such as Quebec or Latin America, one still finds mainly the New Testament in English as well as French or Spanish as the case may be. In Switzerland and Austria it is trilingual with the inclusion of German. This is not a rejection of "God's word" but simply recognition of the differences in philosophical outlook between the two texts. Should we be dominated by the Old Testament legacy of fear, hate and revenge towards others, or the New One which orders us to strive for forgiveness and good will, if not love, towards all rather than only members of one's ethnic group or religion? This is the question for our age which we need to ask ourselves.

It is obvious that the Christian ideal as laid out above has foundered on the shoals of human nature. The Catholic Church was not content with representing the kingdom of Heaven as a spiritual domain but aspired to worldly power and modeled itself after authoritarian terrestrial kingdoms. There was an emperor who commanded princes, dukes, etc., to whom the populace owed obedience. For the Catholic Church the emperor was the Triune God; below Him was the Pope, the cardinals, bishops, and so on. Caesar had to be obeyed and so had to be the Pope. As long as the Pope and the emperor respected each others' turf some degree of harmony was present. But power struggles were unavoidable leading to wars also over the extent of the Papal States in Italy. This was the state of affairs, as well as rampant venality by members of the clergy, which Dante so eloquently condemned in his *Divina Commedia*. Reformation was urgently necessary but no one listened to his warnings. It took another more than 200 years before Luther nailed his 95 Theses on the door of the Wittenberg church which unleashed the Reformation. This split in Christendom had been avoidable if the ecclesiastical powers had shown more concern for the wellbeing of their flocks rather than for their own material gain.

But the Protestants in their search for truth and purity also had a problem. It was easy to abolish the authority of the Pope and his hierarchy but what was to take the place of authoritative teaching? The answer was to declare the Bible i.e., Old and New Testament as the inerrant word of God. All of it, without exception, was God's word and had to be obeyed. This stance, while necessary to save the faith, produced numerous splinter groups within Protestantism and the "Body of Christ" became hopelessly fractured. It was the problem, which had been posed originally by the Gnostics, as to the "true" interpretation of Christian doctrine, which has returned with a vengeance and new denominations are still springing up, with each one declaring itself as the possessor of the final truth. This, obviously, engenders strife and Jesus now gets figuratively crucified over and over again because love of neighbor, let alone the enemy, is nowhere in sight.

Luther thought that by eliminating the Pope and embracing the Old Testament, the Jews would flock to his Reformed Church, but he was sorely disappointed. When they did not accept the role Luther had envisioned for them, the well known anti-Jewish diatribes were the result. Luther's experience had actually been foreshadowed by that of Muhammad not quite a thousand years earlier. He had likewise originally assumed that the Jews of Arabia would receive the Koran with gladness, but when they not only remained steadfast in their belief system, but actually sided with his enemies during the siege of Medina, verses with anti-Jewish content were added.

Christians, regardless of denomination, will have to face another fundamental fact about Judaism which I have more fully discussed in *The Moses Legacy*. While Christianity was intended as a religion for the nations of the world, Judaism never regarded itself as merely a religion. It represented a system of laws designed to build an enduring nation. The nation might intermittently be forced to reside in exile but, by following the precepts of the Torah, it would continue wherever its people might be found at any given time in history. Thus the Law, which St. Paul fought so valiantly against, is the cornerstone and cannot be abrogated lest the nation disappears. The sooner Christians, of all denominations, realize that observant Jews will never be able to accept the Christian belief system the better off all of us will be. We will have to learn to respect each other on our separate turfs rather than striving for an unattainable amalgamation. To paraphrase the gospel, "leave to the Jews what belongs to the Jews, and leave to Jesus what belongs to Jesus."

Let us now make a detour and go back to the Multiple Choice Test as laid out in the Introduction. As far as choice a) is concerned an effort should be made to discourage the use of Jesus' name as an expletive especially in movies and on TV shows. It is offensive to Christians who take their faith seriously and serves no purpose. It may come as a surprise but choice b) "a prophet of God" was taken from the Koran and reflects Muslim belief. Choice c) is endorsed by individuals who have been reared on popular culture and in their busy lives have not yet had the opportunity to clarify for themselves why they hold this opinion. Choice d) "a dangerous false prophet" is problematic, requires more discussion, and is the reason for this detour. The words were taken from the website www.noahide.com which represents the views of a growing subgroup of orthodox Jews. Christians, especially those of the Evangelical persuasion, would be well advised to visit the site. It provides, "A Comparison of Judaism and Christianity," explains "Who is the Son of G-d" and, "Who was Jesus?" It is true that only a minority of Jews subscribe to the tenets of the "Lubavitchers," but it is equally true that among orthodox Jews they represent an increasingly influential segment.

We hear a great deal about the intolerance which is taught in Muslim religious schools but I have yet to find concern expressed about what is taught to the children of the disciples of the late Lubavitcher Rebbe Menachem Mendel Schneerson and in other yeshivas. I am raising this question because on March 5, 1991, Congress passed Public Law 102-14, H.J. Res 104 (available on the

Internet) which honored the Rabbi at his ninetieth birthday for his "educational efforts." Our Christian law-makers obviously had no idea what the Rebbe really taught and what his organization stood for. They would probably have been exceedingly surprised had they been told that the Rebbe's program included the abolition of all religions apart from Judaism. This is a typical example of what can happen when one talks glibly about the Judeo-Christian tradition. The example also shows that Fundamentalism, regardless whether it is of the Jewish, Christian or Muslim variety, cannot be expected to lead to an accommodation between religions and people.

There is an additional problem which Christians should face squarely and be able to explain to others. That is the cross as the symbol of Christianity. Its potential divisiveness should never be underestimated. How can a symbol which depicts a man hanging in agony from a cross be anything but repellent to non-Christians? Even The Church of Jesus Christ of Latter Day Saints (Mormons) does not use it. For Jews there is the additional complication of the Christian charge that they killed Jesus and are now condemned by God on account of it. The accusation has recently been withdrawn, but the idea somehow lingers on and has to create mixed feelings, to say the least. I am sure that there was a good reason why the Church fathers adopted this symbol but I have not yet come across it. My personal opinion is that it may have come from Egypt where the early Church was prominent and where the *ankh* had always been the symbol for life. What would be more natural than to condense the oval above the crossbar into the upright beam? While an Egyptian provenance may or may not be the correct interpretation for the Christian cross *per se* we still have to ask ourselves why a display of a tortured human being should have been chosen to propagate the "good news?"

I never thought much about it and mindlessly wandered by the numerous crucifixes which I saw in my life. They are especially prominent in Austria where practically every little path through fields is graced by a "*Marterl,*" a little shrine which depicts Jesus' agony. In addition a crucifix was displayed in every classroom at school before Hitler had it removed when he annexed the country. But a few years ago, while I sat in Bishop Niederauer's antechamber waiting to have a meeting with him, I looked at the ubiquitous crucifix and the thought hit me, "does he [the Bishop] know that this is the symbol which illustrates Gautama's first noble truth?" I did not ask the Bishop because it would have been pointless but the insight was correct. The world is indeed full of suffering and mankind keeps crucifying itself on a daily basis. All we have to do is to open a newspaper or watch TV to know that this is a fact. As such it is quite appropriate that we should be reminded not only that suffering is ubiquitous but that we should use our best efforts to prevent disasters and mitigate their effects instead of creating new ones.

Although suffering is inevitable it does not need to be meaningless, it can ennoble the soul. An example was provided by one of my professors, Viktor Frankl, whom I have discussed in *War & Mayhem* and on my website. For being a Jew he was sent to a number of concentration camps, including Auschwitz, but was able to return to Vienna in the summer of 1945. Not only had he retained his soul intact by not succumbing to hate or thoughts of revenge, in spite of having lost his wife and family, but he had acquired authenticity for the books he wrote thereafter. While Frankl helped me in my personal search for meaning, I also came to appreciate Goethe's words, which when slightly abbreviated read, *"Wer nie sein Brot mit Tränen asz, wer nie durchwachte schlaflose Nächte, der kennt euch nicht ihr himmlischen Mächte."* Who never with bitter tears his bread did eat, condemned to many a sleepless night, awareness lacks of heaven's might. This is true, and there was an occasion in my life when during sleepless nights tears flowed freely in desperation. But then came the liberating thought, "tears are sperm for the soul." They certainly can be, but one needs to recognize them as such rather than just bewail one's misery.

When we are confronted with all the anguish which exists in our world we can justifiably ask what is our purpose in the midst of all these afflictions? To eat, drink, be merry and propagate is not enough for some of us, and for our sex-crazed culture a paraphrase of Schiller's words comes to mind, *"Wollust ward dem Wurm gegeben, doch der Cherub steht vor Gott."* Orgasm was granted even to the worm but the Cherub stands in the face of God. The verse occurs in his *Ode to Joy* and I took the liberty to add the word "even" and change the original word *und* to *doch*. It is useless to argue over the purpose of this world or the universe but we can endow each one of our actions with a purpose and no one can hinder us from doing so. We have free will, not unlimited but, as statisticians tell us, there are "degrees of freedom." We do not have total control over our lives, the only control we do have, as the sages of the past have pointed out, is over our minds and, therefore, our attitude towards misfortune. This control we should exercise with utmost effort and it will let us rise above our bodies, their frailties and passions which we share with animals, so that we may be of benefit to others who are less fortunate.

In this context we need to recognize that we live in two worlds, or more precisely in two states of consciousness. One is the eyes open condition where we interact with the world around us, and the other the eyes closed condition in which we are alone with our thoughts, visions and dreams. Our materialistic society tends to disregard the eyes closed condition as being irrelevant, yet it shapes our basic world view and thereby our conduct which then becomes reality for others. This internal world is especially important when we close our eyes for the last time. During the process of dying we are on our own and become either a powerless toy of our brains, which conjure up desirable or undesirable visions, or we can call and rely upon the mercy of God. "*Quid sum miser dunc dicturus? Quem patronum rogaturus? Cum vix justus sit securus,*" we hear in the Catholic Requiem Mass. Standing alone before the judge: "What shall I poor soul say then? To whom can I appeal, when even the just person is hardly safe?" Since we are likely to die as we have lived, our habitual daily conduct may well come to the fore in our final visions when words have ceased, as has been pointed out in the chapter on St. Mark.

Can these be shaped while we still have will power? Possibly, because our brains are programmed to learn, and remarkably enough the previously mentioned *Tibetan Book of the Dead or The After-Death Experiences on the Bardo Plane*, provides a clue. The Tibetan title of the book is *Bardo Thödol* or *Liberation by Hearing* and is the corollary of the Catholic Requiem Mass. Its main message is, however, not only for the deceased, or the relatives, but for the living so that we may die properly. As one of the quotes prior to the Preface states, "Against his will he dies who has not learned to die. Learn to die and you shall learn to live, for there shall none learn to live who has not learned to die." The message of the book is the Christian "fear not," but it is predicated not on divine intervention but on the statement that all the visions of heaven and hell, which are experienced by the deceased (for which I would prefer to substitute the words "dying person"), are not external events. They are purely products of the person's own consciousness and have no objective reality.

According to this text, the soul which, through lack of concentration, has been unable to remain in the primordial light, which dawns after the last exhalation, will eventually be reborn. If this birth were to be in the human world, it will see two people having sexual intercourse and an ardent desire will arise. If one is to be reborn as a female, attraction for the male and aversion towards the female partner will be experienced, and vice versa in the case of being born as a male. Anyone who is familiar with the rudiments of psychoanalytic ideas will immediately recognize that Freud's Oedipus complex is prefigured here. But this is not the point. For the Buddhist, rebirth has to be avoided because it leads to further suffering regardless of what station in life one is born into, and the way to "close the womb door," as it is referred to, is by reciting to oneself, "Henceforth I will never act through attraction and repulsion." With other words I shall not be swayed by a desire merely to reject it immediately afterwards but yield to it later or to another one.

As a neurologist I was fascinated by this statement because our nervous systems are electrochemical machines which function precisely on the principle of attraction and repulsion. All of our sensations and movements are based on electrochemical laws where opposites attract and likeness repels. This was the puzzle the neurophysiologist in me was confronted with. Since our physical bodies act on the principle of attraction and repulsion how can we do otherwise? What other force exists beyond electrochemistry which controls us? I wondered. The answer is radiation, and this is what makes Jesus and the ancient Buddhists so relevant for us today. "Make of yourself a light," Gautama had said and Jesus told his disciples, "You are the light of the world [Mt.5:14]." And what is this light which gives, and gives, and does not ask for anything in return? *Agápe* - Love!

It is the recognition of having a choice which distinguishes us from the rest of the animal kingdom. We can act on the passions of electrochemistry which make us desire something but immediately reject it for something we regard as better; or we can act on the principle of radiation which does not concern itself with opposites but like the sun, dispenses its warmth to everyone. As Gautama said to his disciples: "The monk radiates loving compassion in one direction, then the second direction, then the third direction, then the fourth direction, likewise to above and below; recognizing himself in all there is, he radiates throughout the world with a loving mind cleared from wrath and defiance." This is the goal but it requires diligent practice because it does not come naturally to human beings.

It may now be asked: why has objective truth, as obtained through scientific work, not been mentioned at all? The question is legitimate and important because it is widely assumed at this time that science can lead us to ultimate objective truth and we do not need to rely on opinions bolstered by faith. Unfortunately, this is also an erroneous assumption.

Science has limits which must be taken into account. It deals with measurable quantities, can only reveal what our senses, aided by instruments, show and the results depend on the question asked. As such a given result is reproducible and, therefore, valid only for the conditions under which it was obtained and all resulting generalizations must be regarded as a theory or hypothesis rather than enduring fact. Furthermore, scientific studies can only answer questions which deal with "how things happen," but are inapplicable when it comes to "why this is the case." These limitations have not yet been properly recognized especially in the United States where the European scientific optimism of the 1850s still rules.

In 1872 Emil Du-Bois Reymond, who is now honored as the father of electrophysiology as we know it today, gave a lecture in

THE JESUS CONUNDRUM

Leipzig, *"Über die Grenzen der Naturerkenntnis"* - On the Limits of Natural Science. It is available on the Internet and well worth reading. In it he referred to a statement, expressed by Vogt in the 1850s that all mental activities are merely functions of the brain. "To put it crudely, thoughts stand in the same relationship to the brain as bile to the liver, or urine to the kidneys." Du-Bois Reymond rejected this thesis as unwarranted because even in regard to some of the most essential aspects of the material body we have to admit to ignorance, *"ignoramus."* While this statement would have been accepted by the audience his final conclusion created uproar and he was severely criticized by the powers of the era. Because of its importance for our time I shall translate the last paragraph of his speech here:

> "In the face of the riddles the physical world presents us with, the natural scientist has for quite some time been accustomed to state with stoic resignation [*maennlicher Entsagung*] his '*ignoramus*'. But looking back upon victorious past achievements he harbors the silent awareness, that what he does not know at present, he may under certain circumstances perhaps come to know in the future. But in regard to the riddle of what is matter and what is energy [*Materie und Kraft*] and how they are able to think he has to admit to himself the much more difficult truth: '*Ignorabimus*.'"

For 21st century Americans *"ignoramus,"* we don't know, is still a reality and acceptable, but an *"ignorabimus,"* we will not know, even in the future, is also still intolerable. The progress the biological sciences have made since that day in Leipzig will be proudly pointed to. Infectious diseases have largely been eradicated and are for the most part treatable. The human genome has been deciphered, animals have been cloned and only ethical considerations prevent human cloning. Stem-cells can be implanted with the hope of repairing damaged tissues and the life-span of human beings has been significantly expanded. So what should stand in the way of solving the remaining riddles?

The answer is: Reality. We are playing god and in our ignorance we are unaware of the problems we create in so doing. For instance in the field of genetics we are playing pool. The idea that gene splicing will eradicate a given disease is based on the assumption that a particular gene controls a particular function, which is erroneous. Genes are multifunctional and by influencing one process we interfere with several others of which we are unaware. We may well create cancers and other illnesses which don't exist at present. I am not saying "stop medical research," all I am trying to convey is: proceed cautiously with prudence and don't get carried away by pride.

Apart from advances in the biological sciences the progress in the field of physics will also be pointed to. We have, after all, split the atom and are now busy splitting it further, which will supposedly tell us how the universe came into being. This is another assumption and strictly "faith-based." The split atom gave us the bomb and we have no idea how to put that genie back into the bottle before it destroys us. But the split atom also presented us with an additional problem, quantum physics, which the average citizen is quite unaware of and atomic physicists are scratching their heads over. I encourage you to type "quantum physics" into Google and the results will astonish you: all the rules we are used to in our world no longer apply in that realm.

Professor Bernard d'Espagnat, a highly respected authority in this field, has published a book in 2006 which he entitled, "*On* Physics *and* Philosophy." In the Preface he stated "Trying to understand what contemporary physics is truly about unavoidably raises philosophical problems," and in the book he presents us with various aspects of "reality" or "realism." The one which he endorsed and intrigued me most was "the veiled reality hypothesis." I do not pretend to understand the book in detail, lacking the necessary foundation, but "veiled reality" struck a chord because it obviously harks back to the B.C. era and the veiled statue of Isis in Sais.

It should, therefore, be obvious that not only are science and philosophy not in conflict but on the contrary philosophical outlook determines which scientific endeavors we pursue in what manner. The current philosophy is that by separating aspects of matter into ever smaller parts we will come to that part which somehow explains the whole. While this process can work on the descriptive level, where we give ever increasing names to the parts we seem to find, the analytic way then requires synthesis either in thought or action to produce some intended result. This will, however, indeed be "synthetic" i.e., man-made, a replica, which has uses but cannot be taken for the original.

Goethe foresaw this process and has Mephisto say:

"Wer will was Lebendiges erkennen und beschreiben,
Sucht erst den Geist heraus zu treiben,
Dann hat er Teile in der Hand,
Fehlt leider! nur das geistige Band.
Encheiresin naturae nennt's die Chemie,
Spottet ihrer selbst und weiss nicht wie."

One might paraphrase this stanza as follows. Whoever wants to understand and describe a living entity attempts first of all to drive out its spirit. He then has the parts in his hand but alas what's missing is the band which held it together in the first place. This lack is excused by referring to nature's "handiwork" (my approximate rendering of *encheiresin*) thereby mocking ones efforts by not realizing what one has actually done.

Goethe was intensely interested in the progress the sciences had made during his long life, but he sincerely doubted that the analytic way in which the questions were pursued would lead to final answers. About three months before his death in 1832 he told a friend that we have to admit to ourselves that the question how nature creates and promotes life, presents us with an unsolvable mystery. In another lecture, 48 years later, Du-Bois Reymond listed the question in regard to the origin of mental abilities as one of the Seven Riddles of the World, and today we hardly discuss it anymore in respectable scientific circles.

The fundamental problem of elucidating, by modern scientific efforts, what awareness, or consciousness, is was formulated by Du-Bois Reymond as, "a statement that awareness can be explained on basis of mechanics needs to be denied, but a statement that awareness depends upon mechanics is undoubtedly correct." With other words our brains, acting on mechanical electrochemical principles, are required for awareness and the content will be shaped by its state in health and disease but that does not mean that mechanical principles, therefore, explain the origin of awareness. He quoted Leibniz for further explanation:

> One is forced to admit that awareness (*Wahrnehmung*) and everything that depends upon it cannot be explained on a mechanical basis; that is through objects and movement. Let one imagine a machine which is so constructed that it produces thought, feeling and awareness. Let us now magnify it to an extent that one can enter into it like a mill. Under these circumstances one would find in its interior nothing else but parts, which push at each other but never anything from which one could explain awareness.

While thinking about this problem, and before having read the Leibniz analogy, another one had occurred to me. Imagine that a UFO from outer space abducts a car from a street and brings it back to its planet where such contraptions have never existed. The scientists and engineers of that planet would then take it apart piece by piece, examine the parts in detail put them together in various combinations but they still would not have the faintest idea how that piece of machinery functioned and what its purpose was.

Another possibly even more relevant analogy might be with the TV set which sits in our living rooms. It receives programs which fill unseen and unheard the ether but when we tune the set to some channel we will receive intelligible sounds and pictures. Depending upon the quality of the set, and how much we want to pay, we can be satisfied with what the local stations produce or we can expand our view via cable or satellite. The informational content a given person receives and upon which he bases his life's view and actions will, therefore, depend on the extent and quality of the programs available to him. But our brain is not only a passive recipient, as the TV set, but also a TV studio which can, to some extent, do its own programming and replay the information it has received in various combinations, especially during dreams. Nevertheless, the fundamental fact remains that input from an external source comes first and it is entirely conceivable that some of us have the ability to receive information from a cosmic channel that is not available to the rest of us. When one considers the implications of all of the foregoing we must conclude that the pursuit of science is likewise based on an underlying faith and as such religious faith based on esoteric information need not necessarily be ridiculed.

So, how can we answer the question which headlines this chapter? First of all let me re-iterate that absolute Truth is a concept rather than an objective fact. It is a word and words are symbols which represent a conceived reality. These conceptions will differ among people and universal agreement will not be achievable. Under these circumstances the important aspect is that we should become more modest and concentrate instead on truthful human interactions. It matters less what a person says, the yardstick should be conduct; regardless of professed motive. "The way to hell is paved with good intentions," says an English proverb and Mephisto's self definition in *Faust* is, "*Ich bin ein Teil von jener Kraft die stets das Boese will und doch das Gute schafft;*" "I am one part of that force which always desires evil yet creates good."

Instead of debating abstract nouns such as Truth and spin mental images we can be more practical in interpersonal relationships. What really matters is honest conduct in our dealings with each other. If we were to regard ourselves as always standing before the judge who demands of us: "the truth, the whole truth and nothing but the truth," we can adjust our actions accordingly. We know experiential truth but frequently find it too unpalatable to admit to. This is why we tend to take the easy way out and use various ways to shade it, thereby deceiving ourselves as well as others. From my personal life I have concluded that the truth is also that which tends to hurt the most to admit to. But once one has reached this realization there is also help in the New Testament as well as the Buddhist injunction "Fear not!" Once the truth as you know it is out in the open you can deal with it; as long as it remains hidden it will fester and the lies will multiply.

The question now arises, should the truth, as one knows it, always be told or is there room for the "kind" lie? It may be argued that in some instances the truth is so terrible that it should not be communicated because it will create harm. I don't believe this to be the case because the truth, difficult to accept as it may be, can be presented in a kind and constructive manner. This is the time when the Buddhists' "Right Speech" becomes paramount. The question should not be whether or not the truth should be told but only in what manner. When we are confronted with a difficult decision, as physicians frequently are, whether or not to tell another human being a highly unpleasant truth we should regard it as similar to medication. It should be presented in the right amount at the right time. I believe that all lies and even exaggerations are harmful. Lies result from fear and exaggerations from pride. These are emotions that ought to be shunned and even so-called harmless lies are likely to spawn others in a never ending cycle.

There still remains the question how to know whether written statements are true or false. In contemporary events one has the opportunity to check the sources of the statements and when these are carefully evaluated a reasonable opinion can be rendered. But best of all there is the test of time. If we read something that was written fifty, one hundred, several hundred, one thousand or several thousand years ago, as for instance in some of the sources mentioned in this book, or in Egyptian Wisdom Literature, and we can say unreservedly "Yes" to it, then we have found a truth upon which we can conduct our lives. The hallmark of truth is that it is eternal. Her devotees transcend time and space; they are found in all cultures, proclaiming what is right, regardless of contemporary circumstances and are willing to courageously defy societal norms for her sake.

This also pertains to esoteric truth. Although it can be shared only partially with others, to categorically deny its existence is inappropriate. As mentioned, all our factual truths are strictly dependent on what our sense receptors allow us to know at a given stage of our lives. But evolution of the human race has not necessarily stopped and mankind may develop additional receptors which will convey information about cosmic spiritual processes. This is Dr. Bucke's thesis in his previously mentioned book on *Cosmic Consciousness*. Certain individuals throughout human history, including Jesus, had these receptors, or the Third Eye, as it is referred to in Indian literature, and they have been the guideposts for humanity. But since all the rest of us still lack it we misunderstand the message or declare it as nonsensical, which is unwarranted.

All of these aspects need to be taken into account when we assess "gospel truth." As has been made clear there is not one gospel but different writers have put forth different ideas about Jesus and his message. Some of them were found to be acceptable for the needs of the moment, during the first three centuries, while others were regarded as harmful banned and burned. In this respect the Christian Church behaved no differently from the Jewish authorities against whom Jesus had fought his, we must admit, losing battle. But God has seen fit, to resurrect his spirit and it is our task to truthfully represent it, without being encumbered by any ulterior motive.

We also need to realize the essential difference between our mechanistic thinking and how nature really operates. The fact that the organic world differs fundamentally from the inorganic is not being taken into account. In the vegetable kingdom the seed makes roots, which gain strength from the moist earth, then raise a stem above it which, with the help of the sun, eventually turns into a trunk with branches and leaves as well as new seeds. But at every stage of development it remains an organic whole. If we take, for instance, the seed apart, put it's components under the most elaborate microscope, in the hope of learning how the tree comes about we will not succeed.

The same applies, of course, to the development of human beings. The sperm and its DNA is just that, an entity. It meets an egg with its DNA, which is another entity. The two mate, become a "fertilized egg," a different entity with different potential than the single cells which were responsible for it. From it develops the embryo, the baby, the child and eventually the adult. But during any of these stages we are not dealing with parts which are added, instead there is a constant unfolding of latent potentialities which can be fostered, harmed or destroyed by the environment in which the developing organism finds itself.

Another aspect is the non-recognition that nature is not only cruel, in the sense that big fish do eat little fish, but that there is also a tremendous amount of cooperation and interdependence. This applies not only within species but across species. What is bad for one is good for another, as the simple example of respiration shows. Without trees we couldn't live because they produce the oxygen we need and we give them our carbon dioxide in return. This is so rudimentary that it would hardly be worth talking about if the survival of the fittest idea and "subduing" nature were not so deeply ingrained in our behavior that we don't think about it and this extends to political life. Although lip service is paid to "consensus building," the attempt by one faction to dominate the other persists.

When we extend "organic" thinking also to the realm of religion, aspects which cannot be understood mechanistically, can also become accessible to rational thought as shown in the Conclusions of this book.

CONCLUSIONS

Our society has again arrived at a crossroads. It did not need the gift of prophecy for Jesus to predict that Jerusalem would be destroyed if the Jews were to persist in their rebellious behavior against Rome. At the present time it is equally obvious that we may be heading towards WWIII unless we change course. The 2009 US defense budget was in excess of $700 billion and amounted to 48 per cent of that of the rest of the world and when one adds the contributions of our Allies it came to 72 percent of the world's total. We spent 5.8 times more than China, 10.2 times more than Russia, and 98.6 times more than Iran. These figures come from government sources and are readily available on the Internet.

The consequences rational human beings should draw from these facts are obvious. What are we going to do with all these armaments? They canot bring peace and do not even enhance our physical security because other countries will not let themselves be intimidated or dominated by us for any length of time. As such our materialistic-technologic society is heading for catastrophe. This is the course we are pursuing and has to be recognized with its full implications.

To avoid this looming disaster a change in philosophical outlook on life would need to take place and remarkably enough, a sentence from the gospel of John, which I have mentioned earlier, provides an insight. When paraphrased it says, "The Law was given by Moses, but Christ brought *cháris* and *alētheia*." I am deliberately using the Greek words because an English translation diminishes their value. *Cháris* is not just charity or grace, but it is that spontaneous outpouring of good will which has no hidden purpose, wants absolutely nothing in return and evokes in the recipient joy and gratitude. *Alētheia* has been extensively discussed in the last chapter. It does not necessarily refer to the absolute truth which supposedly governs the universe but to that experiential truth of daily life, honesty, which human beings can distinguish from a deliberate lie or other deceptions.

When we look at today's world from this point of view we must conclude that, up to now, in the struggle for our minds and souls, Moses has won and Jesus has failed. Our society relies on laws and these have to be obeyed out of fear from adverse consequences. "Thou shalt fear the Lord thy God" is the commandment repeated throughout the Old Testament and especially in Deuteronomy. That the Lord has been replaced by the State does not change the basic situation. There is no need to belabor the fundamental differences between Judaism and Christianity because they have been dealt with in previous chapters and in *The Moses Legacy*, which can be downloaded free of charge from my website on the Internet. The point to be made here is that the philosophy which undergirds the Old Testament is indeed the one which governs our society today. We are ruled by fear and Jesus' teachings are not heeded. This is, of course, not surprsing because a doctrine based on fear, hate, and cohesion of the tribe is much more congenial to human nature than one which demands selflessness and puts the needs of others above those of one's own.

Yet, it is important to realize that the Old Testament commandments, as applied today by chauvinistic Zionists in Israel, are about to create havoc for all of us. America has committed itself to the defense of the State of Israel, regardless of its policies towards some of its own people and its neighbors. This is the direct result of the identification by many of our citizens with the Old Testament rather than the New. But most of the unquestioning supporters of the State of Israel have not even read the Torah (Pentateuch, Five Books of Moses) properly and would, therefore, be astonished by its political content.

Chapter 7 of Deuteronomy should be required reading; not from a Christian point of view that sees itself as the "New Israel," but in the literal sense that is today enacted by Jewish settlers in the Holy

Land. The chapter should be read in toto but two verses suffice to illustrate the problem:

> And when the Lord thy God shall deliver them [the inhabitants of Canaan] up before thee, and thou shalt smite them; then thou shalt utterly destroy them; thou shalt make no covenant with them, nor show mercy upon them [Deut. 7:2].
>
> But thus shall ye deal with them: ye shall break down their altars, and dash in pieces their pillars, and hew down their asherim, and burn their graven images with fire. [Deut. 7:5]

These sentences were taken from the *Soncino Chumash* and as such represent authentic translations from the Hebrew. When one reads this it is clear why the Arab-Israeli "peace process" has not yielded concrete results. It is literally against the Jewish religion.

Hamas is regarded unacceptable as a negotiating partner because its charter does not recognize the legitimacy of the State of Israel; yet Israel's sacred charter, the Torah—the State does not have a Constitution—does not allow for the presence of any other people in the land but Jews. Under these circumstances we have to ask ourselves: How long will that segment of Israeli society that has been reared on the Torah, and regards it as God's word that has to be obeyed, be able to tolerate a Jerusalem skyline which is dominated by the Dome of the Rock and the Al Aqsa mosque, before some fanatics violate them? But even if these sacred structures were to remain intact how long are the Palestinians expected to live under a repressive occupation? These are aspects which we Americans ignore at our peril, and which make a meaningful, sincere agreement between Zionism and the non-Jewish population of Palestine so difficult. As long as Americans aid and abet chauvinistic Zionism we are co-responsible for the evils which convulse this unfortunate land at present and will do so in the future.

The irony of our current situation is that we are supporting a secular regime in Israel, which bases its claim to the land on an ancient religious promise. God has promised us this land say the religious, yet "God is dead" has been proclaimed since the beginning of the so-called "Enlightenment," and a separation of Church and State is the law in Western democracies. The consequences for the Jewish State are predictable because it is becoming increasingly apparent that its days are numbered unless a radical course change were to take place. If the current policies are continued where lip service is payed to Peace, but the possibility of enactment undermined, no good can come. Time is not on the side of the Jewish State because the very idea is anachronistic and the population dynamics are heading towards Muslims. The only question is whether we and Israel's leadership will recognize the anachronism of the Zionist idea and work on an accommodation, which takes the rights of all of Palestine's people into account, or continue on the militant course which has leveled Jerusalem three times in the past. The Middle East was the birthplace of our culture, it may now become the cause of its demise.

In order to avoid this catatrophe a truly new spirit in the leadership of the U.S. would be required which goes beyond what our politicians are currently able to provide. I am emphasizing the U.S.A. because we are the only country, apart from Israel, which keeps the Zionist dream alive and are supporting it regardless of the consequences. Thus, a change in mental outlook will not occur in Israel unless America takes the lead. The responsibility clearly lies, however, to a large extent with the Jewish American community because when Gentiles point out the problems which the policies the State of Israel are creating for the world, they are defamed as anti-Semites and nothing can be achieved. Before "hearts and minds" can be changed abroad we have to start right here at home and that will require a truthful public assessment of what the various factions which make up "the American people," and their respective spokespersons, really stand for. Whether or not our media, upon whom this responsibility falls, will be able to take up this task is, of course, another question.

Apart from the challenges the Middle East presents us with, there is an additional one which Science, the new god, will be unable to solve. The unbridled optimism of the past three centuries in regard to material progress, as discussed in the previous chapter, has led to great technologic advances and, in some parts of the world, greater prosperity, but this is beginning to unravel even in the US. Greed, the ancient evil, is now threatening the foundations of capitalism and thereby America's birthright, "the pursuit of happiness." Nobel prize winners in economics are scratching their heads and cannot come to an agreement as to the best course to pursue under dramatically changed circumstances. Therefore, the time is right for some soul searching.

As mentioned, the Enlightenment has brought the "God is dead" thesis in its wake which neglected, however, a remarkable property of the Deity. We can kill Him but He refuses to stay dead! That was the lesson not merely from the New Testament but even from the Soviet Union. For more than seventy years atheism officially ruled, but God could not be eliminated from its hard-working, suffering people. As such, the real question should not be, "Is there a God?" but "What does this word mean for us?"

At this point we also have to address the question: Can Man live without God? Obviously, the answer will depend upon what we mean by "God." I shall, therefore, be more specific because there is no unanimity on the concept. But before doing so let me digress for a moment to a personal experience. During my training at the Mayo Clinic I was invited to a Sunday Service at the Rochester Unitarian Church which many of the senior staff physicians were members of. The wife of one of them gave a presentation and the words which riveted my attention were about "the spying eye of God" which she abhorred. As a Viennese Catholic where the "eye of God" not only adorns churches but is also the name of a well known restaurant, this viewpoint was entirely foreign. I had always regarded the "eye of God," which in all probablity is of Egyptian provencance as the eye of Horus as well as *Maat*, as the symbol for a power which watches over all my steps so that I don't make any fatal mistakes. For me it was benevolent while apparently for others it is regarded as a hostile intrusion into one's private realm. My immediate reaction was: what is she so ashamed of that she needs to hide?

The Lady was not alone in her interpretation because it was also that of one of the most prominent atheists, Friedrich Nietzsche. This is not the place to discuss the merits of his philosophy and the illness which in part was responsible for some of its aspects. The point is that if one only reads his books a wrong impression will be gained. To obtain an insight into this profoundly unhappy soul one also needs to study his letters. In August of 1886, somewhat more than two years prior to his mental collapse, he wrote to his most devoted friend Franz Overbeck:

> Oh, if I only could give you an inkling of my sense of lonesomeness. There is no one, neither among the living nor among the dead, with whom I feel any sense of kinship. This is indescribably dreadful; only the training in tolerating this sentiment, and its stepwise development since childhood, allow me to understand why I haven't succumbed to it yet.

This utter sense of abandonment is terrible and tragic. The scion of a long line of Protestant pastors had called out to God with all his soul in his adolescence and early adulthood. When he was met only by silence and after he had read Schopenhauer and Strauss, he not only turned his back on Christianity but attacked it with ever increasing virulence. His overt mental collapse was the result of organic brain disease and herewith enters again the irony of history. The proud "Antichrist" who had defied God and the world, who had codemned compassion as weakness and decadence, was rendered as helpless as a small child. Only the unstinting, selfless, loving care of his pious Christian mother allowed for his prolonged survival from an invariably fatal llness. This tragic fate in turn contributed in no small measure to his subsequent world-wide fame.

Another aspect, which comes through loud and clear in his letters is that he didn't even fully believe everything he himself had written and was astounded when he re-read some of the material. The books he wrote in the summer and fall of 1888 and which are the most vituperative ones, were the result of a manic phase of his illness. The first physician who had been asked by Nietzsche's sister to evaluate her brother's illness for the general public, P. J. Möbius, concluded his assessment in 1904 with this warning:

> People read Nietzsche's works but they do not do so with discernment, by only keeping the best. Instead they take those aspects which please them as single pieces, in the assumption that the reason for them is contained in the

whole. They are confirmed in this belief by a number of male and female litterati who glorify the great philosopher en bloc and assure the public that these single pearls are connected by an invisible string. But who is capable to render such a judgment? At maximum one among a hundred readers. To those other ninety-nine one has to say: If you find pearls, do not assume that you are dealing with a string of pearls. Be suspicious because this man suffers from brain disease.

Needless to say Elisabeth, Nietzsche's sister, was greatly disturbed by this unexpected verdict and she tried to suppress and/or invalidate it. But in my opinion Möbius was correct. His warning was not heeded; some of Nietzsche's most radical ideas were incorporated into Nazi ideology with WWII and its crimes the result. One wonders what the Nietzsche of 1886 would have done had he been privy to the outcome of his fantasies? Would he have burned the books?

So the answer to the question if living without the help of an unseen benevolent power, which we like to call God, is possible, we have to say: yes. But living in mental harmony throughout all of life's vicissitudes is not likely. One conception of Nietzsche's *Übermensch*, "the blond beast" devoid of moral scruples, was tried in the Nazi era, and since we are in love with technology to the exclusion of what eludes our senses, it may well be tried again. The more so because it appeals to our pride while God reminds us of our insignificance and responsibility. But the Nietzsche type *Übermensch* is not the only conceivable one.

In the previous chapter and that on St. Mark I have mentioned Bucke's book on *Cosmic Consciousness* and that Jesus' baptismal experience of the Holy Spirit descending upon him, may have been the phenomenon Bucke had been talking about. The subtitle of the book, which was originally published in 1901, is: *A Study in the Evolution of the Human Mind*. The main thesis is: as our organisms have evolved to their present state so did our minds, but evolution has not stopped! This concept should be kept in mind. We are not a final product; we have the potential capacity to develop further. This is vouchsafed by the fact that mystic experiences of other realities exist and these, although rare now, may be the harbingers of what may become the rule in the future. Just as language has developed from rudiments, so our five senses need not remain the only ones; the sixth one, the mind nourished by the spirit, may come into full bloom as a common property of all.

One may think of this in analogy to cosmic radiation. Our atmosphere shields us from its lethal effects but may also block genuine, intelligent spiritual information. This turns us into Plato's famous cave dwellers who see the shadows and take them for ultimate reality. Some gifted individuals have already left the cave and shown us another reality but since they are truly few and far between at this time, and we cannot partake of their experience, we either scoff at it or regard it as irrelevant for our lives.

The fundamental questions of this type are far from modern. In the discourses of Gautama we find that they were debated 2500 years ago. He was asked to decide between statements by priests who said, "Finite, temporary, is the world; only this is the truth." While others said, "Infinite and eternal is the world; only this is the truth." Some additional questions were in relationship to: the existence or nonexistence of worlds without form; identity or separateness of life and physical body; complete disappearance of one's being or not; is there a beyond or not; do actions—good or bad—have consequences or does predestination rule. In all of these instances he was asked to render a definitive verdict as to which one of these opposing viewpoints contained the final truth.

While most of us might have been inclined to choose one answer over the other, Gautama asked the questioner, and I have to paraphrase now, "Do you hold the opinion which you regard as truth, because you have personally examined it? Have you carefully considered the pros and cons of your opinion as well as their consequences? Have you come to the conclusion you hold true through your own personal experience or are you merely acting upon hearsay and dogma?" Furthermore, he intimated that: Unless you are willing to undergo the rigors which are associated with trying to come to a truthful conclusion on these matters, which require earnest meditation in solitude, do not concern yourself with these questions but instead work on controlling your mind in daily life and root out the passions which enslave you.

This is an example that can be followed. No fruitless discussions, arguments and wars over unverifiable opinions and religious dogmas but patient and consistent examination of oneself and one's motives. "Know Thyself" was the inscription over Apollo's temple in Delphi and this commandment is neglected. Unless and until we have explored the motives of our own actions we will never be able to understand those of others.

The essential problem of our society is our relationship to "the other." We feel ourselves as "self" and the "I" is always confronted with the "you." This is rooted in our biology; the immune system rejects foreign tissue. But as pointed out previously we need not be entirely dependent on the laws which govern our physical bodies; our minds are capable of transcending them. We tend to believe that our scientific endeavors have shown us all there is to the physical universe and as it relates to us. But even neuroscientists don't know what a thought is and how it can be produced at will. We know some concomitants of the process but not its essence. We, therefore, have no right to deny the possible existence of mental-spiritual forces we are currently unaware of.

This is the area where Jesus and the sages of ancient India can be our guide. If someone had told Jesus that the answer to human willfulness, and thereby distress, is *tat tvam asi*, he would have said, "what are your talking about?" But although he would not have recognized the words, his life was based on them, through the Holy Spirit. Literally translated the three Sanskrit words stand for: You are That! This is not necessarily meaningful unless one realizes that the intent behind the words is to establish the relationship of the person to the rest of the world. The message is: You are not only your personal self but also all of that which the world is composed of. Furthermore, the sense of being an individual, separated from the whole, is a delusion; a trick of the mind. The correct understanding would be that, as one part of the whole, what you are doing with, to, or for others, you are really doing to and for yourself. For most of us, these are just words, psychobabble, but some people can not only intellectually agree with it, but have deeply felt it. The *tat tvam asi* experience allowed Jesus to truthfully say, "The Father and I are one." On the other hand since we lack the experience we tend to relegate it to fantasy or to mental illness.

The *tat tvam asi* experience cannot be willed but falls under *cháris* and has been granted to very few individuals, as discussed in the previous chapter under Cosmic Cosciousness. "Many are called but few are chosen," Jesus told us. So how does this help the rest of us? Although we cannot go all the way towards that realization we can go part way. The fundamental insight is that "I," am the "you" to "you." This is a fact which we should keep in our minds at all times. I am not viewed in the way I see myself but only in the way you see me. This is, of course, a trite statement when one limits it to physical appearance which keeps the cosmetic industry and plastic surgeons busy. But we are not talking appearance here, rather the attitude we project and what we do to others. The "I am you," "You are me," is the basis for the Golden Rule, which is universal. Seeing yourself, and him, in "the other," is Jesus' message in the gospels. This is Jesus' relevance for our age and why his message transcends dogma and the legends which have grown around his person. It is also the challenge for our age, and if we can meet it successfully, all will be well. But science cannot help us in this endeavor, we have to open ourselves to the Holy Spirit and thereby allow the possibility of *cháris* to flow into our lives.

I have used the term Holy Spirit throughout this book without having defined it. In the literature one also finds at times the term "Holy Ghost" which compounds the difficulty further. The word "ghost" usually refers to disembodied apparitions of the dead, while spirit animates the living. In the German language the words are "*der heilige Geist*," where *Geist* covers both meanings depending on context. While the Christian religion has personified this cosmic vital force as one aspect of the Trinity, the term antedates it, as has been shown in the chapter on St. Mark, and it is the opposite of the lie and deception. It transcends all cultures and was referred to by Socrates as his *daimon*. In the New Testament the Holy Spirit is also, at times, referred to as "the Paraclete," which is that spiritual force which animated Jesus and took his place when he was no longer physically present. The term is derived from *parakaleo*, and stands for: to comfort, encourage, exhort, as well as "one who comes forth in behalf of another." Its secular meaning in Greek literature was: an aid or legal advisor at a court of law. The latter aspect may come into play at the final judgment of the soul where, as has been mentioned earlier, Satan is the accuser and prosecutor while the Paraclete would act as defense attorney.

The names, that are given to this spiritual force are irrelevant, but the recognition of its existence is important. We cannot see gravity, we only know of it by its effect on us and the same applies to the Holy Spirit. But in contrast to gravity, which is apparent to all at all times, spirit is more subtle. It is perceived by minds which are prepared for it and attuned to its reception.

In the 1960s the hippie slogan was: turn on, tune in and drop out. They tried to achieve higher awareness by drugs, but this was precisely the wrong way because psychoactive drugs remove whatever will power we can exert over our minds. There are no shortcuts and the parable of the sower is most appropriate in this context. Only after we have diligently plowed our minds, possibly watered them with tears, is the seed going to bear fruit. This is also the meaning of the statement, "to him who has will be given, but to him who has not will be taken even the little he has." With other words in the person who, in Gautama's words uses "right effort," the spirit will grow in strength, while others who may have received a smattering of insight and proudly proclaim it as "the only truth" are going to come to grief.

What are the practical consequences for daily living? The most important is that, as has been mentioned previously, we should avoid lying under all circumstances and we should not tolerate being lied to. The "Right Speech," aspect of Gautama's Noble Path is difficult, and requires practice, but is clearly one of the most important aspects of our relationship with others. In this connection it is worth while to point out that in Buddhist discourses even the adversary who defended an opposing viewpoint was always referred to not simply by his name, but with the prefix "Venerable." The personhood of the other was recognized and his views were simply regarded as mistaken which might be correctable by appropriate explanations. What a difference this would make for our world if our politicians began to think in these terms and more importantly really feel them.

Once we accept that the human being consists of body, mind (intellect) and spirit we are on the way to genuine inner sight upon which we can base our conduct. If we neglect one of the three aspects it will atrophy and the consequence will be dis-ease. But when they are fully integrated, a degree of inner harmony can be achieved which will allow one to face with equanimity all the difficulties the material world presents us with. Humankind will never agree on ultimate Truth because as parts of the Whole we cannot comprehend the Whole, or the All. What we can and should do instead is to act truthfully in our daily lives, coupled with respect for those who do not share our opinions. We will always make mistakes but these should be involuntary and we should shun deliberate deception. Imagine for a moment if all of us could read each others thoughts at all times. It would be the end of wars and hypocrisy because they depend on secrecy, greed and fear. The kingdom of God would have arrived. Since this is not in the offing for the world at large we can at least create it in our own limited circles by following the consensus of the ancient teachers to the best of our abilities and stop blaming others for one's own failings. The Catholic "*mea culpa*" is a good starting point.

There is another thought which we should hold clearly in our minds: We live on death row! From the moment the sperm and the egg mated and produced our body it is doomed to die. The only questions are when and what we do in the interval. Over the when we have some limited influence because suicide is an option. The more important aspect, where we have greater choice, is how we conduct ourselves once we have reached the age of reason. If we recognize the fact that all of our thoughts, words and actions have consequences which, although they may not be immediately apparent, can haunt us in years to come we may become more insightful. If we also accept the possibility that we have a soul for which we are responsible, we can become even more circumspect in regard to what we do. The Zoroastrian thought of meeting the soul at time of death can serve as a warning because no one would want to be confronted with one's personal version of Oscar Wilde's *Picture of Dorian Gray*.

As mentioned erlier, the Christian Churches, as institutions, have failed in their task to create a better world. As a matter of fact some of them adhere more to Old Testament "fire and brimstone" rhetoric than to Jesus' message. This also applies to some of our "born again" Christian politicians and preachers who promote hate and revenge rather than love and forgiveness. They may be well advised to consider these words:

> Not everyone who says to me, 'Lord, Lord,' will enter the kingdom of heaven, but only the one who does the will of my Father in Heaven. In that day many will say to me, 'Lord, Lord, did we not prophesy in your name, and cast out demons in your name, and do many deeds of power in your name?' Then I will declare to them, 'I never knew you, go away from me, you evildoers (Mt. 7:21-23).
> And everyone who hears these words of mine and does not act on them will be like a foolish man who built his house on sand. (Mt. 7:26).

In addition the various Christian religious groups still cannot agree on a common ground and jealously guard their respective turf. Some even feel the necessity to proselytize for their version of Christian truth from members of other established Christian denominations. Furthermore, Jesus' message has been overlaid by dogma which conflicts with reason. In former years mysteries and miracles were readily accepted but our age prefers a more sober approach to the problems of mind and spirit. This is the reason why church attendance is dwindling. Nevertheless, the human spirit yearns for more than it receives from society at present and this accounts for the burgeoning interest in Eastern religions.

"Familiarity breeds contempt," is a well known proverb and those of us who happen to have been born into the Christian religion know some of the externals and the rituals but have, by and large, not come to grips with Jesus' message. We are more interested in the messenger and what he supposedly has done than what he tried to teach us. This is the reason for widespread disenchantment with the Christian Church and the search for esoteric doctrines. The message was clear and is indeed the only way to prevent the slide into the abyss I have mentioned in the beginning. We were told that, "The meek/humble will inherit the earth." Will they be human beings who have learned humility from previous disasters, or will it be cockroaches which can survive even an all-out atomic war?

The essence of Jesus' message has been presented in admirable form by Beethoven in his "*Christus am Ölberg,*" "Christ on the Mount of Olives." He said that he had composed it within the short span of 14 days but the work had obviously incubated for a much longer time. It was first performed on Palm Sunday of 1803 and depicts Jesus' agony in the face of a certain cruel death. We hear his pleas that the Father might spare him this fate, but when told by the Seraph that this was indeed the only way for mankind's redemption, he willingly accepted the necessity. We then hear the approaching soldiers, the fear of the disciples about their own fate and Peter's rage and yearning for revenge. But he is admonished by Jesus with: *Du sollst nicht Rache üben, ich lehrt euch bloss allein, die Menschen alle lieben, dem Feinde gern verzeihn.* You must not pursue revenge, I always only told you to love everyone, to gladly forgive the enemy. Whereupon the angels and Jesus sing: *Oh Menschenkinder fasset dies heilige Gebot: liebt jenen der euch hasset nur so gefällt ihr Gott!* Oh humankind, grasp this holy ordinance: Love the one who hates you; this is the only way to please God. The oratorio ends with the heavenly Chorus: *Welten singen Dank und Ehre dem erhab'nen Gottessohn. Preiset ihn, ihr Engelchöre, laut im heil'gen Jubelton.* Worlds sing thanks and honor to the exalted son of God; praise him angel choirs with sacred jubilation.

This is the message which can prevent us from sliding into disaster but it will immediately be objected that to follow it is an impossible task. It need not be when we realize that we have become prisoners of words! As has been explained earlier "loving the enemy" is a translation from a language, Greek, we no longer understand. The message becomes clearer when we realize that, as mentioned earlier, the Greek language has three words for "love" while we have only one. Only *agápē* and *phílos* show up in the New Testament; *eros* i.e., sexual love is absent. While *phílos* denotes friendship, *agápē* is love, as for instance, by parents towards their children, which carries with it a sense of responsibility. The word is also used in the sense of esteem, benevolence and compassion, as well as in relation to God. The important aspect in the current context is, that in regard to "loving your enemy" the word *agápē,* rather than *phílos* was used. We are not ordered to befriend our enemies but to understand their viewpoint and try to arrive at mutually agreeable solutions.

The policy of the George W Bush administration of not talking to our adversaries, which is still advocated by some, was, therefore, thoroughly mistaken. This attitude is the complete opposite of the *Maat* concept, as discussed previously, which orders us to listen to each other. If we only react with fear and hate then we have reduced ourselves to the level of beasts of prey. The fact that somebody may hate me does not require that I have to reciprocate in the same manner. Adversaries can be dealt with in a deliberate and rational manner provided that we first subdue pride, fear, greed and anger. It is a difficult task but essential for the survival of our species.

In our day and age we cannot afford cynicism and an honest re-appraisal of our spiritual heritage is urgently needed. This ought to also include, as pointed out earlier, a fuller appreciation of ancient Egyptian spiritual ideas. The fundamental concept of *Maat,* cosmic order and justice, as explained in the previous chapter is still highly appropriate. Since Egypt has played a profound, but underappreciated, role in the development of Christianity I have tried to draw attention to it on the cover page of this book. It depicts the dove as a symbol of the Holy Spirit descending from the cosmos to earth and in her beak she brings the feather of *Maat.* As mentioned earlier *Maat's* statue still resides in our Court Houses as *Justitia.* But she has been shorn of her divinity through loss of wings and feather. In addition, her all-seeing eyes have been blindfolded. As such, the scales she holds can be filled with lies by prosecutors and defense attorneys whose only object is "to win the case." Our legal system prides itself on the use of the adversarial principle without realizing that we have, thereby, opened the door for Satan, whose name translates into Adversary. With the removal of *Maat's* feather, to balance the scales, truth and justice have frequently become the losers.

When we look at the ethical essence of the messages the great sages of our world have sent us, we find remarkable similarities, and with those as our base we could construct a more humane

CONCLUSIONS

society. East and West are no longer incompatabile but the best ideas
of both can be taken to form a worldview which will benefit all.
Yet, organized religions, as they exist today, have historical roots
in different countries and cultures. They are burdened with past
histories of conflict and are not likely to become universal in their
present form. The currently established Churches would be well
advised to reflect on the original teachings, their origin and their
purpose. They could subsequently retain the universal aspects and
gradually discard the parochial ones. This will not occur over night
but is a process that ought to be set in motion. The world has become
too interconnected and what now hurts one hurts all. We will either
live together in relative harmony or die together in distress. While
organized religions divide, the "religious experience" unites. It is
universal and can be tapped into.

As mentioned earlier the privilege of the human being is
inborn faith coupled with a degree of free will upon which our
Weltanschauung (how we view the world) depends. As materialists
we may chose to believe Macbeth's conclusion that life is "a tale
written by an idiot, full of sound and fury signifying nothing," or we
can see ourselves as having been granted an opportunity to grow in
mental and spiritual stature. The choice is an individual one but this
is how we shape our karma (consequence of all our thoughts and
actions) for the rest of our life.

Furthermore, we ought to clarify for ourselves what our individual
specific role in this world is. Are we condemned to a penal insitution
and is this already purgatory? Are we soldiers who have been drafted
and reluctantly fulfill our duty? Or are we volunteers whose job it
is to help wherever we perceive help is needed without, however,
needlessly meddling in affairs we have not been asked to involve
ourselves in. Those are individual viewpoints and choices which
depend only upon our ourselves, but will inevitably be reflected in
our conduct. We do have a degree of free will over our conduct. It
is currently used to a large extent to gratify sensual demands but it
can be redirected towards greater awareness of the spiritual forces
which move us.

Jesus and Gautama, have shown the way to avoid the snares and
pitfalls of life; now it is up to each one of us to follow it. Although

Jesus died on the cross, his spirit rose and is with us today. Some of us experience his presence in church services while others, whose nature is less gregarious, can take comfort in the promise, "Where two or three are gathered in my name, I am there among them [Mt. 18:20]." We can invite him into our home and if we discuss our problems in his presence we will not be led astray. We, therefore, don't have to wait for a physical Second Coming because his spirit can be with us at any time. Under these circumstances the "historical" Jesus, what he looked like, what he "really" did, and whether or not there was a physical resurrection, becomes irrelevant. The truth we have been seeking resides in his spirit which urges us to look beyond our material world and will provide help when help is needed. All we have to do is to ask with humility and sincerity, and we should not be disappointed when it is not immediately forthcoming, or in a form which does not conform to our expectations.

While Jesus presents a challenge to our materialistic "rational" society, Hindus have no problem welcoming him as an avatar, incarnation of a God, or Buddhists as a *Bodhisattva*. But even in the West Jesus could become a friend, to those of us who are estranged from dogma. If we simply concentrate on the message, rather than harping on those aspects of the messenger, which we find unbelievable, a beneficial effect can be experienced. There is a critical passage in the Gospel of Matthew in Jesus' reply to the Pharisees when they accused him of "casting out demons by Beelzebul [12:22]". When translated into colloquial English he might have said: "I don't care one bit what you say about me, but my words are true because they are not mine. It is the Holy Spirit which dictates what I say [12:32]".

I have called this book the Jesus Conundrum because for many of us in modern Western Society, who feel that they can no longer adhere to official religious dogmas, he represents a vexing problem. We don't know what to do with him because he just doesn't seem to fit in with our sophisticated day and age. Part of the reason is that his picture as presented in the gospel of St. Mark is the antithesis of the one we are confronted with in St. John. Mark shows us a human being who undergoes a process of spiritual development which leads to self-sacrifice and subsequent redemption by God. John uses the physical form of Jesus only as background for explaining the nature of the Christian religion, which was an entirely separate goal.

As such there is no "gospel truth," but each of the evangelists and subsequent editors, who produced the final documents we now have, presented their view of Jesus' life and its meaning. The greatest confusion arises, when the gospels, especially that of John, are taken literally in a materialistic sense, rather than as an invitation to think about the hidden spiritual meanings. There is truth in all of the gospels but to find coherence among them requires insight and effort. Furthermore, Jesus, the rebel against Jewish dogma, has been nailed to a new set of Christian dogmas. These differ among the various denominations Christianity has split and Christian love is frequently sadly absent among them.

An additional and major reason for the conundrum is our mechanistic thinking. This has placed a creator God somewhere out there, "in heaven," Whose designs are inscrutable and Who may or may not listen to petitions. If, however, we abandon this model and use nature as our guide, we can gain an entirely different perspective. As mentioned in the chapter on, "What is Truth?" nature is always a Whole; an entity with latent potentialities and different forms at various stages of development. Nature unfolds! This was the concept used by the Chinese in the Tao; the Hindus called it Brahman in the Vedas, and the Egyptians used the name of *Atum*. Names differ but the thought behind them is the same. This is also precisely what Jesus taught and which was not comprehended. In his parables he had compared the kingdom of God to a seed which has the potential to grow and unfold into a mighty tree which produces abundant fruit.

This seed, with the potential of developing into the kingdom of heaven, a synonym for inner peace and good will towards others in daily conduct, is inborn in all of us as the essential aspect which makes us human. It is our job, as human beings, to create the conditions within us which will allow latent potential to become actuality. This has to be achieved first in the individual and the nuclear family from where it can spread to neighbors, co-workers and eventually to society at large, which re-establishes *Maat*.

This model also allows us to understand the concept of the Trinity, which is incomprehensible from a mechanistic point of view, or even that of St. Paul who compared Christianity with a branch which is grafted onto the tree of Judaism. A clue to the meaning of the Trinity is expressed in the German language as *"die heilige Dreifaltigkeit."* If *Dreifaltigkeit* were to be transliterated it would come out as "threefoldedness," with the emphasis on folds, or aspects, of one entity. We could, therefore, visualize the Father as the roots and trunk of the tree, the Son as the flowers and the Holy Spirit as the seed which is transmitted to all. Vision is the dominant sense in the human being and we have become addicted to forms, but Eastern religions have always de-emphasized form as changeable and illusory. They have instead insisted that we look beyond form to the formless essence and this is also where Christianity's future may be found, once it has rid itself of unsustainable dogma.

There is an additional way to address the Jesus conundrum. The Romans had a saying, *"nomen est omen."* The name we have been given foreshadows our life because unconsciously we strive to live up to it. This is another problem of our society. Names and words have become largely meaningless and this is why we have so many disagreements on most every aspect of life. It need not be, we can clean up language, and thereby thought, which will then restore meaning. To further understand Jesus and his message one can play a word game with his name. Officially, the name in English is Jesus Christ, or Jesus Christus in Latin; the Church language. Jesus was derived from the Hebrew Jeshua or Joshua while Christ is the Greek translation of the Hebrew word for anointed which was used for kings in general and the expected Messiah in particular. Christos in Greek, or Christus in Latin is, therefore an honorific title rather than a name. The Hebrew Yeshua, which was an abbreviation of Yehoshua (Joshua), meant "Yahweh is salvation." As Father McKenzie has pointed out, Moses had derived the name from Hoshea (Num. 13:16) which simply meant "salvation." As such Jesus' task, as "the savior," is indeed contained in his name.

The method how we can help in this task becomes apparent when we realize that the Latin, as well as German pronunciation of the letter J corresponds to the English Y. When one, therefore, pronounces the first three letters of the name in Latin or German and the last two in English one arrives at: Yes-us! This idea provides an unequivocal Yes to life; not only in its beauty but also during all its challenges and vicissitudes. Even under extreme circumstances one can "*trotzdem Ja zum Leben sagen*"; "to say yes to life in spite of everything," which was the title of Victor Frankl's book where he described his concentration camp experiences. The "us" part reminds us that life is to be lived as members of a community who care for each other, rather than reluctantly drudging through life's difficulties as isolated individuals. This caring takes place first, as mentioned above, in the family, it is then extended to friends and co-workers to eventually encompassing society at large. The task for those of us, who call ourselves Christians, has been clearly enunciated: to recognize Jesus in the stranger! Under those circumstances we have no enemies; fear has been banished, and the door to joy has been opened. Playing a similar word game with the name Muslims use for God we could pronounce it in English as All-Ah! The All is experienced with reverence, astonishment and gratitude.

Unfortunately, esoteric thinking has always been limited to relatively few individuals and has not yet entered the mainstream of humanity. Furthermore, and this is the most important aspect, our governments, regardless of type, have always pursued their own narrow interests in our names without moral considerations. Murder, property destruction, theft and rape are justified as War, and lying is condoned under the name of "National Security." But the leadership only expresses our worst instincts. If we as a people would no longer tolerate being lied to, the world would change for the better. All the crimes for which individuals are prosecuted are allowed to governments, albeit under noble names such as defending freedom, or the nation. This allows for the exploitation of greed, fear and hate. We are currently confronted with the results of this type of thinking and can only expect more of the same and worse. World Peace is not in the immediate offing but another World War is still avoidable. This would, however, require a change of mind from Old Testament doctrine, where: domination of others, an "eye for an eye" and a "jealous" God rule; to the much more difficult patient daily practice of Jesus' message:

ALĒTHEIA, AGÁPĒ AND CHÁRIS

BIBLIOGRAPHY

Anonymous. *Zoroaster Zoro-Tushtra. Leben und Wirken des Wegbereiters in Iran*. Alexander Bernhardt: Vomperberg, Tirol. 1957.

Assmann Jan. *Ma'at. Gerechtigkeit und Unsterblichkeit im Alten Ägypten*. Beck'sche Reihe: München. 2001.

Beck, Roger. *Planetary Gods and Planetary Orders in the Mysteries of Mithra*. E. J. Brill: Leiden, New York, København, Köln 1988.

Bennett, William, J. *Why We Fight. Moral Clarity and the War on Terrorism*. Doubleday: New York. 2002.

Berry, Paul. *Correspondence between Paul and Seneca A.D. 61-65*. Ancient Near Eastern Texts and Studies Volume 12. The Edward Mellen Press: Lewiston, Queenston, Lampeter. 1999.

Bin Gorion, Micha, Josef. *Die Sagen der Juden*. Parkland Verlag: Köln. 1997.

Breasted, James Henry. *The Dawn of Conscience*. Charles Scribner's Sons: New York. 1933.

Brenton, Sir Lancelot C.L. *The Septuagint with Apocrypha: Greek and English*. Hendrickson Publishers. 1997.

Brodie, Thomas L. *The Quest for the Origin of John's Gospel.* Oxford University Press: New York, Oxford. 1993.

Brown, Raymond E., Fitzmyer, S. J., Murphy, Roland E. Ed. *The Jerome Biblical Commentary.* Prentice-Hall, Inc: Englewood Cliffs, New Jersey. 1968.

Bucke, Richard Maurice MD. *Cosmic Consciousness. A Study in the Evolution of the Human Mind.* University Books, Inc: New Hyde Park, New York. 1966

Bultmann Rudolf. *Jesus Christ and Mythology.* Prentice Hall: Upper Saddle River, New Jersey. 1958.

Bultmann, Rudolf. *The Gospel of John. A Commentary.* The Westminster Press: Philadelphia. 1971.

Carter, John; Ross and Mahinda Palihawanda. *Sacred Writings. Buddhism: The Dammapada.* Oxford University Press; Book of the Month Club: New York. 1992

Charles, R. H. *The Book of Enoch.* S P C K: London. 1962.

Clauss, Manfred. *The Roman Cult of Mithras. The God and his Mysteries.* Translated by Richard Gordon. Routledge: New York. 2001

Cohen, A. The Soncino Chumash. *The Five Books of Moses with Haphtaroth.* The Soncino Press Ltd.: London, Jerusalem, New York. 1983.

Cohen, A. and Rosenberg A.J. *The Twelve Prophets. Hebrew Text & English Translations with Introductions and Commentary.* The Soncino Press, Ltd.: London, Jerusalem, New York. 1994.

Cooper, John A. and Procopé, J.E. *Seneca. Moral and Political Essays.* Cambridge University Press: New York. 1995.

Cumont, Franz. *The Mysteries of Mithra*. Dover Publications, Inc.: New York. 1956.

Dawood, N. J. *The Koran*. Penguin Books Ltd.: New York. 1980.

d'Espagnat Bernard. *On Physics and Philosphy*. Princeton University Press. 2006.

Dieterich, Albrecht. *Eine Mithrasliturgie*. B.G. Teubner Verlagsgesellschaft: Stuttgart. 1966.

Donfried, Karl P., Richardson, Peter. Ed. *Judaism and Christianity in First-Century Rome*. William B. Eerdmans Publishing Company: Grand Rapids, Michigan / Cambridge, UK. 1998.

Douglas, J.D. Editor. Brown, Robert K. and Comfort, Philip W. *The New Greek-English Interlinear New Testament*. Tyndale House Publishers, Inc.: Wheaton, Illinois. 1990.

Dummelow, J.R. *The One Volume Bible Commentary*. Macmillan Publishing Co. Inc.: New York. 1908.

Evans-Wentz, W. Y. *The Tibetan Book of the Dead*. Oxford University Press: London, Oxford, New York. 1957.

Feldman, Stephen M. *Please Don't Wish Me a Merry Christmas*. New York University Press: New York and London. 1997.

Frankl, Victor E. *... trotzdem Ja zum Leben sagen. Ein Psychologe erlebt das Konzentrationslager*. Deutscher Taschenbuch Verlag: München. 1982.

Frazer, Sir James George. *The New Golden Bough*. Ed. Theodore H. Gaster. Anchor Books. Doubleday & Company: Garden City, New York. 1961.

Fredriksen, Paula. *From Jesus to Christ. The Origins of the New Testament Images of* Jesus. 2nd Ed. Yale Nota Bene, Yale University Press: New Haven and London. 2000.

Frend, W. H. C. *Martyrdom and Persecution in the Early Church.* Oxford University Press: London, Oxford. 1965.

Funk, Robert W., Hoover, Roy and the Jesus Seminar. *The Five Gospels. What did Jesus really say?* Harper: San Francisco. 1993.

Gibbon, Edward. *The Decline and Fall of the Roman Empire.* Great Books of the Western World Vols. 40-41. Robert Maynard Hutchins; Editor in Chief. Encyclopedia Britannica Inc. William Benton, Publisher: Chicago, London, Toronto.1952.

Grimes, John. *A Concise Dictionary of Indian Philosophy. Sanskrit terms defined in English.* State University of New York Press: Albany. 1996.

Hadas, Moses. *The Stoic Philosophy of Seneca. Essays and Letters.* W. W. Norton & Company: New York, London. 1958.

Hippocrates. Great Books of the Western World Vol.10. Robert Maynard Hutchins; Editor in Chief. Encyclopedia Britannica Inc. William Benton, Publisher: Chicago, London, Toronto.1952.

H. H. the Dalai Lama Tenzin Gyatso. *The Opening of the Wisdom~Eye.* Quest Books: Wheaton, Ill., Madras India/ London, England. 1991.

Hoeller, Stephan A. *Gnosticism. New Light on the Ancient Tradition of Inner Knowing.* Quest Books: Wheaton, Ill.., Chennai (Madras), India. 2002..

James, William. *The Varieties of Religious Experience. A Study in Human Nature.* The Modern Library: New York. 1994.

Janz, Kurt Paul. *Friedrich Nietzsche Biographie*. Carl Hanser Verlag: München, Wien. 1978.

Jaspers, Karl. Bultmann, Rudolf. *Myth and Christianity. An Inquiry into the possibility of religion without myth.* Prometheus Books: Amherst, New York. 2005.

Jervell, Jacob. *Jesus in the Gospel of John.* Augsburg Publishing House: Minneapolis. 1984.

Jung, Emil. *Die Herkunft Jesu Im Lichte freier Forschung.* Universitätsverlag Wagner: Innsbruck. 1922.

Lüdemann, Gerd. *Virgin Birth? The Real Story of Mary and Her Son Jesus.* Trinity Press International: Harrisburg , Pennsylvania. 1998.

Kushner, Harold S. *When Bad Things Happen To Good People.* Avon Books: New York. 1981.

Lichtheim, Miriam. *Ancient Egyptian Literature. A Book of Readings.* Volume I: The Old and Middle Kingdoms. University of California Press: Berkeley, Los Angeles, London. 1975.

Maier, Paul L. *Eusebius. The Church History.* A New Translation with Commentary. Kregel Publications: Grand Rapids Michigan.1999.

Mann, Thomas. *Joseph und seine Brüder.* Fischer Taschenbuch Verlag: Hamburg. 1971.

McKenzie, John L. *Dictionary of the Bible.* Macmillan Publishing Co., Inc.: New York. 1965.

Meier, John P. *A Marginal Jew.* Volume two: *Rethinking the historical Jesus.* Doubleday: New York, London, Toronto, Sydney, Auckland. 1994.

Meyer, Marvin W. *The Ancient Mysteries. A Source book. Sacred Texts of the Mystery Religions of the Ancient Mediterranean world.* University of Pennsylvania Press: Philadelphia. 1987.

Mylius, Klaus. *Wörterbuch. Sanskrit-Deutsch.* Langenscheidt Verlage Enzyklopädie: Leipzig, Berlin, München, Wien, Zürich, New York. 1992.

Nestle, Eberhard. *Novum Testamentum Latine. Textum Vaticanum.* Deutsche Bibelgesellschaft: Stuttgart. 1952.

Nietzsche, Friedrich. *Sämtliche Briefe. Kritische Studienausgabe.* Deutscher Taschenbuch Verlag de Gruyter: München. 2003.

Neumann, Karl Eugen. *Die Reden Gotamo Buddhos. Aus der Mittleren Sammlung Majjhimanikayo des Pali-Kanons zum ersten Mal uebersetzt.* R. Piper & Co.: München. 1922.

Pagels, Elaine. *The Gnostic Gospels.* Random House: New York. 1979.

Pagels, Elaine. *Beyond Belief. The Secret Gospel of Thomas.* Random House: New York. 2003.

Philo, The Works Of. Translated by C.D. Yonge. Hendrickson Publishers Inc. 1993.

Plutarch's Moralia. Vol V Translated by E.C. Babbitt. Loeb Classical Library Harvard University Press: Cambridge, Massachusetts. 1984.

Rahner, Hugo S.J. *Greek Myths and Christian Mysteries.* Burnes & Oates Ltd.: London. 1963.

Ratzinger Joseph -Benedict XVI. *Jesus von Nazareth.* Herder: Freiburg, Basel, Wien. 2006.

Renan, Ernest. *The Life of Jesus*. Charles Edwin Wilbour transl. G.W. Dillingham, Publisher: New York. 1868.

Robinson, James M. *The Nag Hammadi Library in English*. Harper: San Francisco. 1990.

Rodin, Ernst. *War & Mayhem. Reflections of a Viennese Physician*. Trafford Publishing: Vancouver B.C. 1999.

Rodin, Ernst. *Whither Zionism?* Trafford Publishing: Vancouver B.C. 2001.

Rodin, Ernst. *The Moses Legacy. Roots of Jewish Suffering*. Booksurge.com.: North Charleston SC. 2004.

Russell, Bertrand. *A History of Western Philosophy and its Connection with Political and Circumstances from the Earliest Times to the Present Day*. Simon and Schuster: New York. 1945.

Russell, Bertrand. *Why I am not a Christian and other Essays on Religion and Related Subjects*. Simon and Schuster: New York. 1967.

Sanford, John A. *Mystical Christianity. A Psychological Commentary on the Gospel of John*. The Crossroads Publishing Company: New York.1993.

Schweitzer, Albert. *The Psychiatric Study of Jesus. Exposition and Criticism*. The Beacon Press: Boston 1948.

Sevenster, Jan Nicolaas. *Paul and Seneca*. E. J. Brill: Leiden 1961.

Speidel, Michael, P. *Mithras - Orion. Greek Hero and Roman Army God*. E. J. Brill: Leiden. 1980.

Strauss, David Friedrich. *Das Leben Jesu für das deutsche Volk bearbeitet*. Alfred Kroener Verlag: Stuttgart. 1905.

Suetonius. *The Twelve Caesars*. Translated by Robert Graves. Penguin Books Ltd.: New York. 1957.

Swami Prabhavananda, Manchester F. *The Upanishads. Breath of the Eternal*. Mentor Book New American Library: New York and Scarborough Ontario. 1948.

The Amplified Bible. Zondervan Bible Publishers: Grand Rapids Michigan. 1965.

The Holy Bible Containing the Old and New Testaments in the Authorized King James Version. Good Counsel Publishing Company: Chicago, Illinois. 1960.

The New English Bible with the Apocrypha. Cambridge University Press: New York. 1971.

The Teaching of Buddha. Kosaido Printing Co. Ltd.: Tokyo, Japan. 1975.

Thera, Nyanaponika. *The Heart of Buddhist Meditation*. Samuel Weiser, Inc.: York Beach, Maine. 1965.

Thich Nhat Hanh. *Going Home. Jesus and Buddha as Brothers*. Riverhead Books a Member of Penguin Putnam Inc.: New York. 1999.

Ulansey, David. *The Origins of the Mithraic Mysteries*. Cosmology and Salvation in the Ancient World. Oxford University Press.: New York, Oxford. 1989.

Van Praagh, James. *Heaven and Earth. Making the Psychic Connection*. Simon & Schuster Source: New York. 2001.

Vollers, Karl. *Die Weltreligionen in ihrem geschichtlichen Zusammenhang*. Eugen Diederichs: Jena. 1907.

Von Wahlde, Urban C. *The Earliest Version of John's Gospel. Recovering the Gospel of Signs*. Michael Glazier: Wilmington, Delaware. 1989.

Whiston, William. *Josephus. Complete Works*. Kregel Publications: Grand Rapids, Michigan. 1981.

Yogananda, Paramahansa. *Autobiography of a Yogi*. Self-Realization Fellowship: Los Angeles. 1959.

Yogananda, Paramahansa. *The Second Coming of Christ. The Resurrection of the Christ within you. A revelatory commentary on the original teachings of Jesus*. Self-Realization Fellowship: Los Angeles. 2004.

Zerwick, Max S. J. and Grosvenor, Mary. *A Grammatical Analysis of the Greek New Testament*. Editirice Pontifico Istituto Biblico: Rome. 1996.

Zodiathes, Spiros Th.D. *The Complete Word Study Dictionary New Testament. For a Deeper Understanding of the Word*. AMG Publishers: Chattanooga, TN. 1993.

INDEX

Augustus 57, 104

B

Ba 203
Baal 34, 35
Babylon(ian) 2, 3, 4, 5, 18, 35, 45, 78,
    146, 149, 152, 205, 221
Bacchantes 98
Baghavad Gita 189, 195
Barabbas 58, 136
Bar Cochba 53, 55
Barnabas 101, 108, 109, 110
Beelzebub (l) 16
Beethoven, Ludwig van 254
Benedict XVI xi, 266. See also Ratz-
    inger
Berry, Paul 261
Bethany 42
Bethlehem 68, 81, 82, 163, 167
Bible xix, xxii, 5, 7, 10, 13, 15, 22,
    27, 35, 45, 51, 53, 55, 58, 84,
    87, 112, 113, 114, 116, 124,
    130, 145, 149, 185, 200, 212,
    213, 225, 226, 263, 265, 268
Bodhisattva 257
Brahman 258
Bucke, Maurice 8, 197, 238, 247, 262
Buddha 8, 16, 19, 29, 42, 69, 185,
    191, 195, 268
Buddhism 16, 185, 187, 192, 194,
    195, 262
Bultmann, Rudolf 219, 262, 265

C

Caesar 46, 104, 136, 142, 146, 155,
    225
Caesarea 100, 103, 108, 142
Cain 214
Calvary 39
Cana 129
Canaanite law 116
Capernaum 10, 12, 130
Carabbas 59

Catholic xvi, 61, 73, 128, 140, 169,
    194, 205, 220, 224, 225, 230,
    245, 252
Cato, Marcus 179
Celsus 162, 163, 164
Cháris 129, 212, 241, 250, 260
Chosen people xx, 4, 36, 42, 150
Christ xvi, xxii, 1, 31, 39, 66, 75, 87,
    92, 94, 97, 99, 104, 108, 109,
    110, 111, 112, 117, 118, 119,
    121, 122, 123, 124, 129, 133,
    139, 141, 143, 150, 152, 170,
    175, 185, 195, 205, 219, 220,
    226, 228, 241, 254, 259, 262,
    264, 269
Christianity x, xxi, 20, 76, 86, 94,
    108, 118, 127, 128, 129, 141,
    144, 155, 162, 168, 185, 195,
    197, 199, 200, 218, 219, 221,
    224, 226, 227, 228, 242, 246,
    255, 258, 259, 263, 265, 267
Church xvi, xix, xxi, 8, 15, 39, 45, 61,
    64, 65, 66, 73, 75, 76, 77, 78,
    79, 80, 81, 87, 88, 94, 95, 96,
    97, 98, 100, 101, 102, 103, 108,
    109, 110, 111, 115, 120, 121,
    122, 124, 128, 129, 131, 139,
    140, 141, 146, 148, 169, 197,
    199, 200, 205, 207, 208, 219,
    220, 221, 224, 225, 226, 228,
    239, 244, 245, 253, 256, 257,
    259, 264, 265
Cilicia 104, 109
Circumcision 82, 100, 101, 108, 117,
    118, 221
Clairvoyance 23, 24
Clairvoyant 23, 24
Claudius 59, 120, 170
Clauss, Manfred 199, 262
Cleopatra 105
Confucius 84
Consciousness 8, 187, 189, 194, 196,
    230, 231, 235, 238, 247, 262
Consciousness, Cosmic 8, 238, 247,
    262

241, 250, 257, 258, 262, 264,
265, 266, 267, 269
Gray, Dorian 252
Greco-Roman xx, 20, 131, 140, 168,
200
Greed 180, 188, 191, 202, 214, 245,
252, 255, 260
Greek xviii, xix, xxii, 6, 7, 10, 11, 12,
22, 25, 27, 33, 34, 37, 49, 50,
51, 52, 60, 61, 67, 68, 69, 71,
73, 75, 88, 90, 104, 107, 111,
112, 113, 128, 129, 133, 134,
140, 145, 146, 166, 167, 168,
200, 215, 218, 241, 251, 254,
259, 261, 263, 266, 267, 269
Gush Enim 144

H

Hagar 115, 116
Hasmonean(s) 52
Heaven ix, 2, 3, 4, 6, 20, 30, 34, 35,
37, 39, 40, 42, 44, 49, 56, 62,
63, 64, 65, 66, 70, 71, 74, 75,
78, 79, 80, 86, 88, 89, 95, 96,
101, 121, 122, 129, 132, 134,
152, 160, 164, 169, 175, 186,
187, 199, 202, 203, 204, 205,
225, 229, 231, 253, 258, 268
Hebrew(s) xix, xx, xxii, 6, 7, 17, 20,
21, 22, 54, 69, 98, 145, 146,
200, 243, 259, 262
Hellenic Christianity 94
Hellenism 110, 168, 221
Hellenistic 76, 82, 95, 104, 106, 111,
124, 145, 169, 221, 222, 223
Hellenist(s) 98, 100
Heraclites 125, 188
Herodians v, 15, 31, 64
Herodias 27
Herod, King of Galilee 69, 163
Herod, the Great 57, 162
Hesiod 168
Hezekiah, King 2
Hillel 85
Hindu xi, 189

Hippocrates 36, 264
Hitler, Adolf 151, 223, 228
Hoeller, Stephan 221, 264
Holy Land xi, xvii, 54, 115, 144, 242
Holy Spirit vii, xvii, xxi, 3, 4, 6, 10,
16, 18, 45, 48, 50, 70, 74, 81,
88, 95, 96, 100, 104, 139, 161,
175, 195, 247, 249, 250, 251,
255, 257, 259
Homer 168
Homoioùsios 140
Homooùsios 140
Horus 205, 245
Hypocrite(s) 28, 78

I

Iliad 71
India 164, 165, 185, 195, 249, 264
Isaac 21, 47, 115, 116
Isaiah 2, 3, 4, 5, 7, 9, 17, 18, 28, 31,
42, 83
Ishmael 116, 117, 118
Isis 127, 205, 206, 218, 234
Israel xx, 4, 5, 7, 9, 14, 15, 32, 35, 38,
43, 47, 69, 74, 78, 85, 87, 101,
116, 118, 149, 151, 165, 221,
222, 242, 243, 244

J

Jacob xx, 7, 20, 21, 47, 48, 131, 132,
265
Jaspers, Karl 219, 265
Jefferson, Thomas xvii
Jerome, Saint xviii, 128
Jerusalem 1, 2, 3, 5, 6, 18, 28, 40, 41,
42, 44, 49, 52, 53, 54, 58, 61,
77, 78, 87, 90, 95, 98, 100, 101,
102, 103, 106, 109, 110, 115,
120, 122, 130, 132, 138, 139,
142, 143, 145, 146, 147, 149,
154, 156, 206, 222, 223, 241,
243, 244, 262
Jesus ix, x, xi, xv, xvi, xvii, xviii, xxi,
xxii, xxiii, 1, 2, 4, 5, 6, 7, 8, 9,

K

Miller, Aaron David 117
Miracle(s) xvi, 12, 19, 20, 22, 23, 24,
    25, 26, 27, 30, 31, 34, 35, 36,
    38, 53, 55, 61, 62, 65, 69, 74,
    83, 84, 86, 89, 96, 97, 100, 126,
    127, 130, 134, 186, 190, 200,
    218, 253
Möbius, P. J. 246
Mormon(s) xxi, 228
Moses x, xviii, xx, 4, 8, 11, 12, 20,
    21, 22, 26, 34, 36, 38, 39, 43,
    44, 45, 47, 52, 55, 68, 69, 75,
    78, 87, 104, 108, 112, 124, 129,
    134, 148, 150, 162, 166, 172,
    181, 200, 204, 206, 223, 224,
    226, 241, 242, 259, 262, 264,
    267
Mount Gerizim 87
Mount Meru 217
Mount of Olives 42, 50, 55, 96, 254
Muhammad 226
Muslim xi, xviii, 88, 151, 174, 175,
    186, 204, 224, 227, 228, 244,
    260

N

Nag Hammadi 219, 221, 267
Napoleon 151
Nathaniel 129
Nazarene 166
Nazareth 6, 25, 26, 66, 74, 81, 83, 84,
    86, 94, 124, 139, 163, 166, 167,
    219, 266
Nazirite(s) 166, 167
Nazi(s) 88, 152, 177, 192, 247
Nazorean 166, 167
Neighbor 47, 48, 87, 117, 226
Nero xviii, 103, 105, 146, 154, 155,
    170, 171, 172
Neuhaus, Richard John 132
New Testament xxi, xxii, 48, 88, 146,
    148, 163, 165, 166, 167, 171,
    182, 190, 215, 219, 220, 221,
    225, 226, 237, 245, 250, 254,
    263, 264, 269

Nicea, Council of 140, 220
Nicodemus 130, 131, 165
Nietzsche, Friedrich 245, 265, 266
Nimrod 21
Novatus 102, 180

O

Old Testament xvii, xix, xx, xxi, xxii,
    1, 4, 7, 8, 18, 36, 38, 49, 69, 71,
    75, 77, 78, 80, 81, 85, 106, 110,
    125, 143, 145, 154, 166, 218,
    224, 225, 226, 242, 253, 260
Ormuzd 2
Orthodox(y) 15, 28, 52, 61, 137, 159,
    221, 227
Osiris 203, 204, 205

P

Pagels, Elaine 128, 266
Palestine 54, 104, 151, 162, 165, 180,
    222, 243, 244
Palestinians 54, 68, 116, 117, 172,
    243
Panthere, also *Panthera* 162
Papias 126
Parable(s) 17, 18, 19, 44, 47, 48, 75,
    76, 77, 79, 86, 87, 88, 89, 90,
    159, 160, 164, 174, 186, 251,
    258
Paraclete 250, 251
Parousia 119
Passover 54, 57, 58, 126, 130, 141
Paul, Saint x, xxi, 97, 104, 124, 165,
    173, 198, 216, 227, 259
Pausanias 200
Pentateuch 45, 242
Pentheus 99, 103
Persia(n) 2, 3, 5, 168, 198
Personality Syndrome 113
Peter, Saint 1, 9, 12, 14, 31, 32, 33,
    34, 41, 44, 50, 55, 56, 64, 65,
    75, 76, 91, 96, 97, 100, 101,
    109, 110, 129, 139, 215, 254,
    263

T

Transfiguration 34, 36
Troy 71
Truth xv, xviii, xix, xxiii, xxiv, 3, 61,
  63, 66, 97, 105, 128, 129, 131,
  132, 135, 136, 138, 141, 143,
  147, 149, 157, 159, 167, 171,
  172, 178, 186, 188, 191, 194,
  196, 202, 209, 210, 212, 216,
  217, 218, 219, 220, 221, 226,
  229, 232, 233, 237, 238, 239,
  242, 248, 251, 252, 253, 255,
  257, 258
Tutankhamen 204

U

Übermensch 247
Upanishads 212, 268

V

Varus, Publicus Quinctilius 162
Vatican xix, 132, 225
Vatican II 132, 225
Vedas 258
Von Wahlde, Urban 126, 269
Vulgata xviii, xix

W

War(s) xi, xv, 3, 16, 50, 51, 52, 53,
  58, 68, 74, 82, 83, 88, 90, 92,
  101, 106, 125, 127, 156, 158,
  163, 172, 179, 194, 195, 197,
  198, 221, 222, 225, 229, 249,
  252, 254, 260, 261, 267
Wilde, Oscar 252
Wittenberg 226
World Trade Center 179

Y

Yahweh 3, 14, 20, 34, 35, 36, 49, 54,
  87, 204, 220, 259
Yogananda, Paramahansa 195, 269
Yoke 42, 75, 76, 112
Yuz Asaf 165

Z

Zacharias 81
Zarathustra 2, 3, 75
Zechariah 147
Zecheriah 138
Zeno 170
Zeus 52, 168, 182
Zionism x, 52, 222, 243, 267
Zodiathes, Spiros 269
Zoroaster 2, 261